DIAMONDS AND DOMINATORS

How to *Feel* Free in a

World of Slavery

JOE GOWERSTREET

To Hallie Joy, my sweet baby girl.

TABLE OF CONTENTS

INTRO

Freedom and Love Will Heal the World

Freedom and love will heal the world.

Your mother keeps asking me, "What's the point of the book?"

That's it.

Freedom and love will heal the world.

This planet is filled with dominators and domination. This is a world controlled by sovereigns, systems, and slavery. These powerful people and institutions *WILL* hurt you deeply. And they will do so in the name of helping and protecting you.

When they do, and you are broken and confused, know that freedom and love will heal you. Freedom and love are healing me.

This is the first book I have ever written. I hope to write several more. But may it always be said that your father's unmistakable message to you, your brothers, your mother, and anyone else who may read this, was encapsulated in his first published words: freedom and love will heal the world.

What is freedom?

Perhaps the deaf community visualizes freedom better than anyone else. In sign language, freedom is communicated by starting with your wrists crossed – signifying that your hands are bound. Then in dramatic fashion, the hands pull apart. This illustrates that the ropes or chains binding the hands have fallen off. The imagery is clear: one has been freed from slavery.

Slavery is being bound by another. Slavery is being dominated and controlled by someone else. Slavery is being owned, ordered, and oppressed against one's will. Slavery is living under the perpetual fear and threat of being hurt by a master.

Slavery is a scenario that we would *never* choose if we were truly given a *free choice.*

And freedom, reduced to its most simple and precise form, is choice. What is freedom? Freedom is choice.

Any and all tests for freedom can be distilled down to this question: "Is the choice mine to make?"

If my answer is "No," then I'm not free. I am only free when I have a choice.

And my choice must be a *free* choice. It must not be a *fear* "choice."

It's never a free choice if someone is threatening to hurt me if I don't make the "choice" they want me to make. It's never a free choice if some dominant person, group, business, government, or religion is threatening me with being burned in hell, killed, caged, shot, gassed, hit, fired, criminalized, censored, shunned, shamed, or having my money and possessions taken if I don't "choose" what they have *chosen for me* to "choose."

Catch that?

These are fear "choices," not free choices. This is force, not freedom. This is coercion, not choice.

The word *coercion* is one I want you to become very familiar with. Coercion is the antithesis and enemy of freedom. Coercion is the malevolent curse and malignant cancer of the world.

What is coercion?

Coercion is being forced to "choose" something against my will out of fear of being hurt.

Don't miss the three parts of coercion. Coercion is:

1. **Being forced** to "choose," think, say, believe, do, be, or become something
2. **Against my will** (I would *never* choose this if given a *free* choice)
3. **Out of fear of being hurt** by a dominate person or group.

Therefore, a second all-important test of freedom is this: "Is coercion being used against me?"

If my answer is "Yes," then I'm not free.

A truly *free* choice is the exact opposite of coercion. It's where I am free to choose something according to my will *without the fear of being hurt.*

A free choice is when neither my will nor my hands are bound. I am in control of my choices.

- I am free to choose what I want.
- I am free to think what I want.
- I am free to believe what I want.
- I am free to say what I want.
- I am free to do what I want.
- I am free to be and become what I want.

True freedom.

And true freedom *feels* free. Something that is exceptionally hard to feel in our world of slavery.

But this is your father's greatest desire: to be free, *and to feel free*. And that my wife, children, grandchildren, and future generations live free and *feel* free.

That we can live our lives in peace – with true inner peace. With our hearts and minds characterized by being consistently at ease rather than constantly on edge. Down deep, in the deepest part of our hearts, I want us to *be* free and to *feel* free.

I'm convinced many people feel this way.

But I must confess that the majority of my life has been spent either being emotionally flat or being controlled at the very center of my being by much darker emotions. Paralyzing fear. Persecuting guilt. Confusing anger. Deep self-hatred. Even extended periods of deep depression, hopelessness, and despair.

Why?

Because my outer world and my inner world are not in harmony. Because outwardly, I am a slave in a world of slavery. And I have been bullied by my dominating masters into bowing, smiling, and pretending that this scenario is ok with me. That I'm ok with them. That this game I am forced to play in is something that I would "freely choose" to play in.

But inwardly, I'm in deep conflict. I know I'm not free – *and I want to be*. I know coercion is being used against me – *and I hate it*. I know if given a *free* choice, this is not the life that I would live.

Powerful individuals and groups that are stronger than I am, whom I will refer to as "dominators" throughout this book, have designed my life *for me*. Dominators who control the details and destiny of my life from the day I was born till the day I die. And if I resist their dominance, they believe they have the right – and moral duty – to hurt me.

Even though most of them can be well-intentioned, dominators always ultimately fail. Because they honestly don't know how to dominate apart from the use of fear, threats, and hurting people.

Why?

Because fear, threats, and hurting people gets results.

Fast.

And what gets rewarded, gets reinforced. Therefore, dominators are always about fear and coercion. They are never about freedom and choice.

I started writing this book around New Year's Day, 2019. I had no idea that in just over a year, COVID-19 would hit our planet. That almost every person on Earth would begin experiencing a whole new level of slavery. That all our tests for freedom would fail at every level of existence.

- What do you mean I must stay home?
- Can I go to work?
- Can I go to school?
- Am I "essential"?
- Can I worship God with the people of God in the house of God?
- Can I travel and move?
- Can I go outside?
- Can I hug someone I love?
- Can I visit my aging mother? Will I ever see her again?
- Do I have to wear a mask?
- If I get COVID-19, can I use *that* drug to save my life?
- What do you mean a vaccine will be potentially *mandated*?
- Why does one human being – an "expert," President, governor, or mayor – get to make choices for millions of individuals?
- Why can't I make my own choices?
- Why can't I live life at my own risk?
- Why do we obey these people?
- Isn't this supposed to be a *free* country?

And those questions represent only a small sample of the ever-tightening chains in our world of slavery. A planet where dominators think they own us. Dominators who evidently believe we were born to be dominated by them. That we supposedly have no other choice than to simply obey what they've chosen *for us*. That we are helpless little children without them.

Earth is at a crossroads. Will COVID-19 be the catalyst for greater human domination? Or will it be the catalyst for the greatest human liberation in history?

For it to be the latter, a freedom movement must be launched. A movement of *FREEDOM LOVERS* who envision a world where you and every single person on Earth can one day take – and pass – the two tests for freedom:

1. "Do I have a choice?" – with the answer being "Yes!"
2. "Is coercion being used against me?" – with the answer being "No!"

But that is not our present world. Not even close.

At present, there are protests all over the Western world condemning police brutality and alleged racism. On May 25, 2020, a Minneapolis police officer subdued an arrested African American man, George Floyd, with a knee to his neck for the better part of nine minutes. Floyd was reported to have repeatedly said, "I can't breathe." The end result: George Floyd died. The literal fires of protest are still burning as I write this.

To be sure, I have 100 opinions from 100 different angles on this incident and its divisive aftermath. But I am going to skip all of them to make one solitary point. A metaphorical one. Hopefully a unifying one.

"I can't breathe."

A dying man has given humanity a succinct message and timeless metaphor for all dominators. "I can't breathe. You don't own me. Get your knee off my neck. I wasn't born to be dominated by you. Stop bullying me through fear and coercion. I want to live and to feel free."

The world you were born into is as broken and wounded as ever. Maybe more than ever.

Why?

Because even though our species is growing smarter, we are not growing wiser. Even though our species constantly advances in doing things better, we – as human beings – are not better. We can build 100 story skyscrapers, nuclear reactors, 5G towers, drones, and artificial intelligence. But we still haven't been able to put it together that fear and coercion will never heal the world.

It needs to be said again and again and again…and again – until it starts to click.

Fear and coercion will *NEVER* heal the world.

It's well into the 21st century, and alpha human dominators still haven't figured that out. They still function by, "Ah-hah! I have an idea that will fix the world…now let me *force* everybody to do it! And, I'll hurt them if they disobey or disagree with me."

How twisted is that? "Let me help you, or I'll hurt you." "Let me protect you, or I'll punish you." "My concern for your safety gives me absolute sovereignty over you."

Dominators are always blind to how dystopian the world becomes when they attempt to force their utopia upon everybody else.

And what's the worn-out, popular definition of insanity? Is it not doing the same thing again and again expecting different results?

No wonder the world is crazy. Our history is simply one of dominators masquerading as liberators using fear and coercion to establish their new utopian societal order.

In our supposedly highly advanced, "enlightened" age, the light bulb has still not turned on in our dark, dumb brains as to the chief moral lesson of our own history. That being this: fear and coercion will *never* heal the world.

Freedom and choice will heal the world.

Freedom *and love* will heal the world.

What is love?

Another shout out to the deaf community. I love their symbol for "I love you." It is simply holding up your hand while dropping the middle and ring finger. The pinky, index finger, and thumb remain extended. I cherish the opportunity of flashing to each of you children this "I love you" sign many times each week.

But what is love? And why do I believe that freedom *and love* as a tandem will heal the world?

The irony of freedom is that it needs to be governed. The quality of choices that freedom will make, depends on the good will or the ill will of the person making the choices. **And only love can properly govern the free choices of an individual.**

I know it sounds delusional, but I believe that fixing the world is really quite simple.

Rule 1: Don't hurt anybody.

Rule 2: Help everybody.

It really is that simple. Don't hurt. Help.

Which brings up a very basic question: *Why do we hurt each other?*

And don't read on until you've pondered the answer to that question.

We all want to be and to feel free. But in the 21st century, we are still using our tiny amounts of residual freedom to hurt each other. When we should be using our freedom to help each other. Because we humans still make choices to hurt others, freedom and choice have to be constantly governed.

But who or what can govern freedom? *So that freedom is still freedom.*

There is only one candidate. One that is perfect, that has no flaws.

Love.

Only love can govern freedom.

Dominators and their so-called "laws," cannot govern freedom. Dominators always – yes always – end up hurting people in the name of helping people. Very few rules made by dominators – if any - have ever been good for all people at all times.

It is almost a *true* law, a universal constant like gravity or entropy, that when dominators make rules to help one group of people, they always end up hurting a different group of people.

All human rules are limited by the tiny number of biased, imperfect, and shortsighted people who make them. Which has made "liberty and justice for all" nothing more than a bogus, hollow sentiment in a world of slavery.

While human rules are always limited, love is unlimited. Love is always good for all people at all times. Love is always the right thing to do. Love is the only candidate to rightly govern freedom.

So what is love?

I define love this way. *Love is the giving of oneself to better another expecting nothing in return.*

Again, don't miss the three aspects to this definition of love. First, love is the giving of oneself. You were born into a greedy world obsessed with taking. Love is obsessed with giving. Love is generous. Love is something you do. And when you love, what you are doing is giving.

Second, love is given to better another person. You were born into a world that is addicted to dominating and to being better than another person. A hyper-competitive planet where you are taught to find meaning and purpose in being smarter, stronger, richer, more attractive, more skilled, more successful, and better than other people.

In contrast, love is addicted to building and bettering *another* person. Love finds meaning and purpose in making the lives of others better. That's why people who use their freedom to love are the real salt of the earth. People who love are the light of a dark world. People who love heal the planet. People who love hold back the rotting corruption of domination, power, and coercion. People who love make life worth living.

Third, love expects nothing in return. Love is unconditional. You were born into a world where most people have a self-serving angle for everything they do. Many people in this world extend fake love and generosity with an angle for themselves. They want something in return.

And usually what they want in return is control and leverage over you. The ability to claim moral high ground and dominance over you because of what they've "given" and "done" for you. That's why conditional love is always impure. Strings are always attached.

True love is different. It expects nothing in return. Which purifies one's motives. There are no strings attached. There are no conditions. Because true love is its own reward.

And this is why only love can properly govern freedom.

Benjamin Franklin said something powerful when he stated, "Only a virtuous people are capable of freedom. As nations become corrupt and vicious, they have more need of masters."[1]

Ben Franklin has a point. It does seem that only "good" people are capable of living free. While I am writing you an entire book on how to live and how to feel free, I must also give a caveat. That being, you need to earn the right to live and to feel free by being a good person.

---

[1] https://franklinpapers.org/framedVolumes.jsp?vol=44&page=605. Franklin's letter to the Abbés Chalut and Arnaud (17 April 1787).

Freedom can only be entrusted to good people who will not abuse their freedom. If freedom is fundamentally about choice, then we must be good people who make wise and responsible choices with our freedom.

Admittedly, this will be the biggest argument *against* my case for human freedom. Historically, humans have sucked at freedom. When it comes to our fellow man, we have consistently made choices to hurt each other instead of making choices to help each other. People who make free choices to help, rather than to hurt, make freedom work.

Good people can be trusted with freedom.

But two obvious questions must be asked.

"What is 'good'?" And "Who is a good person?"

10,000 religions have been started attempting to answer these two questions. Hundreds of nations have come, gone, and still presently exist attempting to answer these two questions.

But there is only one consistently right answer to the "What is 'good'?" question. Love.

There is only one consistently right answer to the "Who is a good person?" question. The one who loves. The one who gives of himself or herself to better another person expecting nothing in return.

Love is the perfect virtue.

- What is truly moral in this immoral world? Love.
- What is truly just in this unjust world? Love.
- What is truly good in this evil world? Love.
- What alone will heal a broken, wounded world? Love.

Love alone can properly govern freedom. Love is the assurance that we will use our freedom to make choices to help, rather than to hurt. Choices to build, rather than to destroy.

In the spirit of *Star Wars: The Rise of Skywalker*, there really is a dyad in the Force. That is, a powerful connection of two joining as one to channel all the liberating, constructive, healing, and life-giving energy that this universe possesses.

And this real dyad in the Force is not Rey Skywalker and Ben Solo.

It's freedom AND love.

If freedom is not combined with love, Earth remains in darkness. It continues to be a world of slavery.

If love is not combined with freedom, Earth remains in darkness. It continues to be a world of slavery.

Only the powerful dyad of freedom AND love can both light and heal our planet.

I love you more than life itself. May this book help you navigate through this crazy world. May it help teach you how to *feel* free in a world of slavery.

Never forget that the point of this book is this: Freedom and love will heal the world.

Never forget, freedom and love will heal you.

CHAPTER 1

You Were Born

You and I will always be connected.

For starters, we were both the unplanned for, unexpected "baby" of five children. From the outset of our marriage, your mother Joy and I always wanted five children. And we already had our four wonderful boys, your big brothers Ray, Lands, Joe Jr., and Max.[2]

However, your brother Lands was born with Down's Syndrome. Then he eventually developed Autism. As you know, he's the sweetest, most loving dude on the planet. But he's a lot of work. To us, he was kind of like having twins. So we thought we were "done" as we were super content with our four boys.

But….

I will never forget the day when I came home after a hard day's work in my lawncare business. As I entered the kitchen where your mother was preparing our supper, she fearfully told me the news that we were expecting.

[2] At my own discretion, and to protect people's privacy, I will frequently be changing names of individuals, organizations, and institutions throughout the book.

Joy was afraid that I would be ticked off. That's how my father responded to the news of my conception.

Don't get me wrong. I had a great dad. And once I was born, he was glad. But when my mother once told me of his initial anger *at her* for being pregnant *with me*, it didn't make me feel good. I promised to myself, that if my wife ever had an unexpected pregnancy, my response would be joy. So needless to say, when your mother sheepishly told me that she was expecting you, I was *so* happy!

However, we just assumed you were going to be another boy. My side of the family didn't do the girl thing. A girl had not been born into our family for 50 years. My family was also four boys and one girl. And on the Gowerstreet side of the family, there were 10 grandchildren before you – all boys.

So we made our plans for Dylan James or "DJ" to come into the world. However, things began to change after the first ultrasound. The technicians predicted you would be a girl.

That was a game-changer. We were in the groove for boys. All of the clothing and toys in our home were for boys. While we wanted a girl, we just assumed that the ultrasound was wrong. We would be having yet another boy, which was great with us.

But a second ultrasound also predicted a girl. So now we were also preparing for the possibility of Hallie Joy.

But your Grandma Kay, now over 80 years old, refused to believe it. She just assumed it would be a boy. You have to understand something, that's how her psychology works. It's her manipulation technique. She uses reverse psychology as a rule. She uses the negative as her personal leverage to accomplish the positive – what she really wants. Hilarious.

We all *really* wanted a girl at this point.

And sure enough, our desires were fulfilled on June 18, 2017 as you, Hallie Joy Gowerstreet, were born into this world. But it was the incredible way you chose to enter this world that forever established our special connection.

A little background. The births of your oldest two brothers were dramatic. Ray, who was nearly 6 weeks early, experienced a doctor prescribed, Pitocin-induced labor resulting in fetal distress resulting in an emergency C-section. He spent the first 2 weeks of his life in the Neonatal Intensive Care Unit (NICU).

Ditto for Lands. He also experienced a doctor prescribed, Pitocin-induced labor resulting in *extreme* fetal distress resulting in an emergency C-section. Lands came out purple, he was so oxygen deprived. He would spend his first two and a half weeks in the NICU. And of course, there was a lot of emotional recovery for your mother and I with the jarring news of having a special needs child. That's another book in itself.

Then about five years later (and after one miscarriage), we were expecting your brother Joe Jr. Even though your mother had already had two C-sections, we knew we wanted to attempt a "V-back" – a natural, vaginal birth. However, no hospital was interested in even letting us try – except for the University of Illinois at Chicago. And of course, they placed us in the birthing room next to the emergency room if she had any difficulties.

But your mother is something else. After her water broke with Joe Jr., she labored 30 hours, with no meds, and delivered him naturally. It was an extraordinary day.

Ditto for Max. After your mother's water broke with him, it was 24 hours of labor, with no meds, before he was naturally born.

Let me state the obvious. Your mom is one tough lady. And the birth accounts of your four brothers gives a little extra context for your extraordinary entry.

At about 10 p.m. on June 17th, your mother told me that she was starting to have contractions. I was so pumped because I knew you would be born on

June 18th, Father's Day. We estimated that we would go to the hospital sometime early in the morning, so I went to sleep while Joy laid down to "rest."

The next thing I remember is being shaken out of my sleep by your mother. It was 2 a.m. She said, "It's time to go to the hospital, my water broke. Call my mom."

Your Grandma Jill was staying at a house nearby that we were fixing and flipping. I walked downstairs, called her, and informed her that it was time for us to go to the hospital. Jill said, "Do I have time to take a shower?" To which I nonchalantly replied, "Oh yeah, it'll be about 45 minutes until we get out of here."

After I hung up with your Grandma, I heard your mom scream for me. I ran upstairs and she was on her knees in our master bathroom. She agonizingly said, "Call 9-1-1! I'm just not going to make it! I mean the baby's so low, it's right here!"

I quickly took my phone and dialed 9-1-1. I ran downstairs and began flipping on lights and unlocking doors for their arrival. Then I heard your mother scream a second time, "Joe!!!"

I ran upstairs and she's standing up and leaning over in agony saying, "The head is right here!" The emergency dispatcher on the phone is trying to talk to me, but I put the phone down on the vanity top.

Not to be crude, but I'm a farm boy who has seen many births. Furthermore, you were baby number five, this wasn't my first rodeo. I reached around your little head, grabbed your shoulder, and - *WHOOSH* - you came right out!

I immediately placed you face down in my hand and we cleaned out anything that might be in your mouth. You began to cry. Your unique voice was heard for the first time on Earth.

The dispatcher could hear what was going on and he said, "That's great, a crying baby is a healthy baby." Joy quickly asked me to hand you to her. I grabbed the phone back and began going downstairs to see if the EMTs had arrived.

As I began talking to the dispatcher again, I said through a dazed laugh, "Holy crap! I just delivered a baby and it's Father's Day!" The dispatcher, who was fantastic through all of this, replied, "Congratulations! That's awesome man!"

What. A. Moment. I was sleeping like a rock at 2 a.m. I was holding you in my hands at 2:11 a.m. And according to your mom, you were born *18 minutes* after her water broke. If anyone deserved a quick delivery, it was your Mom.

As soon as I ran downstairs four EMTs had just arrived. They all ran upstairs to attend to your mother and you. *Your four brothers slept through all of this*. When your grandmother arrived, you and your mother were already in the ambulance and an EMT said to her, "Do you want to meet your new granddaughter?"

The ambulance took you and your Mother to the hospital. Your chosen entry into this world made us legends at the hospital. After two days at the hospital confirmed that you and your mother were both beautiful and healthy, you came home.

If I live to be a hundred-year-old man and someone will ask me, "What were the top five moments of your life?" "Delivering my own daughter on Father's Day" will undoubtedly be near the top of the list.

We are both the baby of 5 children. You were born on Father's Day. I was the first set of human hands to hold you. We will always be connected.

Since your birth, I jokingly tell everybody that you've absolutely "ruined" my life. After four boys, I had no idea that a little girl would take my 6-foot 3-inch frame and wrap it tightly around her little pinky. Needless to say, I am madly in love with you.

My greatest joy was bringing you into this world. Now, my greatest responsibility is preparing you for the world I brought you into.

And the first thing you need to know is that you were born free – with two diamonds in your hands!

CHAPTER 2

You Were Born Free – With Two Diamonds in Your Hands

Diamonds are incredibly beautiful. And in this world, humans have chosen to make them valuable – and even invaluable, priceless.

If you study any top 10 list of the most expensive diamonds on Earth, the top two are usually the same. One is the Cullinan Diamond which was found in South Africa in 1905. The rough, uncut version of this diamond was later cut into 9 smaller diamonds. The other is the Koh-I-Noor Diamond, believed to have been discovered in India in the 1300's and is now part of the British Crown Jewels.

While other famous diamonds, such as the Hope Diamond, have estimated values of up to 350 million dollars, the Cullinan and the Koh-I-Noor are borderline "priceless." Diamonds like these two, once they're in your possession, you don't give them away. You don't sell them. You don't trade them out. You protect them with your life from being stolen. They are precious jewels, not to be parted with at any cost.

You were born free. That moment in our master bathroom, where I held you in my hands for the first time, was the freest moment of your life.

And you were born holding two priceless diamonds – one in each hand.

In your little right hand was the rough, uncut diamond of *your identity*. Who you are. Who you will be. What you will desire. What you will create. What you will bring to the world. Your unique personality. Your unique appearance. Your unique DNA. Your unique giftedness. Your unique voice. You. The real you.

You were born with the diamond *of the power of your identity* in your right hand. Your *individual* identity. There is no one else like you on the entire planet. You cannot be replaced.

Throughout history, the right hand has been a picture of authority and power.[3] You were born with the power to define your own identity firmly in the grasp of your right hand. It is a priceless diamond. Way more valuable than the Cullinan or Koh-I-Noor diamonds. Never give it away. Never sell it. Never trade it. Protect it with your life from being stolen. It's yours.

Then in your tiny left hand was the rough, uncut diamond of *your inner peace*. How you will feel about who you are. Your inner person. Your inner life. Your inner freedom. A free mind firing with curiosity and capable of free thinking and innovation. Free will. Honest emotions. Your inner calm. Your inner rest.

The power of your inner peace.

Your left hand is closest to your heart. Throughout history, the heart has been a picture of the very seat or throne of your inner life. It is the place where mind, will, and emotions converge at a single point. It is where choices of direction, devotion, and destiny are made.

You were born *with the power to determine your own inner peace*, firmly in the grasp of your left hand.

---

[3] For example, Christianity makes much of the "right hand" of power and authority imagery. The New Testament repeatedly refers to Jesus being seated on the "right hand" of God. See Acts 7:55-56; Romans 8:34; Ephesians 1:20; Colossians 3:1; Hebrews 1:3; 8:1.

Inner peace is an extremely rare, priceless diamond. It is a heart at rest instead of a restless heart. It is a soul consistently at ease instead of a soul constantly on edge. It is an inner calm that lives above all paralyzing fear and persecuting guilt, not below them.

The diamond of your inner peace. This diamond is also way more valuable than the Cullinan or Koh-I-Noor diamonds. Never give it away. Never sell it. Never trade it. Protect it with your life from being stolen. It's yours.

The exact moment you came into this world, you were holding the diamond of your identity in your right hand and the diamond of your inner peace in your left hand. Rough. Uncut. Undeveloped.

But yours.

And at birth, for this briefest of moments, you were free.

You were born free.

But....

CHAPTER 3

"They" Want Your Diamonds

There is a nasty history connected with diamonds, even the most famous ones. Many thieves attempt to steal them. And have succeeded in doing so. The Hope Diamond that I alluded to has a spectacular history of changing greedy hands.

The Koh-I-Noor diamond is greatly disputed. Afghanistan, Pakistan, India, and England all claim that the jewel belongs to them. They all believe they have the exclusive "right" of ownership over the diamond.

And it's no different for the two diamonds you hold in your hands. Within minutes after you were born, there were thousands of individuals and groups who wanted to claim ownership over your two diamonds.

"They" would love the opportunity to get close to you. "They" want the chance to pry open your little hands in order to steal your diamonds. "They" want to *claim* ownership over your identity and then program your inner peace to be their slaves.

But who are "They"? Why do "They" want your diamonds so bad? And why do "They" need your diamonds in order to make you their slave?

"They" refers to any person or group who wants to dominate you.

"They" are dominators.

And a dominator is anyone who wants to control your life, remove your freedom, make choices *for* you, design you, mentally and emotionally program you, enlist you, and enslave you for their own purposes.

You might want to read that again.

And dominators will hurt you in a thousand ways – even kill you – if you don't submit to their domination. Dominators, whatever form they may take, all have this same method and motto: "I'm stronger than you. Be afraid of me. Give me your diamonds, or I'm going to hurt you."

All dominators do this. Some with an intimidating snarl. Others with an artificial smile. But "They," dominators, are all the same.

Dominators can take the form of large-scale power groups like:

— **the religious class** (Christianity, Islam, Hinduism, etc.)
— **the ruling class** (global, national, provincial, state, county, local government, etc.)
— **the rich class** (the world-shaping wealthy).

I call the religious, ruling, and rich classes the *power classes*. The unholy trinity of power on Earth. These three dominators have used their power to steal the diamonds of nearly every person on the planet. And all three want yours.

But dominators can also take the form of the *practical classes*. That is, smaller-scale groups or individuals who dominate your tiny corner of the planet. People on a local level who will want to bully you until you submit to their control. Examples of this would be friends, neighbors, teachers, coaches, employers, jerks at school, evil predators, a romantic interest, your own siblings, your mother – and, if I'm humble enough to admit it – even me, your own father.

Unfortunately, you will discover that the people closest to you can be dominators. Dominators who also will attempt to seize either a cut of, or entire control over the two diamonds of your identity and inner peace.

That is who "They" are. "They" are dominators. And these dominators are coming for your diamonds.

But you are two years old as I write this. You're probably closer to 12 years old as your read this. Perhaps your diamonds have already been stolen. Perhaps now as a young lady, you can't even imagine a time in your life when you were free from the tyranny of "They." From dominators dominating you. From control freaks controlling you.

If you already need to reclaim the diamonds of your identity and inner peace, I need to remind you of what you were like at two.

CHAPTER 4

A Mind Free from the Fear of Dominators

It's New Year's Day 2020. When I look at you right now, as a two-year-old, ignorance is indeed bliss. You are the happiest little girl. You are truly the princess of our home. You are the apple of everybody's eye. Not just mine. You also light up your mother. Your brothers adore you (except for maybe Max, your arch-rival and chief competitor). You melt us all to butter with your megawatt smile, dancing brown eyes, and flyaway brown curls. Oh, and your voice. When you speak, we're all "done."

As a two-year-old, life is so simple for you. It's all about adventure and discovery. It's one big party. Everything is new and exciting. You love to wear pretty dresses. You love to learn, look through books, and explore anywhere and everywhere. You love to empty cabinets. You love helping Mom and Dad with any project we are working on. And, of course, you love to play with, fight with, and manipulate your brothers.

At two, your responsibilities are few. Rules are few. You feel protected and provided for, which you are. Life is good.

But there is something way beyond all that. Something I find myself insanely jealous of.

It's how free you are. How much the diamonds of your identity and inner peace are still in your own hands. How wonderfully ignorant you are of "They," the dominators who want to take your diamonds. At two, you have almost no dread – extreme fear – of these dominators.

But as you read this at 12, or whatever age you are right now, you may have tears welling up in your eyes. Tears because you no longer feel like the two-year-old Hallie. Tears because you don't feel free anymore. Tears because you feel you have little control over the details of your life. Tears because you already live with so much fear and dread.

Unfortunately, you may have tears because you don't feel very adored by others. You have been awakened to a cruel world where *everybody* judges you *all the time* about *everything.* And this incessant judgment constantly makes you feel like you are not good enough, pretty enough, obedient enough, smart enough, talented enough, etc.

Maybe you have tears because you feel like everyone else defines your identity. Tears because you cannot even imagine possessing inner peace. You've been "wised up" on how the real-world works.

Hallie, I want to take you on a time travel journey. I want to show you what the two-year-old Hallie was like – and *is like* – from my present perspective. What an extremely free individual looks like. What you acted like when the diamonds of your identity and your inner peace were in your own hands.

When you possessed a mind free from the fear of dominators.

First, as a two-year-old, I see someone with a mind almost entirely free from the fear of dominators in the form of the religious class. At two, no religion has your diamonds. You have no real knowledge of the concept of God. You're not scared of burning in a lake of fire for all eternity. You don't know that there are 10,000 religions in the world – all of which would gladly take your diamonds and dominate you.

And perhaps no group is more zealous about stealing a baby's diamonds than the religious class. Jews circumcise "their" Jewish babies on the 8th day of life. Babies born into Jewish families have their diamonds taken away immediately. These babies already have an identity given to them by their religious dominators. And their Jewish dominators will be sure to program the child's inner peace to match the identity that was forced onto the child.

Roman Catholics usually baptize "their" Catholic babies in the first months of life. Babies born into Catholic families have their diamonds taken away immediately. These babies already have an identity given to them by their religious dominators. And their Catholic dominators will be sure to program the child's inner peace to match the identity that was forced onto the child.

Muslims whisper to Shahadah (There is no God but Allah, and Muhammad is his messenger) to "their" Islamic babies immediately after birth.

Are you seeing a pattern here?

Babies born into Muslim families have their diamonds taken away immediately. These babies already have an identity given to them by their religious dominators. And their Muslim dominators will be sure to program the child's inner peace to match the identity that was forced onto the child.

Religious dominators will take your diamonds while you are in the cradle, and they will *never* return them to you. You will spend a lifetime under their domination. The one life you have for sure, will be spent living in fear of displeasing your religious dominators. You will be terrified of ever resisting their domination.

You were not born into any of the religious scenarios given above. But hundreds of millions of babies have been, are being, and will be. We will talk later about the religious background of the family you were born into.

For now, I return to the point at hand. At two, your mind is free from fear of religious dominators. You do not suffer anxiety concerning the big questions of God.

- Is there one God?
- Is there a Trinity?
- Which version of God is correct?
- Is it the Muslim God?
- Is it the Jewish God?
- Is it the Christian God?
- Are all these the same God?
- Which of the 34,000 versions of Christianity is the right one?
- Which holy book is true?
- Is it the Koran?
- Is it the Torah?
- Is it the New Testament?

These questions are not on the radar of a happy toddler.

Must be nice.

Let me state something without apology. Nothing has ruined your father's sense of inner peace more in life than religious class dominators.

And what amazes me is this: as a two-year-old, you don't even feel religious guilt – *at all*. You have no knowledge of the 613 rules of the Torah, even the 10 commandments. You know nothing of the hundreds (perhaps thousands) of rules written and unwritten in Christianity and Islam.

At two, you don't battle the perpetual guilt that has plagued me for the majority of my life. You weren't born feeling guilty. Your mind and nervous system haven't been programmed yet to feel ashamed for your inability keep all the hundreds of rules that the religious class can force feed an individual.

Imagine that. The diamond of your inner peace is currently in your own hand. You feel no fear of hell. You don't feel like you deserve to be punished for being born. You have never felt any guilt for breaking a religious rule. You feel no need to spend hours confessing or sacrificing.

What's that like?

Let me state something else without recantation or apology. Everything religious class dominators use to terrorize the identity and inner peace of a human being – their endless rules, dogmas, creeds, guilt, blame, shame, threats, condemnation, etc. – ALL OF THESE THINGS originate from outside the person.

ALL OF THEM.

Watching how free you are as a two-year-old confirms my bias. None of the fear, internal guilt, inadequacy, and condemnation that a person can feel from religious training originates inside a child. It all originates from outside the child and is programmed into them by religious class dominators. Almost none of it is nature. Almost all of it is nurture.

Every child is born free from this.

This is critical to understand for those of us adults seeking to reclaim our identity and inner peace. Those of us who had our precious diamonds stolen from us decades ago by religious class dominators.

ALL of this religious coercion must be learned. Again, a baby's diamonds must be stolen soon after birth. Then as a toddler and young child their inner peace must be programmed and automated by the religious class dominator.

A religious "conscience" must be created. Fear and pain training are the surest way to burn into the child's nervous system the fear-based triggers, conditioned cues, and programmed promptings that a religious dominator wants them to feel.

But the two-year-old you that I am observing in the writing of this, is currently free. The diamond of inner peace is still in your left hand.

And the diamond of your identity is still in your right hand. At two, you don't have a religious identity or affiliation. You haven't been forced to identity as "Baptist," "Jewish," "Muslim," "Hindu," "Buddhist," "Mormon," "Catholic," "Orthodox," "Jehovah's Witness," "Atheist," or "Agnostic."

None of these terms mean anything to you. And you're so happy. Ignorance is bliss. You are currently free from these things. You are still in possession of your two diamonds.

Before I move on, let me clarify one thing. Believe it or not, this book is not an anti-God or anti-religion book. It is a pro-human book. It is a pro-freedom book. It is an anti-coercion book. That being said, you must be prepared. Dominators in the form of the religious class are coming for your diamonds. And they will attempt to take them by force.

Second, as a two-year-old, I see someone with a mind almost entirely free from the fear of dominators in the form of the ruling class. The government. As a toddler still in diapers, you are not political. You are not loyal to any one country, culture, party, or people group on earth.

You don't know how to hate people different than yourself. You don't have any sworn enemies. Those who look different. Those who think different. Those who talk different. Those who worship different. Those who live different.

At two, your mind is free from all this drama. You don't know about a tiny percentage of our population who make up the ruling class. A small group of individuals who operate on the assumption that they have the right to "represent" and make choices for everyone else.

At two, you're not aware that the ruling class gathers in important looking buildings and meeting rooms to design your life *for you*. You have no knowledge of any of the thousands of rules they have invented to control almost every miniscule detail of your life.

And at two, you don't know how cruel the ruling class can be. These dominators believe they have the "right" to hurt you if you don't submit to their domination.

To the ruling class, the worst "crime" on Earth is to resist their domination. It never occurs to them that the real crime *is their domination*. And if you resist their domination, they believe it is their "moral" duty to separate you from the love of family, the beauty of nature, and the adventure of life to be thrown into their cage for as long as they decide.

The cage of the ruling class, prison, is their ultimate weapon of fear. You must obey, submit to their domination in all points, or it's the cage for you. The religious class uses hell. The ruling class uses the cell.

At two, neither one of these scare you.

But even in this "woke" age, ruling class dominators still love collecting the diamonds of identity and inner peace from the masses. And they even get the masses to pay for their own domination. The masses actually pay for their own slavery. Ruling class dominators force their dominated to give them money.

And what does the ruling class do with this money? Whatever they want. Primarily, they enter into their meeting rooms and conduct social engineering experiments on the dominated. They make rules for the dominated and call them "laws." And they write down these rules on official looking paper.

Ruling class dominators then use these rules to justify using coercion against people. People who would rather have a free choice. Ruling class dominators force those under their domination to involuntarily submit to:

- the compulsory education (indoctrination) of their children
- their healthcare decisions
- military drafts and war, fighting for the dominators
- resource stealing and terrorism of other countries
- federal tax
- state tax
- county tax
- city tax
- property tax
- sales tax
- occupancy tax
- tariffs

- tolls
- permits
- licenses
- inspections
- punishment for profit schemes
- confiscations
- surveillance
- prisons
- police
- lawyers
- judges
- juries
- plea bargains
- executions
- extortion
- and all forms of government coercion.

And all for “the greater good” of the dominated masses who “want” to be “represented” by these ruling class dominators. A tiny few who make the choices for a massive many. How ironic that the “collective good of all” is always determined by a chosen few.

And never forget, these elite ruling class dominators are not to be resisted or rebelled against. It’s a deadly thing to say “no” to the ruling class. In the 20th century alone, it is estimated that 100 million people were killed by their ruling class dominators. Not by disease. Not by war. But by direct execution at the hands of their “public servants.”

You’re two. You know nothing of this. None of this scares you. None of this robs you of inner peace. None of this burdens you down. You’re not frightened of their cage. You have never felt any guilt for breaking a rule invented by the ruling class. You have never felt stressed that these dominators will catch you doing something of which they disapprove or that they decided, apart from your consent, to make "illegal."

And you are not looking for alcohol, drugs, or something else to give you temporary relief from this fear and oppressiveness. Your mind is almost completely free from this.

Again, what is that like? A mind free from the fear of dominators in the form of the ruling class.

Let me knowingly repeat myself. Almost verbatim.

All of the rules, indoctrination, coercive taxation, fines, imprisonments, guilt, threats, condemnation, criminalization, shame, etc. from ruling class dominators that terrorize the identity and the inner peace of a human being – ALL OF IT originates from outside a child.

ALL OF IT.

ALL the internal misery connected with one's government indoctrination, originates from without. It does not originate from inside a child. It all originates from outside a child and is programmed into them.

Every child is born free from this.

ALL of this government coercion must be learned. A baby's two diamonds must be stolen soon after birth. Then as a toddler and young child their inner peace must be programmed and automated by the ruling class dominators.

A civil "conscience" must be created. Again, fear and pain training are the surest way to burn into the child's nervous system the fear-based triggers, conditioned cues, and programmed promptings that a ruling class dominator wants them to feel.

But the two-year-old you that I am currently observing, is free from the fear of ruling class dominators. The diamond of inner peace is still in your hand. It doesn't belong to the ruling class.

Nor does the diamond of your identity. At two, you don't identify as "American," "British," "Mexican," "Chinese," "Russian," or "South African." You don't identity as "Republican," "Democrat," "Libertarian," "Globalist," "Nationalist," "Liberal," "Conservative," "Left," "Right," "Socialist," "Communist," "Marxist," or "Capitalist." None of these terms mean anything to you.

And you are so happy. Ignorance is bliss. You are currently free from these things. Your diamonds are still in your own hands.

Let me make another clarification. This is not really an anti-government book. It is a pro-human book. It is a pro-freedom book. It is an anti-coercion book. But be prepared, ruling class dominators are coming for your diamonds. And they will attempt to take them by force.

Third, as a two-year-old, I see someone with a mind almost entirely free from the fear of dominators in the form of the rich class. And the rich class is arguably the most powerful class. The religious class and the ruling class will often sell their soul to them.

However, the rich class frequently is the religious class and/or the ruling class. In fact, sometimes it is difficult to differentiate between the religious, ruling, and rich classes. And which of the three evolved first in human history?

In some scenarios, the religious, ruling, and rich classes really are like the Christian Trinity. They are three, but they are one. They are an unholy trinity of power. They are the collective *power class* who rule over the *powerless class*. The dominators in a world of domination. The masters in a world of slaves.

In any scenario, the rich class are the humans who have the most "things." Things such as land, houses, slaves, and money. They are rich in possessions. They are rich in power. Most are rich because they inherited their wealth from powerful parents. Some are rich because of hard work and ambition. No matter how they became rich, many are dependent upon them for survival which only tightens the chains of their slaves.

If we are honest, all of us have a way we want the world to be. We all believe we have ideas that could make Earth a better place. And if we are incredibly honest, we *would* remake the world in our image if we had the power and influence to do so.

Some do have this power. They are the rich class.

Monopoly is not just a board game. It is reality. The rich class dominators have designed a real-life Monopoly game that benefits themselves above all. Like the board game, you want to own. You don't want to be owned. You want to be the lender. You don't want to be the borrower. You don't want to work for money. You want money to work for you – as you charge interest. You want to be the landlord. You don't want to pay rent. You want to own the strip mall. You don't want to sign a lease for an individual space.

On Earth, the real-life Monopoly board is controlled by the "I get to start life ahead," rich class. And the game is rigged in their favor. The rich class dominators have created a "You must start life behind" world for everybody else.

These rich elites have deceived the dominated masses into believing that the way to get ahead in life, is to start way behind. The way to build a life to the sky is to first dig yourself a deep pit that you must climb out of.

A world of debt. A world of servitude. A world of slavery. A world of endless striving for "success." To "dream big." That one day you too can be a rich class dominator. One who has liberated yourself from the dominated, enslaved class.

And the rich class dominators have perfected their real-life Monopoly game. You must borrow from the rich class to rent or buy a house, making you a slave to your shelter.

Let me state that again. You are a slave to your shelter. Don't read on until you let that sink in.

To pay off your slave debt to your shelter, you must work. In order to work, you must drive to work. In order to look respectable, you must drive a nice car. In order to afford a nice car, you must borrow more money from the rich class and create another slave debt. You must borrow from the rich class to secure a car to get to work. You are now a slave to your transportation.

To pay off your slave debt to your shelter and transportation, you must be sure your work pays you well. In order to get a good paying job, you must have impressive sounding credentials. In order to obtain these credentials, you must go to an impressive sounding university to confer impressive sounding credentials upon you. In order to afford the classes to obtain these credentials, you will need to borrow more money from the rich class. A lot more money. You are now the slave of your education.

It's all so brilliantly designed, isn't it? At least for the rich class dominators. This truly is real life Monopoly. Fun for the winner. Hell for the losers.

Forced to play in this elaborate game created by rich class dominators are real people. Real people born free. Real people born with the diamonds of identity and inner peace in their hands. Real people who quickly see how the game is played that has been designed *for them* by the rich and ruling classes.

To survive, out of self-preservation, and to be accepted, real people quickly dedicate their lives to "learn how the game is played." They give the diamond of their identity to the rich class. They too aspire to be labeled and identified as "rich," "famous," "great," "powerful," and "successful." They give their lives to play this game.

And while they are at it, real people also hand over the diamond of their inner peace to rich class dominators. And as a result, they live their lives constantly stressed and driven to win the game created by the wealthy.

Forced to play in this real-life Monopoly game, real people develop a tragically toxic mentality. The mentality of: "I must work 60 hours. I must sacrifice my family. I must take my children to daycare. I must pay my bills.

I must pay my debts. I must look respectable. I must look successful. My house must look successful. My car must look successful. My wardrobe must look successful. My wife and children must look successful. Even my hobbies must look successful. And above all, my credentials, titles, and accomplishments must sound successful."

And it's never enough. Real people who have sold their soul to rich class dominators carry the constant burden of debt, money-making, and a successful appearance. Their soul is constantly on edge.

Inner peace? Their soul is never at ease. The diamond of their inner peace has long since been given to the rich class. Just to sit at the table of the rich class dominator and to play in their game cost them dearly. They slid their two diamonds to the center of the table. And they were gone forever.

But you're two. You still throw food from your highchair. You know nothing of this. You haven't learned yet to identity yourself as rich or poor. You don't view yourself as valuable or invaluable, worthy or unworthy based on: the house you live in, the car you drive, the clothes you wear, the phones and computers you use or don't use, the university you attend or don't attend, or the type of job you can secure.

At two, you're not drowning in the sea of materialism and consuming in order to look successful and acceptable. And you feel no burden of debt. You may not own much. But currently you don't owe anything. You are not currently playing the real-life Monopoly game designed by rich class dominators.

The diamonds of your identity and your inner peace are still in your hands. But be prepared, the rich class dominators are coming for them.

At 12, or whatever your present age, you no doubt have already felt some fear of dominators in the forms of these *power classes* – the religious, ruling, and rich classes.

And we haven't even discussed the fear that can come from dominators in the forms of the *practical classes*. That is, your family, friends, schoolmates, neighbors, etc. That's the vast majority of us in your everyday life who are not part of the power class. We also like power and control. We also – sometimes unknowingly – like to steal diamonds.

But as we've traveled in our time machine back to the two-year-old Hallie, she is free from this. She has a mind free from the fear of dominators in most all of these forms. She wasn't born to be anyone's slave.

And neither were you.

How do you feel free in a world of slavery? Step one is being awakened to the FACT that there was a time your mind was free. Regardless of how brief that moment of time was, you were free.

Let's briefly recap.

You were born. You were born free. You were born with two diamonds in your hands. The diamond of the power of your identity was in your right hand. The diamond of the power of your inner peace was in your left hand. But "They," thousands of individuals and groups, want to steal these diamonds from you. These dominators want you to be their slaves.

Which stimulates many, many questions.

- Why does the world you were born into work this way?
- How did it get this way?
- Why do so many on this planet believe you were born to be dominated by them? That you were born to be their slave?
- What's wrong with this world?
- Why is it filled with coercion and slavery?
- Why is it so crazy?

The answer to all these questions is exactly the same.

The world you were born into is nothing more than one, big *dominance hierarchy*.

Huh?

A domi...what?

I'm sure you must be saying within yourself something like, "Dad, I was following almost everything you've been saying…until now. A *dominance hierarchy*? I can barely pronounce it. You just sailed something about 20 feet above my head."

Be patient. If you are to feel free in a world of slavery, you must know that, 1) there was a moment in time that you were free, and felt free, and 2) how and why Earth became a world of slavery – one, big dominance hierarchy.

Let me cut this massive steak of a *dominance hierarchy* into several smaller pieces so it's more easily digestible for you. When you understand the concept of a dominance hierarchy, you'll never see the world the same way again.

CHAPTER 5

What is a Dominance Hierarchy?

This may be hard for you to believe, but your dad used to be an ordained Baptist minister. Yes, me – the one with the infamous Irish mouth and temper. I'll save more of the details of my religious past for later in the book.

At any rate, when I was going through my ordination to become a Baptist minister, and as I was sharing my personal philosophy of ministry, one of the officiating guest pastors made this gentle criticism of me. He said, "You are an idealist, my friend."

Guilty. I definitely romanticize about the "ideal" world. The way the world should be. The way I want it to be. Honestly, I resonate with many of the lyrics contained in John Lennon's iconic "Imagine" song. I do imagine such a world.

And when I look at the world, the idealist in me wonders what is really so hard about fixing the world.

- Why can't we love instead of hate?
- Why can't we unite instead of divide?
- Why can't we build each other instead of destroy each other?
- Why can't the world be marked by voluntary cooperation instead of involuntary submission?

- A world of choice instead of coercion.
- A world of freedom instead of fear and force.
- A world of helping instead of hurting.
- A world where we are our brother's keeper instead of our brother's king.
- A world of love-based transformation instead of fear-based conformity.
- A world where the highest goal for society is wholeness instead of order.

The ideal world, the way the world should be.

But that's not reality. That's not the world you were born into. You were born into a world where "They" – thousands of groups and individuals – want to steal your diamonds. Dominators who want the power to define your identity and to determine your inner peace. Dominators who want you on their "team." Dominators who want you as part of their "tribe." And dominators who will hurt you – maybe even kill you – if you resist.

This is the real world. The way the world is. It's all one, big dominance hierarchy.

So what is a dominance hierarchy?

Let's start with the word *hierarchy. Hierarchy* simply means *a ranking*. A hierarchy is a ranking from best to worst, from the most superior to the most inferior, from the strongest to the weakest. Hierarchies are human power rankings.

And humans have a ranking, a hierarchy, for everything. And I mean *everything.*

Humans rank physical dominance, who's the strongest and best, reflected through athletic skill. If you want to know the best Division I Men's Collegiate basketball teams, there is a ranking from 1st to 350 something, from the best team to the worst team. Within these rankings are sub-rankings.

You can find team and individual rankings for scoring, rebounding, assists, steals, blocks, free throw percentage, field goal percentage, 3-point field goal percentage, etc. from 1st through infinity.

And that's just Division I. Never mind Division II, Division III, NAIA, etc. And don't forget the women's teams of all the same divisions.

You can look up similar team and individual player rankings for soccer, baseball, football, tennis, swimming, track and field, lacrosse, UFC fighting, boxing, wrestling, etc. In all of these, you will find a hierarchy, ranking teams and individuals from best to worst.

In each of these sports there will be tournaments to determine champions, who is the best, the undisputed top (temporarily) of that sports' hierarchy. And when one has reached the "Mt. Everest" of their respective sport, they usually flash the universal symbol of their dominance by holding up their index finger declaring, "I'm #1, the top, the best, the winner."

I am not saying this is good or bad. I'm just saying it's so. I would even lean towards saying it's a *somewhat* good thing. It shows progress. In some areas of life, humans have stopped killing each other, and they are at least now engaging in friendly competition. A handshake at the end is certainly better than death to the loser.

Humans also love to rank wealth, from the richest to the poorest. If you want to know which nations are the richest, you will find a hierarchy, a ranking from 1st to 195th, from the richest nation to the poorest nation. If you want to know the 500 richest people in every country, you can find a money hierarchy, a literal ranking of the wealthiest to the lesser wealthy.

Money is power and dominance. And the more you have, the more influence – and control – over others you usually have.

And this world makes every attempt to rank intelligence. It wants to document hierarchies reflecting smartest to dumbest. Schools have grade systems and test scores to reflect intelligence in given subjects. Every public school in America is forced to take standardized tests to measure the ability of students to grasp their predestined curriculum. If you want to know the "smartest" schools in this country down to the "dumbest" schools in this country, this information could be obtained.

Being the "smartest person in the room" usually means you have the most influence, control, and dominance over the others in the room. When choices are made in the room, usually your opinion will carry the most weight.

And certainly, physical beauty is not beyond the human affinity for hierarchy. While you may not find official rankings on beauty, all 50 states in our country have beauty pageants that also factor in intelligence, skill, and grace. Winners from all 50 states then compete against each other to determine who is the "best." Make no mistake, those who look good and sound good usually have a great power to influence, control, and dominate others. Others who sees themselves as inferior on the physical beauty hierarchy.

So again, a hierarchy is simply *a ranking* from best to worst. Humans have a ranking or hierarchy for everything. *Everything.*

Which brings us to the word *dominance. Dominance* simply means to dominate, to bring another under your control. This control means you can tell another what to do and they will obey you. If they don't obey you, you have the power to attack and hurt them until they submit to your will. The superior, dominant one controls the choices of the inferior, subordinate one. The stronger controls the weaker.

If you are the one being dominated, all of this is the opposite. The dominator, the one who has brought you under their control, tells you what to do and you must obey them. If you don't obey them, the dominator will attack and hurt you until you submit to their will. These attacks will start with varying levels of threatening vocalizations to get you to obey. If the vocalizations do not prompt your obedience, dominators will use physical violence.

Dominators will let you know that you are not in control of your own choices, they are. You are the weaker. They are the stronger. You are not free. You are their slave.

So, put it all together. A dominance hierarchy is a ranking of the most dominant to the least dominant, from the strongest person or group to the weakest person or group.

And this is at every level of existence on planet Earth. The stronger control the weaker. The weaker must obey the stronger or the stronger will attack and hurt the weaker so that they will obey.

Planet Earth is world of slavery. Our planet is nothing more than one big, dominance hierarchy.

Still a little fuzzy on the whole dominance hierarchy thing? Let me give you two basic examples to shed some more light on this concept.

CHAPTER 6

The Wolf Pack: How Dominance is Gained and Maintained

When I was growing up a zillion years ago, we played a "king of the mountain" type of game on the school playground. It went like this. There is one large stone that 5 boys are trying to be the king of. All 5 boys wrestle, pull, shove, kick, punch, bite, and ultimately push down each other in a struggle to get on top of the "mountain." Finally, after a struggle, one boy gains dominance and a superior position by getting to the top of the stone. The other four boys are in the inferior, dominated position on the ground.

But this isn't the end of the game. Once the one boy gains dominance, he now must maintain dominance. He fought to get on top. Now he must fight to stay on top. The other four boys all will be tugging and yanking to pull him down while he must kick and push to keep them down. This "friendly" playground game is a picture of a brutal reality in animal and human nature.

Perhaps no other animal species more clearly illustrates the concept of a dominance hierarchy than a wolf pack. One wolf gains dominance as the alpha, the "king of the mountain," by putting down the other wolves by biting, clawing, snarling, scratching, and ultimately rising above the other wolves.

Once the alpha establishes dominance over – let's say 9 other wolves – it will not be an egalitarian setup where all 10 wolves now have equal standing and live together in mutual love and respect. How the alpha gained dominance is how he will maintain dominance – fear, force, and the threat of punishment.

And this "societal order" organized through fear will govern every relationship within the hierarchy from wolves 2 through 10 – the "underdogs.". Again, the pack is not one alpha and nine equals. To use chicken dominance hierarchy terminology, there will be a pecking order. Even wolf 9 will be dominate over wolf 10 and use fear and intimidation to keep him in his place.

But back to the alpha. How did this one wolf become the dominant wolf who makes the rules and controls the other 9? How was this dominance gained? How did the alpha become the alpha?

- Was it because he was the smartest wolf?
- Was it because he was the biggest wolf?
- Was it because he was the oldest and most experienced wolf?
- Was it because of a genetic pre-disposition, that it's just in his DNA to be a born leader of wolves?

I believe it's a combination of these things. But I will summarize it this way. **One wolf becomes the alpha by being the most spiritually dominant.** That is, he has the strongest spirit, disposition, attitude, aura, or energy. He has the most forceful personality. He has the strongest mind and will. He has the ability to impose his mind and will upon the others.

This is the number one attribute of the dominant. They have the strongest spirit. They can control weaker spirits. They have the strongest will. They can control weaker wills. They have the strongest mind. They can control weaker minds.

Now, to be sure, many times it is the biggest, physically strongest wolf who has the strongest spirit. He has a strong spirit because he has been awakened to his physical dominance. And his physical dominance strengthens his confidence, enlarges his intelligence, and increases his courage to conquer. All of this strengthens his spirit and makes his personality even more forceful.

This powerful wolf will gain dominance and become the alpha by using fear and intimidation. He physically intimidates. He will bite the other wolves and sink his teeth into their ears, muzzle, or body. He will inflict physical pain. He will forcefully stand over them. He will put his head or paw on them with downward pressure. Every physical act of intimidation will accomplish his end objective: "You will obey my orders, or I will attack and hurt you."

Along with the physical intimidation is the emotional and psychological intimidation. The alpha's purpose in using forceful growling, snarling, and barking is clear. It is a manipulative power play to say to the weaker, "Be afraid of me. Know your place. Don't even think about challenging my dominance and my authority over you."

At this point, it could be said that the alpha has in his possession the diamonds of identity and inner peace from every single wolf in the pack. He defines their identity. The other wolves exist to fulfill his will, not their own. He dictates and determines their inner peace. Their inner peace can only be found in submission to the alpha. To the other 9 wolves in the pack, the alpha is their "They," their dominator.

And, again, it's not just the alpha who operates this way. There is a dominance ranking from 2 to 10. Even between low ranking wolves such as numbers 9 and 10, the higher-ranking wolf will be sure to bully (to borrow dominance hierarchy terminology of cattle) the lower-ranking wolf to remind him of his superiority and that this superiority is not to be challenged.

About two years ago, I remember showing your brothers a brief YouTube video on a wolf pack in captivity. One low ranking wolf had the scent of a caretaker on him. To the judgment of a jealous, higher ranking wolf, this was unacceptable and out-of-line. The higher-ranking wolf immediately began to re-establish its dominance. It kept placing its head and paws above the other wolf.

Initially, there was temporary resistance from the wolf being bullied. But ultimately, the incessant manipulation techniques of growling, biting, pushing, and holding down, helped re-establish dominance in this individual relationship within the pack. This was the dominance hierarchy in action, and not just at the top, *but in every single relationship within the pack.*

By the way, is your mind drawing any parallels yet? Do you see how humans treat each other just like wolves treat each other?

The wolves are most instructive. They teach us that dominance is gained and maintained at every level by spiritual and physical dominance. By using the psychological tools of fear, intimidation, and bullying.

But they also teach us the hideous hypocrisy of the dominance hierarchy. That being, there are two sets of rules: one for the dominator, one for the dominated. One set of rules for the strong. One set of rules for the weak.

You will observe:

- The dominant wolf is the judge. The dominated wolf is the judged.
- Therefore, the dominant wolf is the punisher. The dominated wolf is the punished.
- The dominant wolf can be mean. The dominated wolf must be meek.
- The dominant wolf can be nasty. The dominated wolf must be nice.
- The dominant wolf gets to raise his voice. The dominated wolf must be silent.
- The dominant wolf can use physical violence. The dominated wolf must "take it" and stand down peacefully.

- The dominant wolf can be proud. The dominated wolf must be humble.
- The dominant wolf is the rule maker. The dominated wolf is the rule follower.

The law of the dominance hierarchy is hypocrisy. There are two sets of rules. One for the strong and dominant. One for the weak and dominated. An unfair setup of "Your accountable to me…but I'm not accountable to you. I can hurt you. But you can't hurt me."

Tell me how this is any different than how all humans behave? In my lifetime, I've observed that humans behave this way in almost every single relationship "in the pack."

Let me prepare you for the world I brought you into. Almost every encounter with another person you will have in your life, will bring with it a wolf-like "sniffing out" moment to sense who is more dominant.

And in most cases, both of you will mystically settle into the roles of the dominator and the dominated. One becomes the judge and the other the judged.

And although these words may not be used, facial expressions (especially eyes), overall body language, and the vibe of spirit will clearly communicate something to this effect:

- **"I'm prettier than you are.** Therefore, I'm the dominator, you're the dominated. I'm the judge, you're the judged. Therefore, I can act better than you and treat you like crap."
- **"I'm older and more experienced than you are.** Therefore, I'm the dominator, you're the dominated. I'm the judge, you're the judged. I don't have to respect you. But you better respect me – or else."
- **"I'm richer than you are.** My clothes are nicer than yours. My parent's houses and cars are nicer than that of your parents. Therefore, I'm the dominator, you're the dominated. I'm the judge, you're the

judged. I'm cool. You're not. I can be proud and condescending to you. But you better be humble in my presence."

- **"I'm stronger than you are.** Therefore, I'm clearly the dominator, you're the dominated. I'm the judge, you're the judged. I can be mean to you. But you better be meek and mild in my presence – if you know what's good for you."
- **"I'm smarter than you are.** Therefore, I'm the dominator, you're the dominated. I'm the judge, you're the judged. I can pretend your invisible…unless you kneel before my brilliance…then maybe I will talk to you – in private. I don't want to hurt my image by being seen with you."
- **"I'm more talented and skilled than you are.** Therefore, I'm the dominator, you're the dominated. I'm the judge, you're the judged. I can make fun of you…but you must compliment me and recognize that I'm better than you."
- **"I'm more holy and virtuous than you are.** Therefore, I'm the dominator, you're the dominated. I'm the judge, you're the judged. I am good. You are bad. God is happy with me. God is unhappy with you. I am worthy of acceptance. You are worthy of rejection…unless you become like me."
- **In summary**, "I'm better than you. So I have the right to bully and belittle you."

If you understand this example of the wolf pack, you will understand much about this planet. You will understand how animal and human alphas rise to power. How dominance is gained and then maintained – through fear, force, and violence. You will "get it" as to why there is constant fighting and killing among animals and people on Earth. Both animals and humans are chronically fighting for a higher position on the dominance hierarchy. They all want to be the dominator, not the dominated. They all want to be the judge, not the judged.

But let's turn to the "king of beasts" for more insight into this concept of a dominance hierarchy.

CHAPTER 7

The Lion Pride: Dominators Have No Right, Just the Might

As we digest this concept of a dominance hierarchy, a lion pride is also enlightening. Let's focus on the pride male who ascends to leadership over 15 other lions.

What is it that gives one dominant male lion the *right* to rule a pride? WHO gave him *the authority* to rule and control the other lions?

The short answer is this: no one.

No one.

No one gives a male lion with an impressive mane the *right* to rule.

Interesting.

From the example of a lion pride I want to point out this irrefutable truth: dominators – any individual or group who is higher on a dominance hierarchy than you – do not have a *right* to rule you.

They only have the *might* to rule you.

The ancient saying of "might makes right" is a fact of life. It's how the world works.

Like the alpha wolf, as long as the male lion is strong enough in its mind, forceful enough in its personality, and powerful enough in its body to keep rival male lions subdued and intimidated, he will remain the leader and law maker of the pride. He makes the rules. He establishes the territory. He determines who eats and drinks first. He has sole breeding rights to pass on his genes.

Temporarily.

One day he will become less, while another male lion has become more. Another lion has strengthened his mind, grown in his physical body, been hardened through more life experience, and he is now ready to challenge the top lion. If the challenger possesses the *might* to win the *fight* against the present "king," he then also wins the *right* to rule the pride.

Might. Fight. Right.

It's the same for humans. The story of human history is the story of wolf-like, lion-like, alpha men which history labels as "Great" men. All over the planet, you will find stories of alpha men such as: Sargon the Great (Akkad), Cyrus the Great (Persian/Achaemenid), Alexander the Great (Macedonian), Constantine the Great (Roman), Akbar the Great (Mughal) Peter the Great (Russia), Frederick the Great (Prussia), among many, many others.

And those not carrying the title "the Great" certainly belong in this category of alpha humans. Examples would be Moses, Buddha, Jesus, Mohammad, Julius Caesar, Genghis Khan, Martin Luther, John Calvin, Kings of numerous people groups, Karl Marx, Gandhi, Adolph Hitler, American Presidents, etc.

You get the point. Alpha humans who lead massive human packs. Dominant humans who lead massive human prides.

Like wolves, these are the alpha men who gained and maintained dominance over other humans. How did they become the dominant "alpha"?

The same way a wolf or lion does, through spiritual power. Their force of personality came through some combination of being stronger, smarter, wiser, more virtuous, richer, more accomplished in battle, or courageous in the face of danger.

Like the alpha wolf, most of them used fear, force, intimidation, violence, cruelty, and brutality to maintain dominance over their subjugated peoples. Any hint of insubordination to their dominance would bring about the swiftest of judgment. Harsh judgment to strike fear into the hearts of any other people contemplating resistance and rebellion. And they constantly were at war and/or work to expand their territory and enlarge their dominion.

But WHO gave these alpha humans the *right* to kill, torture, subjugate, plunder (tax), intimidate, and enslave other humans?

God?

Some believe so. The Old Testament frequently presents Yahweh as being behind all the rising and falling of human kings and kingdoms (Isaiah 45:1; Ezra 1:1-2; Daniel 2:21). The New Testament presents God as ordaining all authority to maintain order in the world (John 19:11; Romans 13:1-2).

Really?

So God ordained the dominance hierarchy?

- Did God ordain perpetual war for the people of Earth to slaughter each other?
- Did he ordain, and even sometimes order, the not-so-unusual ancient practices of killing every man, woman (even pregnant ones), child, and baby during conquest (Joshua 6:21; I Samuel 15:3)?
- Did the Creator ordain the extreme normality of the raping of wives and daughters during invasion and conquering?
- Did God ordain the common practices of burning homes and villages and then displacing peoples from their homelands?
- Did the loving Heavenly Father ordain the subjugation and slavery of dominated peoples?

- Was the slave trade and thousands of years of subduing, selling, separating, and humiliating black people part of his predestined plan?
- Was it God's plan for Europeans to come to the Americas, kill millions of Native Americans through disease and war, seize their land, put them in concentrated areas, and make rules *for them* to govern their lives?

And how do Christians holding firmly to Romans 13:1 answer these following questions?

- Did the Triune God ordain the rise of your arch-rival Islam?
- How about the Ottoman Empire?
- Does the Christian God ordain all the Muslim rulers in Muslim nations today?

What about the last 100 years?

- Did God ordain Hitler's rise in Germany and the eventual Holocaust?
- Did God raise up Joseph Stalin and ordain the formation of the Soviet Union?
- How about Mao in China?
- Pol Pot of Cambodia?
- Did God really ordain the killing of 100 million people at the hands of their ruling classes in the 20th century? Was that his plan? Does God ordain genocide?

How about the leaders of the United States?

- Did God raise up Barack Obama? Was his election God's act of deliverance for the liberal left wing? Or was it God's judgment on the conservative right wing?
- Did God raise up Donald Trump? Was his election God's salvation for the conservative right? Or was it God's judgment on the liberal left?

It begins to be a very infuriating conversation when you believe God rules the world through *his* ordained rulers, tyrants, and oppressors. Is God really pro-freedom, or is he actually pro-slavery? Did God ordain the dominance hierarchy?

I don't know. If there is a God, I sure hope not.

But what I presently believe is this. As I observe history and the present world, I see a more natural explanation. It all looks like one, big battle for survival. It all looks like one, big dominance hierarchy. And dominant humans were/are like the male lion. Most alpha humans in history simply had the *might* to win the *fight*. Which in their minds gave them the *right*.

Temporarily.

Like a male lion, one "great" man's supposed right to rule lasts only until he loses the fight against an even more dominant "great" man. And in these fights for dominance, let's not forget the respective soldiers and subjugated peoples under the control of these men. People who are forced to live in the drama created by the alpha humans dominating them.

Take King George III as prime evidence that it is only the *might* to win the *fight* that gives the supposed *right* to rule. Who gave King George III the right to rule the 13 original colonies of America in 1775?

Did his right to rule come from God? If so, was declaring independence from George III's rule actually disobeying God? Was the American Revolution actually an act of Satanic rebellion?

Then how did King George III ever lose his God ordained right to rule the 13 colonies in 1781?

What changed?

- Was it actually God's judgment on George III?
- Was George III really that tyrannical, any more than any other leader in history?

- What did George III do to cross the line in God's mind that he ultimately lost the right to rule the 13 colonies?
- And why did God allow George III to continue ruling England? Why didn't God remove his right to rule there also?
- Was any of this supernatural narrative really taking place?

I don't think so. It's pretty simple. The whole world is one, big dominance hierarchy. This is the true "natural law." Might makes right is natural law. The dominance hierarchy is natural law.

King George III had the right until he lost the fight. When he lost the fight, he lost the right of ruling the 13 American colonies whose leaders had declared independence from his rule.

Starting to get the picture of what a dominance hierarchy is, and how it works?

Perhaps we are getting a little lost in the details. Let's take some time to rise above all these details. Let's attempt to see where the concept of a dominance hierarchy fits in the big picture of our universe.

CHAPTER 8

A Forest View of Planet Earth

There is an old saying, "Don't miss the forest for the trees." It's a simple way of saying don't miss the big picture (the forest) because you are so caught up in the details (the trees).

Think Water Rock Knob. You know that's one of our favorite places to go as a family. But it's a little bit of work to get there. As we travel through the entry gates of the Blue Ridge Parkway, we have to ascend for nearly 30 minutes until we arrive at Water Rock Knob. The elevation is nearly 6000 feet. Once we get up there, it feels like you can see everything. It seems like you can see the whole forest.

Literally.

It feels like from Water Rock Knob you can view the whole of Nantahala National Forest. You are also looking at the Great Smokies National Park, the most visited National Park in the country. And you are so high that you can even see another state. You can see Tennessee's highest peak, Clingman's Dome.

It's absolutely gorgeous to be that high and see the "big picture." To just step back and "see it all" from the single, unified perspective of Water Rock Knob.

The forest.

But imagine that we were 3000 feet lower somewhere in the middle of Nantahala National Forest and its over 500,000 acres. And as we were hiking on a trail, you became interested – nay, obsessed – by the millions of trees.

And not just the trees. You've now trained your mind to become so detail minded, you've also become preoccupied with the hundreds of millions of branches, limbs, leaves, veins in the leaves, and bug-eaten holes in the leaves.

As a result of becoming so lost in the billions (maybe even trillions) of details, you lose the "big picture" perspective. You forgot when, where, and how these trillions of details even fit in the overall setting of the forest they live in.

The trees.

"Don't miss the forest for the trees." Don't miss the big picture because you are lost in billions of details. Take some time to rise above all the details and see the overall view.

So far in this book, we've looked at a lot of trees. We talked about your birth. How you were born to be free – and with two diamonds in your hands. In your right hand was the diamond of your identity. In your left hand was the diamond of your inner peace.

But in your lifetime, there will be thousands of individuals and groups who want to steal your diamonds. Dominators that can take the form of massive power groups like the religious, ruling, and rich classes. And dominators can take the form of smaller practical groups and individuals like friends, neighbors, siblings, and parents.

Dominators want to control you. Dominators will threaten to hurt you if you do not submit to them.

Why?

Because the whole world is one, big dominance hierarchy. It's all about being the alpha in any scenario of life. It's about being the dominator, not the dominated. It's about being the judge, not the judged.

One gains and maintains dominance like an alpha wolf – through fear, force of personality, and the threat of violence. And like the dominant male lion of a pride, one has no "right" to control others this way, they just have the might.

At this point, it sort of feels like we are in the middle of Nantahala National Forest walking around wondering if we are lost. Not knowing how the world got this way, or why it is this way.

The point of the next few chapters is to go to Water Rock Knob. To get the "forest view." To climb to a place where we can "see it all." To get the big picture. To rise above the entire history of our planet, it's bloody battles for survival, the many forms dominators may take, the cruel dominance hierarchies that have evolved, and all of the pain, suffering, slavery, and confusion that its billions of inhabitants have felt – and still feel.

We are going to briefly rise above all that. And I'm going to give you my worldview. Literally, how I view the world. My big picture.

I'm old enough to know that there will be holes and shortcomings in my perspective. Perhaps significant. And in ten years, my ideas of how the world works may be far different than today.

But shortcomings aside, I'm at least going to be painfully honest. Dominators – both great and small – would hate this content. So be it.

If you understand what I'm about to say, it will help you better understand our world of slavery. And you will be better prepared to survive within it.

What I've done is given you a "How the World Works from A to Z." It is actually the foundation for another book I hope to write, "Why the World is Crazy from A to Z: A Prescriptive Path to Sanity." That book will be much more in depth than what I share here.

Each of the points will be intentionally brief. But its content belongs in any advice I would give you on how to live and how to feel free in a world of slavery.

Let me end this chapter by giving you the "forest view of my forest view" before I break it down into more detail in the next three chapters.

How the World Works from A to Z

Letters A to F – Life on Earth is one, big battle for survival.

A – **Alive** – I am alive. How? Why? Doesn't matter, because…

B – **Burden** – I carry a heavy burden to stay alive, to survive.

C – **Competition** – The biggest challenge to survival is competition.

D – **Dominance** – The key to survival is to gain dominance over a territory.

E – **Enemies** – An enemy is anyone who threatens my survival and dominance.

F – **Fighting** – Living means constant fighting for food, survival, and dominance.

Letters G to L – Survivability has a child: the dominance hierarchy.

G – **Group** – To increase one's chances of survival, many times groups are formed.

H – **Hierarchy** – Within the group, a dominance hierarchy or power ranking is formed.

I – **Intimidation** – Fear and intimidation is how group order works from top to bottom.

J – **Judgment** – Judgment comes to anyone challenging the order of the hierarchy.

K – **Killing** – Killing anyone challenging our survival, domination, or hierarchy.

L – **Law** – The law of the dominance hierarchy is hypocrisy.

The dominator lives by one set of rules. The dominated lives by a second set of rules.

Letter M – Survivability has another child: morality.

M – **Moralizing** – At some point in our history, humans moralized the dominance hierarchy.

Letters N to Z – Human moralization of the dominance hierarchy.

N – **Nobility** – dominant humans create the rich class and moralize it.

O – **Oligarchy** – dominant humans create the ruling class and moralize it.

P – **Priesthood** – dominant humans create the religious class and moralize it.

Q – **Quarantine** – the quarantine effect, separation of elites from enslaved.

R – **Regulation** – how the elites justify and moralize their domination.

S – **Subjugation** – how the elites maintain their domination.

T – **Taxation** – how the elites make the enslaved pay for their domination.

U – **Unquestioned** – how the elites never allow anyone to question their domination.

V – **Violence** – the only way the elites gain and maintain dominance.

W – **War** – how the elites spread their dominance and increase power.

X – **Xenophobia** – how the elites justify and moralize the spread of their domination.

Y – **Yoke** – All humanity is living under the heavy yoke of elite domination.

Z – **Zoo –** We're all slaves on display in some zoo created for us by the elites.

Now that I've given you the "forest view of my forest view," let me explain it more fully.

CHAPTER 9

How the World Works from A to Z

(Letters A to L)

Now in my mid-forties, I'm down to this statement when it comes to understanding this crazy world and empathizing with every person and group I encounter. Slowly read the following statement.

Everybody is, what he or she is, because they had to become that – in order to survive.

I recommend you re-read that a few more times.

I have found very few (if any) exceptions to this statement.

Remember this statement if you want to understand your mother. Why is she such a "tough cookie"? Why is she so confrontational at times? Remember that she had three older brothers. A couple of which could be physically abusive at times. Your mother is, the way she is, because she had to become that – in order to survive.

If you want to understand me, remember this statement. Why did your Dad use to be a preacher, but no longer is? Why does he not go to church with us? Why does he now do lawn care, flip houses, and attempt to write books? Because I am, the way I am, because I had to become that – in order to survive.

- Why do some people get out of religion? They had to become that – in order to survive.
- Why do some people get into religion? They had to become that – in order to survive.
- Why do some people adopt diverse lifestyles? They had to become that – in order to survive.
- Why do people usually conform to the culture they were born into? They had to become that – in order to survive.
- Why do some people become obsessed with rule-keeping and obedience to the power classes? They had to become that – in order to survive.
- Why do some men become woman haters? Why do some women become man haters? They had to become that in order to survive.

Everybody is, what he or she is, because they had to become that – in order to survive.

And I believe that this is not just true at the individual level. I believe it is also true at the collective, group level. Every religion. Every nation. Every tribe. Every people group. They are, the way they are, because they had to become that – in order to survive.

And I can make this a global argument as well. The Earth is, the way it is, because it had to become that – in order to survive. In the past, and in the present.

As I give you letters A to L of my forest view of how the world works, I must tweak something I've been saying so far. I've repeatedly been saying that the whole world is nothing more than one, big dominance hierarchy. That's true. But it's incomplete.

It is true that the cause and origin of Earth's pain, suffering, and oppression is a dominance hierarchy governing every level of existence. But what

I have not shared with you yet is this. The dominance hierarchy is not just a cause, it is an effect.

What caused the dominance hierarchy? Where did it come from? How did it form? Why did it form? Who or what is the parent that gave birth to the dominance hierarchy?

I'm going to add a layer to what I've been saying so far. More specifically, Earth is nothing more than one, big battle for survival. Which *caused* Earth to become nothing more than one, big dominance hierarchy.

Earth is, what it is, because it had to become that – in order to survive.

As I give you my forest view of how the world works, you will see that living on this planet is nothing more than one big battle for survival which gave rise to dominance hierarchies.

Here are letters A to L of your father's "How the World Works from A to Z." Letters A to L are true for BOTH animals and humans.

Letters A to F – Life on Earth is one, big battle for survival.

A – **Alive**.

I am alive.

I exist.

How?

Why?

Don't know. *No one* does.

Most think that there is one God who created all that we see.

Some think it was gods.

Some think it was purely chance and natural processes.

A few think it was an advanced species from another world that created life on this planet.

But the harsh reality: *no one* really *knows*.

Which leaves all of us with *belief* instead of *knowledge*. We all believe something as to how we got here. But none of us truly *knows* how or why we are alive.

And it doesn't really matter because…

B – Burden.

I have a burden on me to stay alive. I am carrying a heavy, heavy load to just to *stay alive* – to survive.

Because of this, I have a natural fear of death. I must survive by eating, avoid being killed, and reproducing myself.

C – Competition.

The biggest challenge to survival is competition. On Earth, there are tens of billions of other living creatures alive. And they are all carrying the same burden to survive by eating, avoiding being killed, and reproducing.

D – Dominance.

The key to survival is to gain physical dominance and ruling control over a territory – whether the territory is land, water, or sky. This is the key to survival, be the dominant one – the one in power. To control the territory is to control the resources – especially food – that can be gathered in that territory.

E – Enemies.

The other living humans and animals competing for territory and resources become natural enemies. You hate them because they threaten your survival. They hate you because you threaten their survival. This is the origin of Earth's problematic "us vs. them" and "we're the good guys…and you're the bad guys" paradigm.

F – Fighting.

Billions of living creatures all trying to stay alive through establishing dominance over a territory to gather resources means one thing: constant fighting. Fighting to gain dominance over the territory. Fighting to keep dominance over the territory. Fighting to kill others for food or as food.

Letters G to L – Increasing the odds of survival.

G – Group.

To increase one's chances of survival, many times groups are formed. Gaining dominance over a territory is easier as a group. Gathering resources, killing for food, and protecting that food is easier as a group. Think back to our examples of the wolf pack and the lion pride. Avoiding being killed is easier as a group. Protecting the offspring is easier as a group. Groups can be called packs, prides, herds, schools, flocks, families, tribes, nations, religions, gangs, etc.

H – Hierarchy.

Within the group, a hierarchy or ranking is formed. One dominant individual, an alpha, gains dominance over the others through fear, intimidation, and sheer force of mind, body, and will. Within the group, individual relationships function similarly.

This is called a dominance hierarchy. It is a power ranking within the group from the strongest to the weakest. This too means even more fighting as individuals attempt to rise up the dominance hierarchy. Despite the chronic tension to maintain the order of this hierarchy, the goal remains constant: work together to survive.

Here is where you find a dominance hierarchy fitting within the big picture of existence on Earth. The dominance hierarchy is the child of survivability. The biggest problem on Earth is actually the battle for survival. This battle of survival is what gave rise to evolving dominance hierarchies.

I – Intimidation.

The dominance hierarchy, from top to bottom, from the strongest to the weakest is characterized by one word: intimidation. You must make another afraid of you so that they will submit to your control. You must fill the dominated one with fear of being hurt by you. The dominance hierarchy attempts to hold itself together by means of fear and intimidation.

In a book written to you about living and feeling free, know that intimidation (fear) always lays the rock-solid foundation for any house of slavery. Destroy the foundation of fear and you collapse the house of slavery.

To use another metaphor, think canned goods in Grandma Gowerstreet's cellar. They have a shelf life. Fear and slavery have the same shelf life. As long as fear remains, slavery remains. When fear expires and is thrown out, so is slavery.

The bottom line: the strong must intimidate and enslave the weak to keep them in their place. If one does not keep his place in the hierarchy....

J – Judgment.

The burden to survive makes living tough enough. The formation of a group organized by a dominance hierarchy was supposed to lighten that burden. However, in many ways, it only adds to the burden of existence. It makes group life one of constant judgment. Being judged all the time by everyone for everything. And judgment in the sense of punishment.

And the biggest "punishable crime" of all in a dominance hierarchy is to challenge a superior. This brings heavy judgment from the superior.

The superior will use whatever force is necessary to bring you back into submission. They will first use harsh, threatening vocalizations. If that doesn't work to get you back in line, they will then inflict light physical pain. If that doesn't intimidate you back into submission, they will become terrifyingly aggressive and inflict severe physical pain. If that doesn't work…

K – Killing.

Throughout its history, Earth has been a dangerous and deadly place to live. Not just because of disease and natural disasters. The biggest killer in world history is the battle for survival and the dominance hierarchy. Living creatures killing each other for food and resources to survive – the food chain. Living creatures killing each other for dominance over territories. Living creatures killing each other for disobedience to superiors within the dominance hierarchy.

L – Law.

The law of the dominance hierarchy is this: hypocrisy. The dominator lives by one set of rules. The dominated lives by a second set of rules. The dominator is the strong and the rule maker. The dominated is the weak and the rule follower. The dominator gets to be judge. The dominated gets to be judged. The dominator gets to hurt the dominated. The dominated is not allowed to hurt the dominator. The dominator is the master. The dominated is the slave.

The only way to change your fortunes in all this is to fight and win – to become the dominator.

We are halfway through.

Letters A-L is how animals have always lived and organized themselves.

But A-L is also how humans have organized themselves for most of human history. What makes human dominance hierarchies any different from animal dominance hierarchies?

One, massive difference. Which brings us to letter "M."

CHAPTER 10

How the World Works from A to Z
(Letter M)

M – Moralizing.

Humans moralize the dominance hierarchy. Something humans didn't always do. Something humans learned how to do.

Something animals have never done. Animal dominance hierarchies are solely about who's weak and who's strong. For thousands of years, human dominance hierarchies seemed to function identically to this.

But at some point in our human history, we created another skill for gaining and maintaining dominance: morality.

Humans learned how to moralize the dominance hierarchy. We learned how to make dominance over another person also a "who's right" and "who's wrong" matter. To make dominance over another human a "who's good" and "who's bad" scenario.

Some time ago, your oldest brother, Ray, asked me, "Dad, what is the worst evil on Earth?"

What. A. Question.

What is the worst evil on Earth?

Hmm…. I do not remember my initial answer to him. But in subsequent week's and month's I continued to meditate on that question. What *is* the greatest evil on the planet?

Sometime later I came back to Ray with this answer. "Ray, I believe the greatest evil on Earth is this: for one person to stand over another person and claim, 'I have the *right* to dominate you. If you submit to my domination…you're a good person. If you resist my domination…you're a bad person, and you deserve to be hurt by me."

This is the greatest evil on earth. To dominate another person, and then to moralize it.

Stated another way, the greatest evil on earth is: 1) to steal another person's two diamonds, 2) to deceitfully claim to be the "moral," rightful owner of the diamonds, and 3) to use the diamonds as the means of controlling that person.

There is nothing more subtilty evil than convincing yourself that you are "good" for claiming authority over someone who naturally desires autonomy. Believing that you are "good" for making someone your slave.

And that you possess the "right" to mentally program your slave. To brainwash your new slave into seeing themselves as "bad" (their identity) and to "feel bad" (their inner peace) if they ever resist your domination and want freedom from your control.

Domination and control that the dominated never agreed to. Domination and control that the dominated *would never agree to* if truly given a *free* choice.

And this claim of ownership and control gets even nastier. In their lust for power, dominators will even put on a highly colorful mask of piety. Dominators may even invoke the name of God in their slave-making process.

- "It is 'God's will' that *I* rule over *you*."

- "It is *my* divine right."
- "Resisting *me*, is resisting *God*."
- "God created *me* to be *your* master."
- "God created *you* to be *my* slave. I was born to dominate you."
- "You were born to be dominated by me."
- "It's the divine order of things. Don't fight it."

As a result, dominators actually convince themselves that they are holy for hurting you. That they have a right to punish you. That as a "righteous" dominator, they are "justified" and "good" for using fear, intimidation, anger, open palms, fists, whips, swords, racks, guns, torture, labels, criminalization, written records, confiscation of possessions and property, separation from family, confinement in cages, and condemnation to hell – all to keep you under their domination and control.

"You didn't submit to my domination. So this is what you 'deserve.'"

Animals don't even do this. That is, the moralizing propaganda part. For them, the dominance hierarchy was, and still is, all about survival. There is nothing moral about it. It has nothing to do with "ethics," "morality," "individual rights" or "what is right."

It's NOT about who's right and who's wrong. It's ALL about who's weak and who's strong. Land animals, birds, marine life, and insects are not labeled as "good" or "bad" because they organize themselves by a dominance hierarchy. And no reasonable human holds animals to any invented human standard of morality.

Think of our example of the dominant male lion.

- Humans do not judge and label the male lion as "immoral," "bad," or "evil" for beating up the weaker lions who are a threat to his dominance.
- Not even 21st century "woke" humans conclude that the dominant male lion is a "corrupt tyrant" and a "perv" who kills lion cubs to bring their mother into heat sooner.

- No human government has imprisoned a "terrorist" pride of lions for committing a "hate crime" against a Wildebeest that they ambush killed for their own survival.
- And you can be sure that the dominant male lion is not afraid of hell, the cell, or karma catching up to him for all of his "bad" behavior.

Again, in the animal realm, this behavior is all about survival. It has nothing to do with "morality." It has nothing to do with who's right and who's wrong. It's all about who's weak and who's strong. Period.

But humans have taken the dominance hierarchy to another level. At some point in our history, humans invented another powerful method of gaining and maintaining dominance.

Morality.

No one really wants to hear this, but it can be effectively argued that all human morality is an invention. Pick any general moral principle or specific moral particular. Even "big stuff" like murder, rape, and robbery. And then layout the history of that moral principle or particular on a homemade timeline.

As "moral" principles, even murder, rape and robbery had starting points. That is, a time in history when external, societal guilt BEGAN to be applied and punished. And a time in history when internal, personal guilt BEGAN to be felt for committing these hurtful actions.

Take murder as an example. Today, murder is almost universally recognized as evil. But for thousands of years, killing was seen only as a matter of survival. Humans killing other humans was as common as lions killing other lions and other competitors like hyenas in a battle for survival.

For millennia, murder wasn't "bad." Just normal behavior by living organisms fighting to survive. Even among humans.

Religions may object to these comments with, "No, the command of "Thou shalt not kill "came from God!"

When?

Even the strictest Genesis timeline reveals morality as being extremely undeveloped and generic in the first 2500 years after Creation.

- Adam and Eve never received any of the 10 commandments before or after their expulsion from Eden.
- The "no murder" command finally came after Noah's Flood at least 1500 years after Creation (Genesis 9:6).
- The 10 Commandments did not come until at least 1000 years after that (Exodus 20:1ff.).

Morality from ANY worldview was a slow developing process. Even the most obvious moral particular of "no murder."

It doesn't take a lot of research to see that for thousands of years, human dominance hierarchies functioned almost on par with animal dominance hierarchies. Where humans had little or no internal guilt when stealing one another's harvested food in order to survive. Where humans had no shame slaughtering whole villages of rival tribes.

In fact, they would even gloriously celebrate such accomplishments. They were not tossing and turning in some guilt-ridden sleep pondering, "I've killed so many people. How will I ever live with myself?"

To the contrary, you can find more evidence that they felt good instead of bad by most of their survival instinct behaviors.

Why did humans begin at some point in their history to start making "moral" judgments?

My answer: the burden to survive.

Survivability has produced many children. The burden to survive gave birth to dominance hierarchies. It is my belief that the burden to survive also gave birth to morality.

Morality is the child of survivability. Both for the dominators and for the dominated. For the strong, morality was (and still is) a survival skill to gain and maintain power. To justify their dominance. For the weak, morality was (and still is) a survival skill for protection against dominators.

Morality is all about survivability from BOTH the perspectives of the powerful and the powerless.

- BOTH the powerful and the powerless use morality to reason: "This is why you CAN'T hurt me."
- BOTH the powerful and the powerless use morality to reason: "This is why I CAN hurt you."

In a world that is one, big battle for survival. In a world that is one, big dominance hierarchy struggle. Morality was developed as a masterful manipulation technique for gaining and maintaining dominance.

That is why religion and government have always been a source of perpetual debate and conflict. "Don't talk religion or politics!"

Why?

Because these are explosive moral debates. These are passionate fights over what is right and wrong, who is good and bad, and who should be punished and hurt. These are modern power struggles to gain the dominant position.

And "winning" the moral debate means you get to be the judge and punisher of other human beings. And history has proven that humans love to hurt each other.

Why?

We hurt, to keep from being hurt. "I will hurt you…to keep you from hurting me."

And humans have learned to use morality as a weapon. An extremely powerful weapon to actually justify hurting another person.

Don't believe this?

It's pretty amazing the stuff that comes out of our mouth when we spout our "moral" indignation and outrage at our enemies.

- "They're going to burn forever in hell!"
- "They should be wiped off the face of the Earth!"
- "Kill 'em all!"
- "Lock them up and throw away the key!"
- "I hope their kids die!"

Such hatred and venom only expose that we are moral frauds. That love is not the gasoline our moral engine is running on. Hatred is. And morality is often used to disguise our lust for power, domination, and desire to hurt others.

It is my belief that morality was created by humans as a powerful weapon for claiming the high ground, the position of dominance. To become the judge, not the judged. To become the punisher, not the punished. To be the first to blame, so that we are not blamed.

Slowly digest what I am about to say. It is my firm conviction that human dominance hierarchies have NEVER stopped operating like animal dominance hierarchies. Humans still organize themselves like wolf packs and lion prides.

But at some point in our history, humans deceived themselves into moralizing the tribalism, bullying, intimidation, cruel judgments, killing, and hypocritical double standard. Humans learned how to morally justify behaving like animals and rationalizing that such behavior was "good," "moral," "ethical," and "right."

In my view, this is why so much evil is done in the name of "good." Why so much immoral and excessive cruelty is done in the name of enforcing "morality."

- As one old time preacher stated it, moralizing dominators always "get the devil in them, getting the devil out of everyone else."
- Moralizing dominators will usually commit 100 sins in their attempt to crusade against 1 sin. Think of our ruling class dominators and the devastating consequences of their COVID-19 lockdowns.
- Moralizing dominators are always wolves in sheep's clothing. The predatory and vicious disguise themselves as the passive and harmless.
- Stated another way, moralizing dominators do not present themselves as grotesque demons of darkness, but as angels of light. Villainous persecutors disguise themselves as virtuous protectors.

But underneath their fake mask (facemask) of piety is their lust for power. A moralizing dominator's desire to hurt is every bit as strong – or stronger – than their desire to help.

Morality is clearly the child of survivability from the perspective of the strong. It has helped the strong gain and maintain dominance. It has helped them justify all manner of cruelty against anyone resisting their dominance. To justify hurting others as a protection from being hurt themselves.

But morality is also the child of survivability from the perspective of the weak. It has helped the weak to survive in a world of dominators.

Interestingly enough, this is why morality has evolved into being THE weapon of choice to claim dominance. You no longer have to be the biggest, strongest, best looking, or smartest to be a dominator.

Moralizing is the "Everyman's" domination tool. All you have to do is: 1) claim to be someone's judge, 2) condemn their words or ways of living, and 3) crusade for them to be disproportionally hurt. Which only makes us immoral in our zeal to moralize. Which reveals our true motive as being dominance, not moral indignation.

We presently call this behavior "virtue signaling." I hate the term. It's so vague and non-impactful emotionally.

"Virtue signaling" simply means that people are attempting to gain dominance through moralizing. That they are the "good" person with the moral high ground. That they are "good" by living one notch stricter in some area of life. That this somehow makes them the judge and punisher of other people. Those not measuring up to their invented standard of virtue and goodness.

"Virtue signaling" is a survival technique that greatly benefits the weak. It's a way for the weaker "Barney Fifes" in this world to feel powerful. It's their way of claiming dominance and being better than others.

But "virtue signaling" will never heal the world. When we moralize to feel powerful and dominant, it merely turns us into hypocritical, self-righteous pricks whose purpose in life is to find meaning in being "gooder" than everyone else. And most people listening to our moral sermons can feel that our vibrational frequency is hatred, not humility. That our intent is to hurt, not heal.

Can you see how morality is the child of survivability – from the perspectives of BOTH the strong and the weak?

Is this the true origin of morality?

I don't know.

But it is what I currently believe, and it makes sense to me. That morality is the child of survivability.

Think of any "moral" law, rule, command, etc. invented by human beings. And then ask "Why?" The survivability of either the weak or the strong is almost always the unspoken answer. Some basic examples would be:

- "Thou shalt not kill." Why? So I can survive.
- "Don't drink and drive." Why? To increase the chances of my survivability.
- In some cities, "Don't use your property as a vacation rental." Why? So Holiday Inn can survive.

- "Don't commit treason against your King." Why? So the royal family can survive and stay in power.
- "Don't leave and apostatize from your religion." Why? So the religion can survive.
- "Apply social distancing at all times." And all the rules surrounding the COVID-19 Lockdown. Why? Every government dominator will claim their rules are to save lives. Survivability is their sole justification for their "moral authority." And therefore, you are a "bad" person" for disobeying or disagreeing with the rules they've invented.

You get the point. Morality is the child of survivability. And in many, many cases so-called "morality" is nothing more than a survival technique to either stay in power, or as a protection from power.

At this point I need to clarify something. I do believe that humans moralizing the dominance hierarchy has had BOTH a positive effect, and a negative effect on Earth.

On the positive side, creating morality helped humans become "civilized." To allow for civilization, for humans to peacefully co-exist – at least in theory. Moralizing human dominance hierarchies made them slowly and progressively appear less like the vicious, bloody, coercive, cruel, and deadly wolf packs and lion prides.

And this seems to be at least partially true when studying written history. It could be argued that Alexander's Macedonian Empire conquering the Persian Empire made that portion of the world one notch more "civil." The result: the world became a little less coercive and a little less cruel. While still remaining very coercive and cruel.

The Roman Empire eventually assumed power where the Macedonian Empire had. The result: the world became a little less coercive and a little less cruel. While still remaining very coercive and cruel.

Monotheistic religions such as Roman Catholic Christianity and Islam eventually assumed power where the Pagan Roman Empire once held authority. The result: it's possible that the world became a little less coercive and a little less cruel. While still remaining very coercive and cruel.

In the last 500 years, Protestant Christianity has made great inroads throughout the world. The result: the world became a little less coercive and little less cruel. While still remaining very coercive and cruel.

In the last 250 years, Democracy has spread throughout the world as Monarchy has minimized. The result: the world became a little less coercive and a little less cruel. While still remaining very coercive and cruel.

Humans moralizing the dominance hierarchy has had a positive effect on the planet. We can all hotly debate as to how much or to how little. And the world is still on a slowly rising upward trajectory of growing a little less coercive and a little less cruel. While still remaining very coercive and cruel.

And I have to be honest enough to admit something else. Someone can effectively argue that failure to dominate some people *would actually be immoral*. That for their own good, less developed people groups with vicious and cruel behaviors need to be dominated by more advanced people groups. That the Catholic Spanish Conquistadors needed to dominate the Aztecs to help shut down their practice of human sacrifice. That England needed to bring India up to the modern era. Therefore, to NOT dominate such groups would have been immoral.

Fair enough. My only problem with this is when we do not recognize at least two IMMORAL by-products of such "moral" domination. First, that dominators masquerading as "liberators" always have mixed motives. Their motives are not pure through and through.

Did the Spanish "morally" dominate the Aztecs out of love with no strings attached? Did the Conquistadors have the sole motive of bettering the lives of the Aztecs expecting nothing in return?

Or were they happy to also steal gold in their Christianizing process? Was it both sharing God and stealing gold that were their motives? If so, can you really call this "moral" domination?

Did the British Empire "morally" dominate the Indian subcontinent out of love with no strings attached? Did the British have the sole motive of bettering the lives of the Indians expecting nothing in return?

Or were they happy to simultaneously rob India of their resources? Was it both modernizing India and stealing natural resources that were their motives? If so, can you really call this "moral" domination?

How about America's recent practice of toppling Middle East nations? Are these acts of "moral" domination done out of love with no strings attached? Or are we happy to also rape these lands of their resources? "To the victor go the spoils!"

Dominators almost always plunder while they are "purifying." A mentality of, "While we're at it, let's rob these lands of their resources, and return them to the king!" Dominators sinfully steal from the people they allegedly are sanctifying.

There is a second immoral by-product of "moral" domination. Dominators usually corrupt as much as they "cleanse."

Dominators aren't perfect themselves. FAR FROM IT. Dominators attempting to rescue people from one set of immoral behaviors always seem to bring their own different set of immoral behaviors with them. Dominators may "cleanse" and "free" a people group from human sacrifice, widow burning, and bizarre sexual practices. Only to turn right around and enslave and corrupt the same "saved" people with their violence, cruelty, bigotry, greed, arrogance, elitism, and oppressive coercion.

And let's face it. The one immoral human behavior that dominators never seem to repent of is coercion.

Which brings us to the negative effects of humans moralizing the dominance hierarchy. The negative effects of moralized domination are clear. The consequences and results are devastating. The pages of written history are filled with explicit details of how dominant, alpha humans and their soldiers, police, rule makers, and judges have "morally" justified using all manner of coercion and cruelty to gain and maintain dominance.

Consider the following types of "just punishments" dominators have historically used against anyone resisting their domination. Notice how badly dominators behave forcing people to be "good."

- "Holy" wars and "Just" wars (notice the terminology, the moralizing of killing)
- Crusades and Inquisitions
- Gas chambers and Holocausts
- Ethnic cleansings and genocides (again, moralized murder)
- Slavery – the kidnapping, auctioning, and owning of other human beings
- Shootings
- Bombings and drone strikes
- Every method of cruel torture and interrogation imaginable
- Forced thirst and starvation
- Isolation and Exiling
- Killing one's family
- Staged mauling by wild animals – think of the Roman Coliseum
- Stealing property as "legal confiscation" or "spoils of war" (moralized theft)
- Fining as a punishment for profit scheme (a favorite in the 21st century)
- Stabbing, impaling, disemboweling, and quartering
- Humiliating by displaying one naked in public
- Electrocuting
- Waterboarding
- Tar and feathering
- Poisoning

- Chemical and Biowarfare
- Intentionally infecting one with a disease
- Boiling and burning alive
- Amputating, maiming and mutilating parts of the physical body
- Raping of women
- Abuse of children
- Burning of villages
- Beheadings
- Hangings
- Dragging
- Crucifixions
- Beatings and whippings
- Stoning
- Dungeons, prisons, and jails
- Gulags, concentration, and "re-education" camps
- Etc. Etc. Etc.

In this present day, if I did any of the above things to our neighbor, I would be viewed as being "immoral" and "evil."

But historically, each of the above human actions and behaviors were/are viewed as "moral," "just," and "righteous," because they were/are being done by moralizing dominators.

This is why power corrupts. Gaining and maintain dominance requires the dominator to act and behave this way and then to moralize it.

How can a dominator NOT begin to rot from the inside out?

This is the very essence of "corruption." Corruption is when a person in a supposedly "good guy" position is doing "bad guy" things.

Can you see why I believe that the greatest evil on the planet is the moralizing of one's dominance?

It is unimaginably and incomprehensibly evil that dominators can convince themselves that they are "good," "moral" and "just" when they:

- Coerce conformity – force their fellow humans against their wills and under the threat of being hurt to think, believe, say, do and be something.
- Maintain order and dominance over their fellow humans through the habitual fear of being hurt, caged, or killed.
- Threaten and terrorize their fellow humans with unimaginably brutal and disproportionate judgments.
- Kill hundreds, thousands, and even millions of their fellow humans.
- Willfully live by an intentional, hypocritical double standard.

The greatest evil on earth is moralizing the dominance hierarchy.

And let me return for one brief moment to the "just punishments" of dominators. Let's also not forget to include Christianity and Islam's biggest threat for those who resist their domination. The "only just punishment" for those who disagree with and disobey their standards of "morality." Their God will throw the "immoral" into a lake of fire where he will burn them alive.

For how long?

Not for 10 seconds – which would be enough. Not for 10 minutes. Not for 10 hours. Not for 10 days. Not for 10 months. Not for 10 years. Not for 10 decades. Not for 10 centuries. Not for 10 millennia. Not for 10 million years. Not for 10 billion years. Not for 10 trillion years. But he will burn the "immoral" alive for endless 100 trillion-year cycles in a lake of fire.

Forever.

In endless starvation, thirst, loneliness, and despair. With no offer of relief. With no intent to reform.

And mysteriously, a line is never crossed by God. Eternal hell is presented by much of Christianity and Islam as being a "just punishment."

Somehow this "just" punishment never transitions into "unjust" torture – like after 10 minutes.

Could you imagine watching someone get burned alive for 10 minutes? Or for a whole hour? How about for a whole day – literally binge-watching someone getting burned alive without them dying or decaying for 24 hours straight? Listening to them continually screaming in anguish and unfathomable misery. Even if it was your worst enemy, wouldn't you say *at some point*, "Yeah, that'll do it. I'm satisfied."

Not for the Christian and Muslim God. Even three consecutive 100 trillion-year cycles of burning someone alive is just "day one" of eternity. And his justice is somehow never satisfied.

Moralizing the dominance hierarchy. "Civilized" and "Moral" humans have made animals look sane and virtuous.

Why have humans become so "immoral" in the enforcement of their "morality"?

The answer: the law of the dominance hierarchy. Two sets of laws. One for the dominators. One for the dominated. The judge and the judged. The punisher and the punished. And at some point in human history, the dominators learned the survival skill of moralizing and justifying their domination.

It just never dawns on dominators how badly they behave forcing people to be "good." It never occurs to the dominator how dystopian the world becomes as they force their utopia on everyone else.

Power corrupts. Absolute power corrupts absolutely. Are you starting to see why that is?

It is utterly remarkable to me just how bad we become trying to "out-good" one another. How we use bad behavior to correct bad behavior. How we use cruelty to defeat cruelty. How we wear a fake moral mask to hide our real lust for power. How we use "virtue" as our justification for violence.

In a very confusing world, this one thing is clear to me: *"advanced" human societies are still organizing themselves like animals.*

Catch that?

What's wrong with the world? We still organize ourselves like animals.

"Progressive" human beings still use all the same methods of control that animals use. Look back over letters A to L of how the world works. Put a mental check mark next to any letter that no longer applies to "enlightened" humans.

They *ALL* still apply. All of them.

In the 21st century, humans still organize themselves like animals. Tribalism. Coercion. Fear. Intimidation. Cruel judgment. Killing. The law of hypocrisy.

IT'S. ALL. STILL. HERE.

And humans are even worse than animals because we moralize it.

Keep this in mind as I now share with you letters N to Z of how the world works.

CHAPTER 11

How the World Works from A to Z

(Letters N to Z)

In recent days, I've come to this realization, "Everything that now is, didn't use to be." Almost everything that exists in the present, did not exist in the past. Everything was created. Everything was invented.

Think of technology created in just the last 150 years.

- We now have artificial intelligence. We didn't use to.
- We now have satellites. We didn't use to.
- We now have drones. We didn't use to.
- We now have the internet. We didn't use to.
- We now have smart phones. We didn't use to.
- We now have computers. We didn't use to.
- We now have airplanes. We didn't use to.
- We now have cars. We didn't use to.
- We now have subways. We didn't use to.
- We now have electricity. We didn't use to.
- We now have televisions and radios. We didn't use to.
- We have refrigerators, ovens, and microwaves. We didn't use to.
- This list could go on and on.

The point is this. All of this modern technology that we now have, we didn't use to have. For thousands of years it didn't even exist on our planet. But at some point in our history, these things had a beginning. Humans invented these things. Now we can't even remember or envision a world without these things.

But the same is true for every other aspect of existence.

- You exist now. You didn't use to.
- Your mother and I exist now. We didn't use to.
- Your brothers exist now. They didn't use to.
- Your living grandparents exist now. They didn't use to.
- The house you live in exists now. But it didn't use to.
- The town you live in exists now. But it didn't use to.
- The county you live in exists now. But it didn't use to.
- The state you live in exists now. But it didn't use to.
- The United States of America exists now. It didn't use to.
- China exists now. It didn't use to.
- Every nation on earth that exists now, didn't use to.
- Heck, animals and humans exist now. But they didn't use to.
- The Earth exists now. But it didn't use to.
- Our sun and solar system exist now. They didn't use to.
- The universe exists now. From the viewpoints of both religion and science, it didn't use to.

At some point in history, all these things were created. They ALL had a beginning. Now we can't even remember or envision a world without these things.

Everything that now is, didn't use to be. Everything that exists in the present, didn't exist in the past.

This must be remembered about the dominance hierarchy.

- The dominance hierarchy exists now. It didn't use to.

- Slavery now exists. Ready for this? It didn't use to.
- Humans now moralize the dominance hierarchy. They didn't use to.
- This moralization has created hundreds of religious and political dominators, along with their systems of dominance, that now exist. They didn't use to.

Think of the religious class.

- Hinduism exists now. It didn't use to.
- Buddhism exists now. It didn't use to.
- Judaism and the Old Testament Bible exist now. They didn't use to.
- Catholic, Orthodox, Protestant, and tens of thousands of other Christian denominations – and the New Testament – exist now. They didn't use to.
- Sunni and Shia Islam and the Koran exist now. They didn't use to.

Every religion on Earth that presently exists. Every religious rule. Every religiously sanctioned punishment (including hell). Every religious leadership position. Every doctrinal belief. Every creed. Every dogma. Every fear-based manipulation technique these religions use to retain their adherents. All these things now exist.

They didn't use to.

All these things were created at some point by religious class dominators. And billions of people who were born into these religious systems can't remember or envision a world where these things didn't exist.

Think of the ruling class.

- Kings now exist. They didn't use to.
- Presidents now exist. They didn't use to.
- Royal families now exist. They didn't use to.
- All forms and systems of government that now exist. Didn't use to.
- Capitalism now exists. It didn't use to.
- Communism and Socialism now exist. They didn't use to.

- Sharia Law now exists. It didn't use to.
- Law creating bodies such as Congress and Parliament now exist. They didn't use to.
- All taxation that now exists. Didn't use to.
- Income tax now exists. It didn't use to.
- Property tax now exists. It didn't use to.
- Sales tax now exists. It didn't use to.
- You pick the tax, toll, license, permit, etc. that now exist. They didn't use to.

And laws in a million forms now exist. They didn't use to.

Not a one.

- Traffic laws now exist. They didn't use to.
- Building codes now exist. They didn't use to.
- Immigration laws now exist. They didn't use to.
- Compulsory education now exists. It didn't use to.
- Name any law that now exists for each and every detail of human existence. It didn't use to.

Every government on Earth that presently exists. Every position of power. Every law. Every punishment. Every judge and law-enforcer. Prisons. Guns. Tasers. Tear-gas. Every fear-based manipulation technique ruling classes use to keep people dominated. These all now exist.

They didn't use to.

All these things were created at some point by ruling class dominators. And all of us living inside these political systems can't remember or envision a world where these things didn't exist.

Think of the rich class.

- The real-life Monopoly game they invented now exists. It didn't use to.

- Money now exists. It didn't use to.
- Banks now exist. They didn't use to.
- Loans charging interest now exist. They didn't use to.
- The Federal Reserve now exists. It didn't use to.
- Stock markets now exist. They didn't use to.
- 30-year house mortgages now exist. They didn't use to.
- Students Loans for college now exist. They didn't use to.
- Life, auto, and health Insurance now exists. They didn't use to.

All these things were created at some point by rich class dominators. And all of us living inside this real-life Monopoly game can't remember or envision a world where these things didn't exist.

Everything that now is, didn't use to be. Everything that exists in the present, didn't exist in the past.

Hallie, remember this. Because this truth will set you free. All the things of this Earth that seem so dominating, monstrous, controlling, and ETERNAL – aren't. The whole world is one, big battle for survival. And this struggle to survive resulted in our planet being nothing more than one, big dominance hierarchy. A dominance hierarchy that humans ultimately moralized as a means of greater dominance, advantage, and control.

Remember, you were born free. No one has the "right" to dominate you. No one has the "right" to make you a slave of their system. No one has the "right" to own you. No one has the "right" to order you around. No one has the "right" to oppress and hurt you.

Learn to stand up straight and look any potential dominator in the eye. And then tell them these two important truths: 1) I was born to be free, and 2) I wasn't born to be dominated by you.

As we finish up the *forest view* of "How the World Works from A to Z," we are going to see letters N to Z. You will see what the world currently looks like – one where humans have moralized the dominance hierarchy.

Earth seems so on "lockdown" and completely dominated by powerful dominators. The whole situation looks hopeless. However, as you read how the world presently works, and how the world presently is, just keep reminding yourself of this fact: *everything that now is, didn't use to be.* And let your hope and mission be this: *everything that now is, one day will no longer be!*

N – Nobility.

Dominant humans create the rich class and moralize it. The human dominance hierarchy now moralized breaks down into two general categories: the nobility and the nobodies. The elites and the enslaved. The rich and the poor. Masters and servants. Sovereigns and serfs. The have's and the have nots.

The rich class has been created. And as a result, caste and class systems.

The nobility controls the ownership and decision making of a given territory and its resources. The nobility is a tiny minority of important somebodies in contrast to the very large majority of unimportant nobodies.

While the nobles will do all in their power to look kind, good, and just in their superiority, they cause humans to continue to organize themselves like animals. These elites wear a moral mask to disguise their lust for power.

Do you want to know if the nobility really are nice people? Disagree. Disobey. Do your own thing. See what happens.

In the 21st century, it's still the dominators vs. the dominated. The elites vs. the enslaved. And the enslaved are at the mercy of the elite.

Historically, the nobility has moralized the caste and class systems as "god's will" and "God's ordained order." They're on top. And it's God's plan. Rebelling and resisting such "divine order" would have been viewed as satanic, evil, and immoral. The nobility love moralizing the dominance hierarchy.

O – Oligarchy.

Dominant humans create the ruling class and moralize it. An oligarchy is created. That is, a few who will dominate, rule, and control the many. And I will put monarchy (rule by one) under the broader heading of oligarchy. It doesn't matter if it's one person or 600, it is still the few ruling the many.

In the oligarchy, the ruling class dominators moralize their domination by declaring it to be "officially" and "authoritatively" justified, legalized, and codified. Societal "order" is established. The few rule the many. The few are "good" for ruling. The many are "good" if they obey the few. The many are "bad" if they resist the few.

This is the formation of the power and punishing class. As a result, you have the punishers and the punished. The judge and the judged. The ruling class and the ruled class. The rule makers and the rule followers. The royal family and the rabble. The king and his kingdom.

Sometimes the rich class and the ruling class are one in the same. Sometimes the rich class simply bosses the ruling class around and tells them what to do.

P – Priesthood.

Dominant humans create the religious class and moralize it. The human dominance hierarchy now moralized finds its most controlling ally in the priesthood. The religious class comprised of God's "priests." Or, many other "p" words could have been used such as "pope," "prophet," "preacher," or "pastor."

The priesthood is anyone claiming to know the mind of God and his allegedly revealed "morality." The priesthood or religious class creates yet another form of dominant elite that the dominated enslaved are forced to submit to.

To be fair, it must be pointed out that many religions were formed – not from the dominate position, but from the dominated position. But whether its Christianity or Islam, once a religion builds up enough momentum and *might* to win the *fight*, their disposition suddenly changes. They now believe they have gained the *rights* that go with being a dominator.

The formerly docile religion inevitably begins behaving like their former dominators. Those who were persecuted in the past, inevitably become the prosecutors of the present. The powerless have become the powerful. And you can be sure that they moralize the dominance they have gained in order to maintain it.

The priesthood and the religious class create a similar divide within humanity that the rich and ruling classes do. You now have the "moral" and the "immoral." The righteous and the unrighteous. The good and the bad. The worthy and the unworthy. Sinners and saints. Clean and unclean. Pure and impure. God's children and Satan's children.

Q – Quarantine.

The quarantine effect is a separation that is made by the elites from their enslaved. A separation is created by dominators from their dominated. The moralization of the dominance hierarchy always creates this quarantine effect within human society. That is, a separation by the nobility *from* the nobodies, of the elite *from* the enslaved.

And this quarantine effect will be symbolized in every way. The quality of life for the elite dominators will be superior in all things. Their lavish housing (usually a protected palace or castle), their exotic food and wine, their colorful and expensive clothing, their elite and powerful friends, and their top-of-the-line transportation all look superior, because they are. The few, elite dominators quarantine, isolate, and make themselves untouchable from the masses they are dominating.

The quality of life for the dominated will be inferior. Their housing, their food, their clothing, their friends, and their transportation will all be inferior to their dominators. In many cases, by an extremely wide margin. And their dominators expect them to rejoice in this quality of life disparity. The dominated are to view their dominator's survival and quality of life as more important than their own.

This whole quarantine effect is a complete sham. The "regal power" that the dominators parade around with, looks far more "civil," "moral" and sophisticated than a lion pride or wolf pack.

But do not be deceived. It's all a lie. Letters A-L of the dominance hierarchy are fully operational. This is the animal dominance hierarchy in a despicable, human, moralized form.

R – Regulation.

How the elites justify and moralize their domination. The chief tool humans use when moralizing a dominance hierarchy is regulation.

Rules, rules, and more rules. And after that, more rules.

Dominators have a way they want the world to be. So they gather in small meeting rooms to decide how to control, employ, and appease the dominated. They create rules that the enslaved must obey. And with each rule they create, they also create a way to hurt the person who disagrees and/or disobeys.

Some of the rules the elite have created are understandable for all human survival (no murder, no rape). But many hundreds and thousands of these rules are complete frauds. They do not reflect what is right and wrong. They simply represent who's weak and who's strong. The will of the dominators. Not the will of the dominated.

These rules simply reflect what is best for the elite and adequate for the enslaved. These temporary, arbitrary, fluid rules are called "laws" to give them more of a fixed, permanent, and intimidating sound. Doing this puts fear into the hearts of the enslaved so that they stay dominated.

S – Subjugation.

How the elites maintain their domination. The tiny number of elites cannot subjugate and control the massive population of the enslaved by themselves. They hire men to threaten with violence anyone who disagrees or disobeys. Police and soldiers with swords, guns, bombs, tasers, gas, clubs and cages carry out the fear, force, and intimidation of their elite masters. Judges are appointed to also enforce the will of the elites.

Positions of punishing power become attractive to many of the dominated because it is ascension upwards in the dominance hierarchy. It makes the unimportant feel important. It makes the unimportant nobody feel like an important somebody. It makes the powerless feel powerful.

T – Taxation.

How the elites make the enslaved pay for their own domination. The elite force the enslaved to pay taxes. They use coercion to make the dominated ones pay for the real-life Monopoly game the dominators have designed for them.

There is no choice. You are not free to opt out. You must play their game. You must pay for their game. You must pay for the services they have chosen for you. And you will be punished severely – even killed or caged – if you resist.

And this coercive taxation is always moralized. Theft is made "moral" and "legal" when the dominators are the ones doing it. Dominators will take by force as much as they want. And after taking your money, they will spend it how they want.

Never say that you live in a free country.

- If coercive taxation exists, you are not free. You are dominated.
- If you do not have a choice, you are not free. You are enslaved.

- If society is no longer one of voluntary cooperation, but only one of involuntary submission, you are not free.
- If refusing to surrender a portion of your money to the dominators – no matter how small the percentage – means that they will forcefully claim ownership over 100% of your life to be placed in their cage, you are not free.

Coercive taxation means that you are owned. You are entirely a slave.

U – Unquestioned.

How the elites never allow anyone to question their domination. A dominators self-assumed right to control their dominated is never to be questioned. It cannot be questioned. It cannot be spoken against. It cannot be criticized.

Dominator's will threaten the masses of their dominated with loud and frequent messages to be afraid of them. To never question them. They hold up the diamonds of identity and inner peace formerly in the possession of the enslaved, and they remind them: "Anyone resisting my domination is 'immoral,' 'evil,' and 'worthy' of the severest punishment."

The rich, ruling, and religious classes, the unholy trinity of power, have always had this in common: "Because I said so." You will be viewed as a rebellious sinner or criminal if you question the authority of the elite dominator.

You will be censored. You will be silenced.

The law of the dominance hierarchy, hypocrisy, is in full effect. The elites demand that the enslaved are accountable to them. The dominated cannot hold the dominator accountable. Here again lies the greatest evil on earth: the moralizing of the dominance hierarchy.

V – Violence.

The only way the elites gain and maintain dominance. Animals have always gained and maintained dominance through fear and violence. Humans have always gained and maintained dominance through fear and violence.

But it is only the humans, not the animals, who moralize this method of violence.

And it is only the humans, not the animals, who act confused as to why the world is so crazy. "Enlightened" and "Civilized" humans still haven't been able to grasp this very basic fact: *the world is tearing itself apart, because dominators try to hold it together through fear.* Fear and the threat of violence.

At some point, maybe humans will think "outside the box," and try organizing a society without using fear, force, and the threat of violence.

A world without violent coercion. Imagine that.

Unfortunately, 21st century human dominators continue to use violence as their primary method for maintaining dominance and control of their territories. Dominators use violence as the weapon of choice to coerce conformity.

And dominators also continue to use violence to invade other territories to expand their domination. More territory means more resources. The surest path of the elite to conquer more, in order to obtain more, is violence. This means constant…

W – War.

How the elites spread their dominance and increase their power. The elites want constant war, 1) to spread their ideology of how the world should be organized, 2) to claim ownership and dominance over more territory, and 3) to gather more resources.

And dominators will force their dominated to do their fighting *for* them. The destinies of the enslaved are always at the mercy of the elites. Elite, alpha humans who threaten other elite, alpha humans with invasion and bombings, etc.

At no time in recorded history has the entire planet been at peace, free from war.

Why?

Go back to letter A and review. Earth is nothing more than one, big dominance hierarchy in one, big battle for survival.

Elites have their armies invade other territories, kill other people groups, and steal their resources. And it is always moralized and sanitized by stating phrases such as "to the victor goes the spoils."

Sounds a lot like a wolf pack or a lion pride.

War, war, and more war.

Why?

Dominators are never satisfied. Power does corrupt. Dominators are always looking to win the global Monopoly game. And as they view the rest of the "board" of the world, they are looking for other people to dominate. This creates…

X – Xenophobia.

How elites justify and moralize the spread of their domination. Humans have always battled xenophobia – fear of other peoples. People groups and individuals who have different skin colors, religions, beliefs, behaviors, and social customs.

The elite, human alphas who are society designers, do not like other elite, human alphas who design different types of societies. Human alphas see themselves as the "good guys," and their rival human alphas and their societies as the "bad guys."

Therefore, the elites like to point out the bizarre behaviors and practices of other people groups (sometimes legitimately) and see an opportunity to impose their rule on that territory. And while they are at it, the elites steal the resources of that territory.

Are you getting this?

Here again is the moralization of the dominance hierarchy by humans. Millions of people who make up the enslaved majority in each of these territories just want to be left alone, to live their lives in peace. But they are all forced into this drama by their elite, human alphas. Dominators who indoctrinate their dominated to hate others different from themselves.

Y – Yoke.

All humanity is living under the heavy yoke of elite domination. A yoke is the wooden device humans created thousands of years ago. The purpose of a yoke was to control the heads of cattle, bind them to other cattle, and force them to collectively plow their master's fields.

Human elites, dominators, have put a yoke on their fellow humans.

Human alphas have taken the way animals organize themselves for survival and perfected it. The elites have moralized the dominance hierarchy. They have created the unholy trinity of the rich, ruling, and religious classes to control the enslaved masses by a permanent external and internal yoke.

The dominated are crushed under a yoke of rules, a yoke of threats, a yoke of destruction and war, a yoke of debt, a yoke of hopelessness and despair. The dominated are made to play in the dominator's game. All the while the dominators moralize it to make it seem "good," and all part of the "greater good."

Something inside the enslaved knows that they want to be free. That they were born to be free. That they were not born to be dominated.

But to throw off the yoke of their dominators, they need relief from all the mental programming. Legions of the dominated look for temporary relief and find it in alcohol, drugs, sex, porn, video games, entertainment, etc. Addictions abound as they do not have the physical, mental, and spiritual power to throw off the yoke of their oppressors. Those in possession of their diamonds of identity and inner peace.

Z – Zoo.

The bottom line: we're all slaves on display in some zoo created for us by elite dominators.

A zoo is often used as a descriptive word for chaos. Perhaps you've heard someone say something like, "It's Black Friday. Don't go to Wal-Mart today. It's an absolute zoo!"

But actually, a zoo is a bad metaphor for chaos. A zoo is the complete opposite of chaos.

A zoo is extreme order. Formerly free and wild animals are now so docile and domesticated that they are a shell of their former selves. Their potential is next to nothing. They are comfortable. They are provided for. They are protected. But they are slaves.

The zookeepers of these animals may even be well-intentioned. If you listen to them, they will certainly moralize the superiority of this type of controlled environment for formerly free and wild animals.

Seeing any parallels to our elite dominators?

In a grand battle to survive, dominance hierarchies were formed. Survivability also gave rise to morality. Humans have moralized their dominance over one another to such a degree, that Earth is nothing more than hundreds of human zoos. Limited mobility. Limited potential. Limited thoughts. Limited speech. Limited ability to defend oneself. Limited choices. Dominated. Slaves.

Is this really the life we would choose if we truly had a *free* choice? If no coercion was being used against us?

This is your father's *forest view* of planet Earth. My big picture. My idea of "How the World Works from A to Z."

How right am I? How wrong am I? What did I overstate? What did I understate? I'll leave that for you to think through.

You can see why I feel such a big burden and responsibility to prepare you for the world I brought you into. You were born free. But you were brought into a world of slavery.

We all deeply desire to live free and to feel free in this one life we have on Earth. But instead we live and feel like slaves.

Why?

Because we are.

Being honest about this is a good start for walking a new path. A path that leads to living and feeling more free.

So how can anyone ever feel free in a world of diamond stealing dominators? How can anyone ever feel free in a world of slavery?

Let me give you a starter kit. Two indispensable survival skills that you will need for walking the path of freedom: 1) learning how to think, and 2) learning how to live above the judgments of others.

CHAPTER 12

Survival Skill #1 – Learning How to Think

In my twenties, and before I married your mother, I was a Bible Professor at Stewart Christian College (SCC).[4] I was trained by them and brought up through their system. This is the same school where I received my bachelors and first master's degree. For six years I taught classes such as Elementary Greek, Old Testament Survey, New Testament Survey, Life of Christ, Acts, Romans, and the General Epistles. It was a good gig and I did well at it.

At some point during my time as professor at SCC, they hired another man onto their Bible Faculty whom I will refer to as Dr. Roberts. A man who was not trained by SCC. But instead was trained by and had an earned doctorate from Dallas Theological Seminary in Texas.

I loved this guy. One of the most genuine, wise, compassionate, and connected human beings I have ever met. Everybody loved and respected him because he knew how to love and respect just about everybody. Funny how that works.

---

[4] Just a reminder that at my own discretion and for the protection of privacy, I have changed the names of individuals, organizations, and institutions. Stewart Christian College is a completely made-up name that I came up with.

One of the things I enjoyed about being a professor was having students line up outside my office door. They were coming to have me answer their questions or give them life advice.

Dr. Roberts had multitudes of students waiting outside his office to talk to him. But he also had many teachers (myself included) lined up to talk to him. He was so far above us in his knowledge, wisdom, and insight that we wanted his perspectives on everything. He was truly a teacher's teacher.

One day we asked Dr. Roberts a very pointed question. "Why are you here" (imagine me holding up my hand to represent a very high level), and why are us SCC trained guys here (holding my hand at a significantly lower level)?"

Dr. Roberts was a humble guy. But when answering this question, he did not hesitate, nor did he give some nauseatingly self-deprecating answer. Instead, he replied without skipping a beat, "Stewart teaches you what to think. Dallas taught us how to think."

Boom.

SCC indoctrinated you guys, they taught you what to think. Dallas Seminary educated me, they taught me how to think.

But before you think I'm completely throwing SCC under the bus, let me say this. Most colleges and universities do this. Again, it's all about survivability.

In the 21st century "institutions of higher learning" still teach young people what to think, instead of how to think. Almost every school of the rich, ruling, and religious classes indoctrinate. They do not educate. They all see their students as a "product" they're trying to "produce" and "put out there." In this day and age, going to college is a prison sentence for your mind.

But all colleges and universities will still claim to educate. That they are free and open-minded. But all you have to do is disagree or disobey. And you will be dismissed, defunded, and disgraced.

Dominators never want you holding the diamonds of your own identity and inner peace. They hold the diamonds. They control all the information. Dominators control how much, and to what extent, your neural pathways can flow and grow. You supposedly need them. You are supposedly helpless without them.

You were born into a world where information is more accessible than at any other point in Earth's history – by far. The internet, magazines, books, etc. abound. It's an exciting time to be alive.

But mere information does not mean truth. Mere information does not mean intelligence. Mere information does not mean wisdom. Mere information does not mean what is whole and healthy.

In the world you were born into, dominators all pass themselves off as "experts." The only springs from which all reliable information flows. Dominators know that it is hard to dominate someone who knows how to think. Their key to domination is to force-feed the dominated with what to think.

Dominators are always indoctrinators. First and foremost, they want to dominant your mind and your thinking. Dominators want to train and program your mind on what to think. It is how they gain and maintain dominance over you. It is why they need your diamonds.

Dominators have all learned the art of 1) controlling the information, 2) programming the minds and emotions of the dominated, and 3) demonizing any dissenting voices. Dominators as indoctrinators can be clearly seen in the following disguises.

- **The press** wants to teach you what to think, not how to think. These press dominators supposedly always get the "official" story right. The press or news media disguises themselves as "journalists" – who only want the truth. As being the real thinkers among us. But most people in the press are merely activists and propagandists for the rich and ruling classes who use them to teach you what to think.

- **The polls** are meant to teach you what to think, not how to think. Polls supposedly reflect the majority view on any subject. And polls carry with them a terrible assumption. That is, that the majority view (51%) on any subject has won the fight, and therefore the right of authority over the minority view. The majority view is in the dominant position on the information dominance hierarchy. It becomes the judge, not the judged. Therefore, it gets to act as judge over the minority view. It can label, condemn, and demonize the "loser" in the polls. Polls are an absolutely horrific approach to thinking and living. They are the very essence of false authority and bad thinking. They are the epitome of humanity's awful and foolish obsession with making large conclusions on small amounts of data.
- **The popular "cool crowd"** want to teach you what to think, not how to think. These are usually rich, famous, physically attractive, socially confident performers such as athletes, actors, and musicians. These cultural alphas supposedly use their celebrity and "platform" to influence others as to "right positions" on various subjects. And of course, these cool crowd dominators believe themselves to be the "right" moral example for all us little people.
- **The professors** definitely want to teach you what to think, not how to think. These "educational" dominators supposedly always organize, interpret and apply the information in a way that is "right." Professors supposedly have no biases, and they bring the clear, level-headed thinking that impressionable 18 to 22-year old's so desperately need. Uh huh.
- **The professionals** want to teach you what to think, not how to think. As long as these trade dominators are licensed and certified, they are supposedly infallible, and their proposed solutions will always be right for you and your family. You are not to think for yourself and seek solutions outside of "trained professionals." You'll mess things up. They never will.

- **The politicians** want to teach you what to think, not how to think. These ruling class dominators supposedly always "represent" what all the people want and always get the rules "right."
- **The preachers** want to teach you what to think, not how to think. These religious class dominators supposedly always represent God "right." Do you want to see an unhappy holy man? Disagree with him. See how he responds.
- **The parents** can also be very guilty of teaching you what to think, not how to think. Parents can even be the core dominators in a person's life. The bigger question is this: who is dominating the parents? Where do the parents get their information from? Who is thinking for the parents? Parents supposedly always know what is "right" for you. I'm holding myself accountable by including this.

If you are going to survive and thrive on this planet, you're going to need the survival skill of knowing how to think for yourself. Because dominators are indoctrinators.

"Stewart taught you what to think. Dallas taught me how to think."

I take this comment made to me, around 20 years ago, very personally. In a good way. I'm exceedingly grateful that Dr. Roberts said this. One crisp, concise line spoken by a wise man has made a profound difference in my life. And as a result, I hope it also makes a difference in your life.

Here's what I hope for you (and myself). That one day you can say to me something to this effect: "Dad, the other day someone asked me, 'Hallie, why are you here (holding their hand high), and why are the rest us here (holding their hand low)?' And Dad, without hesitation, I answered them, 'The press, the polls, the popular 'cool crowd,' the professors...all taught you *what to think*. My Mom and Dad taught me *how to think*.'"

Let me do that right now. I was indoctrinated. I know first-hand what it means to be taught what to think. But over the last 15 years or so, I have been learning how to think. And in this process of progressively learning how to think, I have created two acronyms.

The first acronym is "S.T.U.P.I.D." The six letters of this acronym correspond to six signs that alert me as to when my thinking is indeed stupid. Literally. The times in my life when I have put my mind and emotions in a position where they are either: 1) slow to grasp or understand something, or 2) presently incapable of grasping or understanding something.

When any or all of these six signs of S.T.U.P.I.D. thinking are present, I am reminded to stop. To quit doing these things. To be smart, not stupid. To be wise, not foolish. To be mindful, not mindless.

Which leads me to the second acronym. The second acronym is "S.M.A.R.T." The five letters of this acronym correspond to five signs that I am being guided by a smarter thinking process. The five signs of S.M.A.R.T. thinking are the polar opposites of the six signs of S.T.U.P.I.D. thinking.

When I find myself living by these five signs or characteristics of smart thinking, life is better. I have put my mind in a position where it is much more capable of grasping or understanding something. I have put my mental and emotional states in a position much more capable of discerning truth.

May these two acronyms help you (and anyone you ever influence) for the rest of your lives. May they teach you how to think. May they protect your mind from dominators acting as indoctrinators.

May these two acronyms guide you into freethinking. Literally, that you are free to think. You are free to doubt. You are free to disagree. You are free to question. You are free to enquire. You are free to investigate. You are free to follow the truth wherever it leads – and whatever the consequences. You are free to say, "I know" when in fact you do. You are free to say, "I don't know" when you truly don't.

Let's start with laying out the six signs of S.T.U.P.I.D. thinking. Let me give you all of them and then I will give you more particulars.

When encountering new information, I know my thinking is stupid when my personal judgments are:

S = **S**nap

T = **T**otal

U = **U**nquestioned

P = **P**assive

I = **I**deologically Filtered

D = **D**ogmatic

S - Snap

Snap your fingers. That fast.

The first sign that alerts me to my own S.T.U.P.I.D. thinking is when I come across new information and I make a snap judgment concerning it.

Making a snap judgment is making a conclusion about something the split second after hearing it. It is when my first impulse is to judge, rather than the vastly wiser "I don't know. I'm not going agree or disagree. I need to learn more."

Snap judgments are when my first trigger becomes my foundational truth. When the first thing my mind triggers in response to new information, becomes what I consider to be true. Snap judgments are simply knee-jerk, immediate emotional responses.

In the two and half years you've been alive, I've observed that snap judgments are being made *by everyone all of time about everything*. It's not the exception. It's the rule.

It's very easy to see how mob violence or a mob mentality gets started. Just start gathering a large group of people and get them to make snap judgments on something. You will see people's first impulse almost invariably to be reactionary, not rational. To be triggered, not thoughtful.

If you want to stir up a human hornet's nest, just go to any Social Media platform like Twitter, Facebook, or Instagram and throw out some explosive sounding judgment on a controversial subject. Make some strong, dogmatic opinion (on *either* side of the argument) about Covid-19, Social distancing, Black Lives Matter, All Lives Matter, Systemic Racism, China, Climate Change, Vaccinations, 5G, Veganism, Socialism, Capitalism, Racism, Identity Politics, Christianity, Islam, Barack Obama, the Clintons, Jeffrey Epstein, Donald Trump, Gender Identification, Gay-Marriage, Gun-Control, Immigration, Abortion, Flat-Earth, the 9/11 attack of 2001, etc.

Then sit back and watch people burn. Watch them lose their minds and begin firing a flurry of tweets and posts expressing their snap judgments. For expressing a contrary opinion, you will quickly be called one of the 4 "I's." That is, be prepared for:

- "You're a complete **idiot**!"
- "You're so painfully **ignorant**!"
- "You're **immoral**! You're a bad person!"
- And always anticipate everyone's favorite power play phrase, "You're **insane**!"

If you want to appear like your "winning" one of these lively and mindless debates – whether in writing or in audible conversation – here's how to do it.

Don't make any real arguments. Just do a bunch of name calling. And always work in that your opponent's views are "idiotic," "ignorant," "immoral," and "insane" in a raged-filled rant of under 60 seconds.

You'll totally rock at debate in the eyes of a weak-minded society addicted to snap judgments. They will make tribute videos about you, and how you "destroyed" your opponent.

And do you know what the reality of all this is? Making a snap judgment is not really stupid thinking.

It's not thinking at all.

Snap judgments are merely emotional triggering. It's actually being mindless and reactionary, not mindful and rational.

Labels are NOT logic.

Name-calling is NOT evidence of neural activity.

Character assassinations are NOT convincing arguments.

Let's face it. All humans are judging machines. And we live in a day where people pretend to be pious and non-judgmental. But what is closer to the truth is this: we all judge everybody all the time about everything. Watch T.V. or listen to the radio. You can fill up 24 hours a day on the judgments of others.

We rarely call them "judgments." Humans sanitize and moralize this too. We call them "takes," "views," "positions," "opinions," "reviews," or "perspectives."

Talk shows even use these words in their names. "The View" sounds more palatable than "The Judgment." But that's exactly what it is. "First Take" sounds more friendly than "First Judgment." But that's exactly what it is.

Humans are judging machines.

Dominators in the forms of the press, politicians, preachers, etc. know that domination is directly tied to information. Telling people what to think is the foundation for control. And dominators know, 1) that the vast majority of people do not think for themselves, 2) that they are waiting for others to tell them what to think, and 3) that they will make snap judgments about what they hear.

The ruling class and the press deliberately play on the human propensity for snap judgments. They use emotional trigger words all the time to activate the stupid, snap judgments of the populace. Listen for it.

- So and so is a "terrorist."
- So and so is a "dictator."

- So and so is "homophobic."
- So and so is “Islamophobic.”
- So and so is a "racist."
- So and so is a "bigot."
- So and so is a "radical."
- So and so is a "criminal."
- So and so is “Hitler.”
- So and so is a “Nazi.”
- So and so is a “Fascist.”
- So and so is “washed up” or “irrelevant.”
- So and so is a “loser.”
- So and so is a.... You get the idea.

You can go through every news headline or political speech and identify the emotional trigger words used to shape public opinion. None of these are arguments.

Don’t make snap judgments. Remember that triggers are not truth. Labels are not logic. Name-calling is not evidence of neural activity. Reactionary people are not rational people.

T - Total

The second sign that alerts me to my own S.T.U.P.I.D. thinking is when my judgments are total. Snap judgments. Total judgments.

In fact, I could almost stop right here. If you want to encapsulate my own personal stupidity and that of the masses, it is this. We make snap, total judgments on almost everything.

Again, go to Social Media and throw out a controversial take on something. The venom that will come back will not only contain people’s snap judgments. They will be total judgments. Look for the totalism. Listen for the totalism.

- "You are a 'total' moron."
- "You're a 'complete' idiot."
- "Donald Trump is 'pure' evil."
- "Nancy Pelosi is 'absolutely' insane."
- "ALL cops are crooked."
- "ALL whites are racist."
- "You're position is 'entirely' immoral."
- "You're 'totally' ignorant on the subject."
- "You know 'nothing.'"
- "You're 'utterly' incompetent to speak on this subject."

Total judgments are a sure sign of stupid thinking. It's lazy thinking. It's not thinking rightly or justly. That is, it doesn't take the time required to think about something *just as it is*. Not worse than it is. Not better than it is. *Just as it is*.

Why do we make so many snap, total judgments?

Because humans have so much on their brains already. As a result, we take shortcuts in thinking. We make snap, total judgments on things. We label something and leave it. Then we go on living under the delusion that we "know about that." We pretend we can make snap, total judgments and hit the bull's eye of truth.

And we even moralize our snap, total judgments. We act virtuous as we boast, "I'm just a 'calls 'em like I sees 'em' type of person." We pride ourselves as being "black or white" on an issue. As though we possess uncommon moral clarity on all issues.

But the reality is that most of us humans are extremely lazy "EITHER…OR" thinkers. To the vast majority of us, something is EITHER 100% true, OR it is 100% false. Someone is EITHER 100% good, OR he or she is 100% evil.

No exceptions. No nuance. No degrees. No spectrum. No shades of gray.

Nope, it's a total judgment one way or another. No mixture of truth and falsehood. No mixture of good and evil.

Because any concession of a mixture requires humility, honesty, hard-working investigation of the real facts, and wisdom. Whose got time for that?

Totalists are rarely, if ever, going to arrive at truth. Again, most people think determining what is true only has two choices. "It's EITHER this…OR it's that." They rarely recognize that truth is usually a wide spectrum. And that there are not just 50 shades of gray on some subjects. But there may be 500, 5000, or 5,000,000.

But why work through a truth spectrum? Being a totalist is just a lot easier. It's a lot less work. Saying Barack Obama's two terms of President were a "complete" disaster is so much easier than saying, "I have extensively studied Obama's Presidency. Here's the 10 things he did that I think were fantastic. Here's the 10 things he did that really hurt our country." One's political tribe and their lack of time do not allow for such reasonable thinking.

Saying Donald Trump is "pure" evil is so much easier than saying, "I have closely followed the Trump Presidency. Here's the 10 things he did that helped America. Here's the 10 things he did that hurt America." Again, one's political tribe and their lack of time do not allow for such even-handed thinking.

And on an everyday, practical level, saying, "That girl is a 'total' idiot," is so much easier than getting to know the person. It's much easier than actually trying to find out why the girl was acting like an idiot in that moment.

Letting your first impulse be to judge, is so much easier than letting your first impulse be to love. Love takes work. It may involve listening. It may involve forgiveness. It may involve understanding. Whose got time for that?

If you guard yourself against making snap, total judgments, you're going to be way ahead of most of humanity.

U - Unquestioned

The third sign that alerts me to my own S.T.U.P.I.D. thinking is when my judgments are unquestioned. Snap judgments. Total judgments. Unquestioned judgments.

Most non-thinking people are just plain gullible. They believe most everything they hear. They never question any messenger of new information. They never question whether the new information is real or fake. Whether it is true or false. Or whether it is a mixture of truth and falsehood.

To survive in this world, you should question everything. To survive in this world, you need to know how to think. You must drill any messenger of new information with a myriad of questions.

- Who are you?
- Why should I believe you?
- Where did you get your information?
- Why should I believe your source(s)?
- What is your worldview?
- What team or tribe are you rooting for?
- What do you *want* to be true?
- What are your biases?
- What is your motive?
- What is your agenda?
- Are you more loyal to tribe or to truth?
- Do you really *know* these things to be true?
- Or do you only *believe* these things to be true?
- Why do people disagree with what you are saying?
- Do critics of your information raise valid points?
- Have you ever been wrong?

Most of humanity just receives information without question. Because they believe they are receiving this information from an "authority" who is smarter or more informed than we are. Someone who has credentials, so we just assume their information must be credible and true.

Yet, most people never take the time to ask if the information IS true. Nor do we question how the information is being organized to manipulate the listener.

Always ask questions. I remember a time when I was in ministry and someone passed on some juicy gossip to me. “Did you hear that Pastor so and so is divorced?” The person saying this did so in a very critical and condescending way. He was the judge. The person he was gossiping about was the judged.

I remember being very troubled by this new information. As a result, I personally called the church of this pastor and found out that the rumor was completely bogus. I was able to pass on this information to the original messenger of the gossip.

If you want the truth, ask questions. A lot of them.

Growing up, I frequently heard this cliché, “Don’t believe everything you hear.” It would be closer to the truth to say, “Don’t believe *anything* you hear.” Question everything. Investigate everything. Exhaustively.

P - Passive

The fourth sign that alerts me to my own S.T.U.P.I.D. thinking is when my judgments are passive. Snap judgments. Total judgments. Unquestioned judgments. Passive judgments.

We don't even realize it, but when we make snap, total, and unquestioned judgments, they are not *our* judgments. We are passive in this process. We have accepted the judgment of *another*. We have outsourced our thinking to someone else. Someone is telling us what to think.

Non-thinking people do not proactively research, interview, and investigate all the available data for themselves. Instead, we take the word of someone else we consider an "expert" or "authority."

And why do we do we put trust in another's take on something? Because maybe they do know more about something.

But how much more?

In my journey, I remember first starting Bible College. As a wide-eyed, insecure, impressionable 18-year-old, the professors and the pastor seemed larger than life to me. They "knew so much." And I devoured almost everything they taught me.

But in time, the knowledge gap between me and my Bible teachers began to close. I was rising up the Bible knowledge hierarchy. In time, I was also a teacher. I was a contemporary and colleague.

And what I'm about to say, is not being as disrespectful as it sounds. When my knowledge began to rival the level of my teachers, I was awakened to a harsh reality. Those I was in awe of as an 18-year-old, were not as smart as I thought they were. They were not the "experts" that I thought. There was so much *they didn't know*. There were so many gaps in their understanding. They had many blind spots in their perspectives. And they had biases.

What is a bias?

Let me give you two more acronyms. A bias is this:

- **B**elieving
- **I**s
- **A**utomatically
- **S**eeing

Or, a bias is:

- **B**elieving
- **I**

- Am
- Superior

I began to notice that the professors who taught me were as human as I was. They were as bias as I was. They were as clouded in their judgment as I was. That for them, interpreting the Bible was *never* a matter of "go to the evidence, and follow the truth wherever it leads" – and whatever the consequences.

Because the consequences of thinking for yourself and having an "out of the box" view could mean many things. Getting fired. Losing your means of money-making and survival. Being branded a heretic. Excommunication from the group. Losing your marriage. Leaving your religion. Having to reinvent yourself. Struggling to find another means of living.

For my professors, humbly studying Biblical data and interpreting it correctly, was NOT a matter of "seeing is believing." But instead, "believing was seeing." Bias clouded their judgment. For them, believing was automatically seeing.

The professors who taught me were more loyal to tribe than to truth. There were "Biblical positions" they HAD to come to if they wanted to stay part of our particular tribe.

SCC was an independent, fundamental Baptist institution. My professors could "prove" from the Bible anything they wanted to in order to make this worldview the truth. They could "prove" that "God was on our side" of given issues. My professors and our pastor knew how to put together a package of verses from the Bible – regardless of context – in order to be "right." They knew how to start with a conclusion, then go to the Biblical data, and then twist and harmonize it to fit the pre-determined conclusion.

What pre-determined conclusions? All of the doctrines and ethics that are dear to independent, fundamental Baptists. My professors' views, perspectives, and judgments were clouded by this bias. Bias that was shaped by their religious tribe. Biases that caused them to begin with conclusions instead of end with them. Biases that caused them to unconsciously twist and harmonize data so our Independent Baptist "team" would win.

Were these horrible men? To the contrary, they were great guys on multiple levels. It's not a "good guy" issue. It's a truth issue. And everybody is, what he or she is, because they had to become that – in order to survive. Including my professors.

I do not question the sincerity of my professors for one minute. I do not question the purity of their intentions. I do not question that that they were "good" men – whatever that means. But I'm not sure I would categorize them as "free-thinkers" or "truth seekers."

Today, I think it is reasonable to say that I know more about the Bible than 99% of the world. That 1% still leaves tens of millions of people who may know more about the Bible than I do. I do not say this to brag. I mention this only to say that I know what it is to be an "expert." To have hundreds of people hanging on my every word. Most passively drinking in all the information coming out of my mouth as the 100% truth.

This is painful. I look back years later and say to myself, "How much disinformation did I spread during my 15 years as a professor and pastor – *IN MY SPECIFIC AREA OF EXPERTISE*?" Someone who was "educated." Someone who was "credentialed." Someone who was an "authority." Someone who was an "expert."

This has been a hard lesson, but a valuable one. I've learned to refuse being passive in the thinking and learning process. To never, *and I mean never*, be intimidated by someone throwing out their impressive sounding titles, educational backgrounds, and credentials. They don't know it all – not even close. Even in their areas of specific "expertise."

Information dominators are human. They have extreme limits in their knowledge. The have wide gaps in their understanding. There are numerous questions they cannot even begin to answer – *in their field of expertise*. They have blind spots. They have biases. They have a subjective side that roots for what they *want* to be true. They rarely, if ever, think critically about their own tribe and the "truths" they have been taught. And they too, have dominators over them. Dominators who pay their salary. Dominators they are dependent upon to survive.

NEVER passively sit back and let someone else do your thinking for you. Dominators are very dangerous people. Because they are always indoctrinators. Their domination depends on their ability to teach you what to think. Dominators want you to be passive in the learning process. They want their positions to be your positions. Their views to be your views. Their judgments to be your judgments.

Never be passive in your thinking or judgments. Make no mistake, attractive, smart, and articulate people can be the most dangerous people in the world. And every rival religious and political group has possessed charismatic personalities. Human alphas who can persuasively and eloquently state the "way the world should be" from their perspective.

But charismatic, attractive, smart, and eloquent does not mean honest with data. Charismatic, attractive, smart, and eloquent does not mean good. Charismatic, attractive, smart, and eloquent does not mean wise. Charismatic, attractive, smart, and eloquent does not mean truth.

Reject being passive in the thinking process. Reject making passive judgments. Never let someone do your thinking for you.

I - Ideologically filtered

The fifth sign that alerts me to my own S.T.U.P.I.D. thinking is when my judgments are ideologically filtered.

In simple terms, an ideology is literally an *idea* of how the world *should* be. Every human on earth is born into an ideology. One that began with an alpha human that popularized their version of how the world *should* be. Buddhism is traced to Buddha. Christianity is traced to Jesus. Islam is traced to

Mohammad. Communism is traced to Karl Marx among others. Democracy is traced to ancient Greece and more recently the signers of the Declaration of Independence in America.

Religion and Government are nearly one in the same in this regard. A single person or a small minority of powerful people have ideas for a better world. Then they create rules to make these ideas an actual reality for the vast majority of people under their domination.

In theory, obedience to these rules will bring about the world imagined by its creators. And of course, disobedience to these rules will bring swift and painful punishment to those threatening this way of life.

Again, whether you are dealing with religion or secular government, the concept is the same. It's all ideologically driven by the idea: "this way of living makes the world a better place."

But the problem with any ideology, is that the majority of the world doesn't agree. It's a sobering reality that: whatever you are, most of the world is not.

- Are you a Christian? Most of the world is not.
- Are you a Muslim? Most of the world is not.
- Are you a Hindu? Most of the world is not.
- Are you a Jew? Most of the world is not.
- Are you an Atheist? Most of the world is not.
- Are you a Buddhist? Most of the world is not.
- Are you American? Most of the world is not.
- Are you Chinese? Most of the world is not.
- Are you Russian? Most of the world is not.
- Are you Indian? Most of the world is not.

I remember when your brother Ray was around eight or nine years old. We were throwing around a football in the front yard. At some point Ray said to me, "Dad, I don't think I'm a Baptist."

I'm sure this phraseology was not original with him. He probably heard me say something similar and was just repeating it. I said back to him, "Ray, you can be a Baptist if you want to be. But you don't have to be a Baptist either. You are free to choose for yourself. Take the time to know what you believe and why you believe it."

Then I had him do something. It was in Autumn, and the leaves were all over the ground. I had Ray gather 100 fallen leaves and told him to place them in 10 rows of 10 leaves – placing them on the cement slab at the front of our home. After all the leaves were collected and organized, I told him to separate 2 of the leaves from the remaining 98.

I said, "Ray, do you know what these two leaves represent? They represent how many people in this world are some type of Baptist Christian. Do you know what the remaining 98 leaves represent? They represent the number of people in this world who are not Baptist. Most of the world is not Baptist."

Then I had Ray separate out two more leaves. Now there were now 4 leaves in one group and 96 leaves in the other. I said, "What do you think these four leaves represent? They represent the number of people in the world who are American. The 96 leaves represent the number of people in the world who are not American. Most of the world is not American."

And I made this point to him: "Ray, your dad was raised in a Baptist American household. In my upbringing I interacted with 2% to 4% of the world's population and information. That means that I rarely interacted with 96% to 98% of the world's population and information. Do not be in a hurry to call yourself a Baptist or anything else. Take the time to know what you believe, and more importantly, why you believe it."

Every person on the planet could tailor this leaf analogy to match their own upbringing. We're all born into an ideology - the way someone thinks the world should be. But the fact remains. Most of the world doesn't fit our view of how the world should be.

So how should we view people with different ideologies? They don't have the same ideas about God. They don't have the same ideas about worship. They don't have the same ideas about women. They don't have the same ideas about sexuality. They don't have the same ideas about money. They don't have the same ideas about....

And each of these ideologies believe they are the ones on Earth who are "good," and who got it "right." Each ideology can never view the majority of the world, who think and live differently from them, as being "good." They CAN'T view alternative ideologies as truth. This would undermine their own ideology which has 5000, 3500, 2500, 2000, 1400, or 250 years of tradition.

All ideologies have come too far to examine their own worldview. They have lived for millennia, centuries, or decades believing they are the ones who are 100% good and 100% true. They are the enlightened ones who have seen the light.

The vast majority of others who live differently are in darkness. Other ideologies are "evil." They are deceived. It is them who need to adopt our way of living. We must take the beautiful utopian world we have created and spread it to them - by force if necessary.

You get the idea.

These ideological conflicts also create a martyr complex. That is, a "victim's mentality," or a "we are a persecuted people" complex. Most all ideologies want to be the "winning" ideology. Therefore, ideologies attempt to force other "inferior" or "outdated" ideologies to live by their rules, for their good.

They will even go to war if necessary. If they win the war, the winning ideology will bring the losing ideology under their domination. The losing ideology must live in fearful submission to the winning ideology.

What is the new mentality of the losing ideology?

The losing ideology now casts itself as a martyr. It's an oppressed remnant. It's a victim.

In my ideological background, it always seemed like Christianity thought it was unique and special because someone wrote "Foxes Book of Martyrs." A mentality of "You know what we believe is true, because of all the people who died for the faith."

But name one religion who couldn't write the same book. Name one political group who couldn't write the same book. Name one people group or race of people on earth who couldn't write the same book.

Here's the point. We are all born into some ideology or ideologies. I was born into a Baptist Christian American Republican household. Get all that?

I chose none of these identifying labels. But these ideas of how the world should be were all forced upon me by well-intentioned parents. I learned very early in life to process all new information through these ideological filters.

By being raised Baptist, if I found out someone was a Catholic – gasp! I learned to make a snap, total, unquestioning, passive, and ideologically filtered judgment on this person. I quickly concluded that this Catholic person (but not me) was going to burn in hell forever. That the Catholic person (but not me) was part of a false religion. That the Catholics (but not us) were bad people. That the Catholics (but not us) were in error. That the Catholics (but not us) needed conversion.

And if I could convert a Catholic, they were to live by our specific Christian rules now. If a Catholic should push back and resist my attempts to convert them, then I would interpret this as me being persecuted for my faith. Therefore, one day, God will punish the Catholic for this. My Baptist team wins in the end. I'm the good guy. The Catholic is the bad guy.

Growing up in a Republican household, I had the same ideologically filtered judgment on anyone I discovered was a Democrat. Gasp. Immediate suspicion. This Democrat must be a liberal (whatever that means), baby killing, sexually immoral, corrupt, and evil person.

For most of my life I did this. Anyone who was not what I was raised to be, would get a similar ideologically filtered judgment from me (like I was their judge). If I discovered someone was a Muslim, a Buddhist, a Jehovah's Witness, a Communist, a Socialist, a Laker fan, etc., they must be a bad person, or at least deceived.

For most of the first 30 years of my life, my thinking was constantly stupid. I consistently made judgments that were snap, total, unquestioning, passive, and ideologically filtered. Anyone who viewed the world differently than my Baptist tribe, they were bad. They were wrong. Because we were good. We were right.

To date, no ideology of how the world should be has gotten it all right. Every one of them is a mixture of good and evil. Every one of them is a blend of virtue and vice. Every one of them mixes truth and error. Every one of them has blind spots. Every one of them uses fear, force, and the threat of punishment to accomplish their will. And the world continues to tear itself apart. Because everyone tries to hold it together through fear and endless cycles of coercion.

That we ALL make ideologically filtered judgments is the point NO ONE wants to concede. Too much is at stake. Other religions are false. Not mine. Other governments are corrupt. Not mine. Other parents were misguided. Not mine.

Why not? Because they loved you and were wonderful people? Because they were sincere? Because they protected and provided for you? Therefore, do you just turn a blind eye to the deficiencies of their worldview?

Let me ask a few questions. Can you point out the errors, evils, and hypocrisy in other religions? Probably.

Have you ever used this same critical thinking ability to judge if there are errors, evils, and hypocrisy *within your own religion*?

Can you point out the errors, evils, and hypocrisy in other nations? Probably.

Have you ever used these same reasoning abilities to locate errors, evils, and hypocrisy *within your own nation*?

Let's get very real.

- If coercion was not being used against you in any way.
- If you were not threatened with being hurt.
- If you were not under the constant threats of execution, caging, ex-communication, disowning, defunding, fining, shaming, etc.
- If these threats were completely removed.
- If you had no threat of family, professional, or societal rejection.
- If your survival and wellbeing was not threatened in any way.
- If you were under no compulsion to conform through "fear choices."
- If you were completely liberated in your life to make *free* choices.
- If you were completely free to think what you wanted to think.
- If you were completely free to believe what you wanted to believe.
- If you were completely free to say what you wanted to say.
- If you were completely free to do what you wanted to do.
- If you were completely free to be what you wanted to be…

Would you still be a Catholic?

Would you still be a Baptist?

Would you still be Muslim?

Would you still be Hindu?

Would you still be American?

Would you still be a Liberal?

Would you still be a Conservative?

Would you still be a…? You fill in the blank with your ideological filters.

This is the problem. These ideological filters keep us from honesty. They keep us from humility. They keep us from love. They keep us from freedom.

They may be keeping us from truth. They cause us to become S.T.U.P.I.D. in our thinking. They keep us from the better world WE ALL want.

None of us are 100% good. None of us are 100% knowledgeable of the truth. None of us have it all figured out.

Have the courage to reject ideologically filtered judgments. Have even more courage to examine your own ideology.

D - Dogmatic.

The sixth sign that alerts me to my own S.T.U.P.I.D. thinking is when my judgments are dogmatic. Snap judgments. Total judgments. Unquestioned judgments. Passive judgments. Ideologically filtered judgments. Dogmatic judgments.

Being dogmatic is when your first impulse is "case closed" rather than "let's open the case." When your first impulse is to yell rather than to listen. When your first impulse is to judge rather than to love. When your first impulse is ego and pride rather than humility. When your first impulse is to attack and dominate rather than to befriend and serve. When your first impulse is to win a debate rather than a mutually profitable discussion.

Dogmatic. My thinking is stupid when I emotionally and dogmatically explode on anyone with a differing viewpoint. My arrogance, my anger, and even my words again reflect the four "I's":

- "You're an **idiot**. Only a stupid person would believe that."
- "You're so **ignorant**. Get an education moron. My IQ is lowering my just being in your presence."
- "You're just **insane!** They should lock you up. You don't even belong in a sane world."
- "You're **immoral**. You're a bad person."

When we respond this way, it is clear that truth is not our highest priority. Domination is. We want the high ground. We want to be the judge, not the judged. We want our team to win.

We fool ourselves into believing that our dogmatic judgments make us right. That we have earned the “right” to explode on people and call them names. Throwing out “power-play” phrases like the four “I’s,” is our manipulation technique to get the dominant position. We must instantly assume the position of the judge before we become the judged. We must blast people with a judgment before they judge us. We must blame them before they blame us.

Therefore, we become dogmatic as quickly as possible. The obsession with being right and having the "high ground," can turn us into pretty nasty people.

And since humans less frequently resolve their dominance hierarchy disputes through physical altercation and violence, it gets settled in a war of words. Hence, the need to be dogmatic. I have to be the smart one. You’re stupid. I'm right. You’re wrong. I will give you a label because it is my wolf-like way of putting "my paw" on your head and declaring dominance over you.

Bad thinking. Being dogmatic exposes your true motives. Truth is not the goal. Dominance and control are the goal. The result is that we all become stupid in our thinking. We become obsessed with being right. We turn into M.A.D. (**M**ean. **A**ngry. **D**isrespectful.) people who scorn any differing opinion that challenges us.

Snap judgments. Total judgments. Unquestioned judgments. Passive judgments. Ideologically filtered judgments. Dogmatic judgments. These are the six signs I can look for in myself when I suspect that my thinking is S.T.U.P.I.D.

The brutal reality in all this: *none of these six things represent thinking at all.* They are simply emotional triggers reacting defensively against information contrary to my mental training and programming. All 6 of these signs reflect an individual who has been taught what to think and doesn't know how to think. Someone who has an indoctrinated mind, not a truly educated mind.

Me, for the first 30 years of life.

Thankfully, for the last 15 years or so in my life, I've been learning how to think. And I'm still learning.

What then are the five signs of S.M.A.R.T. thinking? Again, let me give the whole acronym and then I will break it down – much more briefly than the first acronym.

When encountering new information, I know my thinking is S.M.A.R.T. when I am:

S = **S**uspending Judgment

— Instead of making **s**nap judgments.

M = **M**iddle in my starting place

— Instead of making **t**otal judgments.

A = **A**sking questions exhaustively

— Instead of making **u**nquestioned, **p**assive judgments.

R = **R**ecognizing biases

— Instead of making **i**deologically filtered judgments.

T = **T**olerant

— Instead of making **d**ogmatic judgments.

S = **S**uspending Judgment

When encountering any new information in life, the first sign that my thinking is S.M.A.R.T. is when I am suspending judgment.

I'm human, I'm going to make snap judgments. When encountering "breaking news," or new information, it's going to happen. My mind WILL trigger some initial snap judgment and emotional knee-jerk reaction about what I've just seen or heard.

But this initial snap judgment will NOT be my final judgment. This snap judgment will not control me. I immediately take control of the snap judgment. After my seemingly unstoppable, initial snap judgment, I will immediately follow this by making a conscious choice to suspend judgment. To put judgment on hold. To never start with a conclusion on any subject.

Smart thinking needs A LOT more information before it forms even an *initial* judgment. Smart thinking refuses making large conclusions on small amounts of data – whether we're talking about new people you meet, current events, controversial subjects, ideologies, etc.

My thinking is S.M.A.R.T. when I am consciously suspending judgment.

M = Middle in my starting place

When encountering any new information in life, the second sign that my thinking is S.M.A.R.T. is when I am middle in my starting place.

Smart thinking rejects snap, total judgments. While most people start with EITHER, "This is 100% true," OR "This is 100% false," smart thinking does not. While most people begin with EITHER, "That person is 100% good," OR "That person is 100% evil," smart thinking will not.

Smart thinking is middle in its starting place. Smart thinking has an attitude more like this: "If this new information is like most of the world's information, then what I just heard is probably *a mixture* of truth and falsehood. I am going to suspend judgment on what I've just seen and heard. And as I begin to research this, I will be middle in my starting place. As though what I heard is 50% true, and 50% false. As I gather more information, I will discern whether what I first heard was more true than false, or whether it was more false than true."

Smart thinking begins from a more neutral position. It refuses to take sides from the start. Smart thinking never begins with a total judgment of something being completely true or completely false. Smart thinking never begins with a person being completely good or completely bad.

Smart thinking is middle in its starting place.

A = **A**sking questions exhaustively

When encountering any new information in life, the third sign that my thinking is S.M.A.R.T. is when I am asking questions exhaustively.

Smart thinking rejects making passive, unquestioned judgments. Instead, smart thinking begins by asking questions exhaustively. Until there are no more questions to be asked. That is, until it eventually thinks of more questions.

Smart thinking never blindly takes another's "authoritative" word for it.

- This applies to the ruling classes and their written laws.
- This applies to religious leaders and their written texts.
- This applies to the scientific community and their studies and peer reviewed journals.
- This applies to the press and their trigger inducing headlines.
- This applies to famous "I have a platform" people and their forceful personalities.
- This applies even to people I know and trust such as friends and family.

Because these dominators say something…doesn't make it true. Because these dominators have millions who agree with them…doesn't make it so. Because these dominators have fame, fortune, titles, credentials, a platform, and a microphone doesn't make them wise. Because some dominators come from old traditions, even thousands of years old, doesn't make their traditions true and good for all humanity.

Smart thinking questions everything and everybody with healthy and courteous skepticism. Smart thinking asks questions exhaustively, without being a jerk about it. Smart thinking is just endlessly curious and asks questions until there are no more questions to be asked – at this point.

Smart thinking will keep asking questions until even the "authoritative" source of the information has to concede, "I don't know." You must probe to see how much an "expert" person actually knows, and what they are merely pretending to know.

Never forget that almost every "expert" can be questioned into an "I don't know" answer within 60 seconds – in their field of specific expertise.

Ask questions. Ask questions. Ask questions. And when there are no more questions to be asked – think of even more questions to ask.

R = Recognizing biases

When encountering any new information in life, the fourth sign that my thinking is S.M.A.R.T. is when I am recognizing biases.

Smart thinking refuses to make ideologically filtered judgments. Smart thinking refuses to allow another's, or even my own, ideological filters to twist, cherry-pick, or harmonize data to fit the story they or I want to tell.

Smart thinking's greatest loyalty is to the truth, not to tribe. Nor to the tribe's ideological filters for viewing and interpreting all the information in the world. The tribe who used the diamonds of one's identity and inner peace to teach them what to think, what to say, what to do, what to feel, what to believe, and who to be.

Every national, local, religious, familial, and religious tribe on earth is biased. They all want their team to win. They all have a way of life that they want to keep intact.

Understandably so.

But loyalty to ideologies always create deep biases that blind people to truths they need to hear, see, acknowledge, and incorporate into their overall body of knowledge. Recognize these biases.

Smart thinking will follow the truth wherever it leads – and whatever the consequences.

T = Tolerant

When encountering any new information in life, the fifth sign that my thinking is S.M.A.R.T. is when I am tolerant.

Smart thinking is open to the very real possibility of being partially, or completely, wrong about something or someone. Smart thinking will humbly, happily, and gratefully change if proven wrong.

Smart thinking welcomes friendly debate and cross-examination. Smart thinking is tolerant of, and open to, differing viewpoints. Smart thinking is teachable. Smart thinking never thinks it "knows it all." Smart thinking is truly enlightened. It has been awakened to its own ignorance.

Smart thinking refuses be dogmatic in its judgments and conclusions. Smart thinking makes judgments that are soft, pliable, and even possibly temporary. Smart thinking never makes judgments that are hard, rigid, and permanent.

Smart thinking is tolerant.

Knowing how to think. If you want to walk the path of freedom in a world of domination and slavery, this is survival skill #1 that you will need. You must know how to think for yourself. You must protect your mind from being indoctrinated in what to think.

Always observe your own thinking and judgments. If you are ever to feel free in a world of slavery, you must know how to think. If you want to keep yourself from being dominated, you must know how to think.

CHAPTER 13

Survival Skill #2 – Living Above the Judgments of Others

Here's a statement my experience has taught me. And a statement I never want you to forget.

I cannot stop you from judging me. But you cannot stop me from living above your judgment.

Hallie, never live below the judgments of others. Live above the judgments of others. This is the second survival skill you will need for walking the path of freedom and for feeling free in a world of slavery. To keep yourself from being dominated by any individual or group, you must learn how to live above the judgments of others.

Many young people your age already hate themselves. They feel like they never measure up. That they are never good enough. That they are never obedient enough. That they are never smart enough. That they are never handsome or pretty enough. That they are never athletic enough. That they are never cool enough.

That they are inferior. That their lives are not worth living.

Why? Because the dominance hierarchy on Earth has produced a world of non-stop judgment.

Non-stop. It never ends.

Everyone wants to be better than the next person. They want to be superior, not inferior. They want to be the dominator, not the dominated. Everyone wants to be the judge, not the judged. Everyone wants to be higher, not lower on the dominance hierarchy. Everyone wants your diamonds, not just the power classes. They want to define your identity and disrupt your inner peace.

Therefore, it is only a slight overstatement to say that young people hate themselves, and hate their lives, because they have been awakened to a brutal reality. That being: *that they are being judged all the time by everybody for everything*. And as a result, their inner lives are in perpetual conflict as they struggle to live above, and not beneath the heavy weight of constant judgment.

Some might object to me making these comments to you. I can almost hear someone saying something like this: "That's a colossal overstatement. That's not true. Teens need to be taught that most people aren't thinking about them at all. They shouldn't be so narcissistic anyways."

Which is a judgment. Which makes teens feel even worse. That they are invisible. That they haven't been judged as being important enough by others to be noticed. That for some unexplainable reason they went from being cute, adored, and delighted in as small children, to being condemned, abhorred, and despised as teenagers.

Let me prepare you for the world I brought you into. You must learn to deal with the absolute fact that most everybody will be judging you all the time about everything.

You already know this. And it's not going away in your lifetime. You will be judged. You will be labeled. You will be called names. You will be bullied. You will be threatened. And all potential dominators have this in common: they want you to live below their judgment. They want their judgment to control you, to keep you in their assigned place for you.

The whole world is one big, battle for survival. As a result, the whole world is one, big dominance hierarchy. As a result, the whole world is one, big ball of judgment.

This is the world I brought you into.

So, let me prepare you for this world. Let me give the second survival skill you will need for your journey. That being: how to live above, not below, the judgments of others.

In what ways will you be judged?

First, in this world, everything – and I mean everything – about your physical body will be judged. In our culture, physical beauty is a fast path to dominance. The physically attractive will dominate the school spirit in every level of your education. The physically attractive dominate social media. The physically attractive dominate advertisement. The physically attractive dominant entertainment. The physically attractive are usually the leaders of society.

In this world, many people assume the dominated position because a more physically attractive person has assumed the dominant position. All the "uglier" people end up listening to them. In this world, less attractive people surrender the diamonds of their identity and inner peace to more attractive people.

A couple of years ago I was chaperoning an overnight field trip for your brother's 6th grade class. During one activity, the group I was overseeing was doing a treasure hunt. They had to solve clues and riddles in order to find the right paths that would lead them to their treasure.

The prettiest girl in the class took the lead. She immediately made her conclusion about the first riddle and started leading the pack down a meadow trail. They all followed her.

Except for one girl. Someone just as smart. But not as attractive and socially confident. In an insecure, weak voice she yelled to the group, "Guys, it's this way," pointing in the opposite direction.

After we chaperones helped the less popular girl, get the mindless pack following the pretty and popular girl to stop, we all re-evaluated the riddle. The one girl who was not as attractive was actually correct. Following her logic lead our group to the right path and ultimately to the treasure.

The point is NOT that physically attractive people are bad and should not be trusted. Or that they will always lead you astray. The point is that physically attractive people are dominators. And that most people will defer to someone who is better looking. They will follow someone who is better looking. They will listen to someone who is better looking. I'm not saying this is right or wrong. I'm only saying it is so.

The physically attractive dominated the public high school I attended. They were the most popular and the cool crowd. They dominated the leadership positions of my college. I see them dominating culture and social media. I see them dominating leadership positions in business and politics around the world.

I'm not against attractive people. You are one. I am just preparing you for something. Physical beauty is idolized in this world. And you will be judged on every aspect of your physical appearance.

And if someone judges some aspect of your physical body to be insufficient according to their judgment – they will vocalize it. If they are "nice enough" to not vocalize it, they will communicate their disapproval through their body language.

I'm not sure I can pinpoint a single aspect of my physical appearance that has NOT been judged to be inferior by someone else. I have frequently been made fun of for my fair, Irish complexion. I always wished I had one of those deep suntans so that people would not make fun of me. Anytime that

I attempted to get a tan, it always resulted in three days of pain from a red sunburn that simply faded in just a few more days.

I've also been told numerous times in my life how parts of my face were unacceptable. I had extremely crooked teeth growing up. Needless to say, many people could not conceal their judgment about how unsatisfactory my teeth were to them. They just had to vocalize their disapproval to me – which was hurtful. Which impacted my identity and inner peace. It was such a relief to get braces in college. Once my teeth were straightened, I avoided the painful judgment of others about my teeth.

With my teeth straightened, judgers looked elsewhere for an opening for dominance. They focused on my nose which had been broken multiple times in basketball. People had no problem vocalizing to my face how unacceptable my nose was to them. Eventually, worn down from all the mean statements from others, I had my nose fixed. My nose is still not a thing of beauty, but it's better than it was. Getting a "nose job" has helped me avoid the painful judgments of others about my nose.

In my first couple of decades of life I was extremely skinny. Many people were happy to tell me how weak, skinny, and inferior my physique was to their judgment. Therefore, I lifted weights diligently until my physique looked more impressive. Gaining some muscle helped me avoid the painful judgments of others about my physique.

Now in my mid-forties, I look back on all this with horror. That so much of my life was lived under the domination of other people's judgments. That I surrendered the diamonds of my identity and inner peace to mean people. That I allowed others to dominate me through their cruel judgments and nasty words. That their judgments drove me to make changes.

I don't regret the changes. They gave me more confidence. But I do regret the motive for the changes. I regret living under the judgments of others. I regret being manipulated through the cruel pettiness of insecure human beings. People who found happiness in my unhappiness. People who found security in my insecurity. People whose judgment said more about them than it said about me.

I have bad news. It's going to be worse for you as a girl. You're already in my eyes a very beautiful little girl. And I'm not just being a glass-half-full person when I say I think you're going to be a very beautiful woman.

But I've noticed something. People already are judging you based on physical beauty. At two, they are already projecting how beautiful you will be or not be. Welcome to the world. It just never ends.

Everything about your physical appearance is going to be judged. They're going to judge your eyes. They're going to judge your skin and its complexion. They're going to judge your nose and ears. They're going to judge your mouth and teeth. They're going to judge your hair color, style, and texture. They're going to judge your neck. They're going to judge your body type. They're going to judge your bone structure and muscle tone. They're going to judge your breasts, your butt, your legs, etc.

Welcome to the real world. It's all one, big dominance hierarchy. And physical beauty is the fast path to dominance. If another girl thinks she's prettier than you, don't be surprised if she's not nice to you.

- In her own mind, she has claimed the dominant position.
- In her mind, she is the judge. You are the judged and you must live under her judgment.
- In her mind, she has the right to disrespect you.
- In her mind, she can justly be mean, nasty, and condescending to you.
- In her mind, she's better than you.

Before I go too far, let me say something. You are beautiful. You are going to be tempted to be the dominator. That you can treat people bad who you judge to be more physically unattractive than yourself.

Don't you dare. Don't judge people, love them. Don't label people, love them. Don't lord over people, love them. Lift people up. Don't put them down.

Second, in this world, everything about your intelligence will be judged. If someone judges themselves to be smarter than you, they will assume the dominant position over you. They will expect you to live under their judgment. They will expect you to submit to their will and decision making. They will expect you to wear their labels for you. They expect you to surrender to them the diamonds of your identity and inner peace.

Your intelligence will be judged in any possible scenario you find yourself in. People will want to know your knowledge and skill level:

- in any sport you participate in
- in any subject you study in school
- in any musical instrument you lay your hands on
- in any job you are working
- in any discussion on video games and entertainment, etc.

Why?

Because if people judge themselves to be smarter, more skilled, and more experienced, they will assume the dominant position. They become the judge. You become the judged.

After leaving ministry, I remember working a construction job for a couple of months. I was low man on the totem pole when it came to building skills.

And the men I worked with treated me accordingly. The loved their area of dominance over me. Were they bigger than me? No. Were they wealthier than me? No. Were they more well-traveled than me? No. Were they more educated than me. No. Were they any better looking than me. Not really.

But they were better at installing kitchens. Therefore, they judged themselves to be dominant. They had the right to be condescending and treat me as though I was stupid. Because I wasn't "smart" in their area.

I have to also add this. One day they were trying to make me feel worthless and insignificant because they had watched more movies than I had. That they were smarter, more worldly wise, and more knowledgeable about modern entertainment. My congratulations to them. They were better couch potatoes than me.

Be prepared. You are in a world where everyone is vying for dominance. People trying to make you look stupid will be a daily occurrence. When it comes to knowledge and intelligence, everyone is looking for the high ground. Everyone wants to know more than you and judge themselves as more intelligent, that way they get the dominant position. They want to be the judge, not the judged. They want the "right" to be mean and nasty. They want to define your identity and disrupt your inner peace.

I should also add, your intelligence will be judged by your ability to speak. If you are clear and articulate, they will judge you to be intelligent. If you are shy, quiet, slow in delivery, or inarticulate, they will judge you to be unintelligent.

Is it any wonder why public speaking is almost always near the top of any "greatest fears" list? Legions of people are extremely smart, but they do not want to expose themselves to the judgmental ears and eyes of a crowd. I get it.

Third, in this world, everything about your possessions will be judged. If someone judges themselves to be richer than you, they will act dominant over you. In their minds, they are the judge. You are the judged and must live under their judgment. In their minds, they are superior, you are inferior. In their minds, they can treat you bad. In their minds, they are better than you.

Recently, we began watching Season 1 of *Little House on the Prairie*. A show I watched growing up. In one of the episodes we were watching, Mary and Laura were nervous about their first day of school. Not only was it their first day of school. They were new in town and had never attended school before. And they were farmer's daughters with plain clothing.

As they arrived at their one room schoolhouse in Walnut Grove, Kansas, the judgmental eyes of all the other students were on them. Like a wolf pack, the students instantly smelled Mary and Laura's fear. They mocked their ignorance and inexperience. They looked down on the fact they were poor and in drab clothing.

And the richest, prettiest girl in school, Nellie Olson, quickly asserted the dominance of an alpha female. She scanned Mary and Laura up and down with her eyes. She then gave them a condescending look and said, "Hmm. Country Girls."

Nellie judged them. Nellie labeled them. Nellie treated them like crap. Nellie attempted to rule over them on the playground. Everyone had to play the games that Nellie decided. Nellie expected them to live under her judgment.

Something Mary and Laura learned not to do. Instead, they learned to stand up to Nellie and to live above, not under, her judgments.

"Nellie Olson's" are a dime a dozen. They are everywhere. In every workplace. In every school classroom. In every sporting event. In every social gathering. In every church. In every family. In every setting. Never be one. Never live under the judgment of one.

The "Nellie Olson's" of the world want to dominate you. They will judge everything about all your possessions. They are looking for an opening to assert dominance. They will judge your clothes and shoes. They will want to know the brand names that you wear or do not wear. They want to estimate in their minds how much your clothing and shoes cost. If they judge you to be inferior to them concerning these matters, they will believe themselves to be dominant over you. And they will treat you accordingly.

The "Nellie Olson's" of the world will judge you by the lunch you pack, the type of foods you eat, and even the lunchbox that it is in. They will judge you by what you drink out of. Even food comparisons turn into dominance hierarchy battles.

And I'm sorry, but you will be judged by your family. You will be judged by the physical appearance, intelligence, and social confidence of your father, mother, and brothers. You will be judged for having a brother with Down's Syndrome and whose Autism makes him uncomfortably stim. You will be judged by the car we drop you off in. You will be judged by the house we live in.

You will definitely be judged by the professions of myself and your mother. You will be asked frequently, "What does your father do?" And, "What does your mother do?"

Hmm. I wonder why they want to know this?

I wish I did not have to share these things with you. But I think it's going to help you survive in this world of slavery. And I want you to have a game plan on how you're going to deal with this.

Just understanding the universal normality of being judged is a great start. Make no mistake, all humans are constantly judging and comparing themselves with one another, because they are trying to see where they fit in the dominance hierarchy.

Be prepared. You live in a world where everyone judges one another all the time about everything. The world is one big, battle for survival. Which caused the world to become one, big dominance hierarchy battle. Which caused the world to become one, big ball of perpetual judgment.

How do you survive in such a world? By not surrendering the diamonds of your identity and inner peace to anyone. NO ONE gets your diamonds. By protecting your mind by knowing how to think for yourself. And by having the courage to live above, not below the judgments of others.

Here's the statement again that you'll probably hear me say a 1000 times in the first 18 years of your life.

I cannot stop you from judging me. But you cannot stop me from living above your judgment.

This is what you must always think, and even frequently say, to the "Nellie Olson's" of the world. Those who want to assume dominance over you. Those who have set themselves up as judge over you. Those who want you to live under their judgment.

There may be occasions where someone tries to make you feel inferior because of physical appearance, intelligence, wealth, skills, etc. Feel free to look at them and say, "I cannot stop you from judging me. But you cannot stop me from living above your judgment."

Let me give you a visual. Make a fist with your right hand. This fist represents you. Then make an umbrella shape with your left hand, palm-side facing downward. Place your right fist beneath your now arched, umbrella-shaped left hand. This umbrella-shaped left hand represents any judgmental person attempting to dominate and control you.

This is what the "Nellie Olson's" of the world want. For you to be living underneath the shade of their judgment. For you to be controlled by the label they have slapped on you. For them to achieve a sadistic inner peace by the knowledge they have disrupted yours.

You can't stop people from attempting to do this. And some might succeed for as long as you allow it. But don't stay there. Don't live under the judgment of another human being. Living free requires that you learn the skill of living above the judgments of others.

Now take your right fist which is below the umbrella-shaped left hand and do three things: 1) pull it out from underneath the left hand, 2) place it above the left hand, and 3) forcefully pound the left hand down. This represents the choice to live above the judgments of others. You can't stop people from judging you. But they can't stop you from living above their judgments.

I want you to remember this visual every time someone comes up and makes some kind of mean, nasty comment. Remember they want dominance over you. They want to let you know that they believe themselves to be superior to you. They want to be the judge. They want you to be their judged. It's just part of man's baser nature.

Let's give a practical, future scenario. Let's say that one day, when you are having a bad hair day, some catty girl sarcastically spouts, "Nice hair, Hallie." And it is abundantly clear that she is just saying it to be mean, and as a means of dominance over you.

In that moment, make a decision. Choose to live above, not beneath the judgment of another. You, not her, have the power over your own identity and inner peace. You have the power to say to yourself, "I cannot stop her from being a jerk. I cannot stop her from being judgmental and cruel. But she cannot stop me from living above her judgment."

Get to the place where you can reply, "I know making fun of me makes you feel like you're more. But it doesn't make me feel like I'm less." In some situations, you might even say, "You'll never earn my respect by disrespecting me."

As I close this chapter, let me clarify two things. First, I'm not talking about being hyper-sensitive about any and all comments that could ever be made to you. I beg you, don't take yourself too seriously.

Get over yourself. Soon. Enjoy good-natured ribbing that may come from one of your friends causing you both to laugh about an unmanageable hair day.

You will need to learn to laugh at yourself. What I'm talking about in this chapter is living above bad-natured put downs coming from people who clearly want dominance over you.

Second, the judgments of others, even those given with bad motives, can occasionally be helpful. Learn to judge the judgments.

- Are these things being said as constructive criticism? Is the person saying this to build and better me?
- Or, are these things being said as destructive criticism? Is the person saying this to dominate and destroy me?
- Can even the words of an enemy, maliciously spoken to hurt me, also be used to instruct and to help me?

Criticism, whether constructive or destructive, is like potential food. Some of it is harmful like poison berries. Don't ever pick it up. Don't ever eat it. It's fatal. Don't consider it for a moment.

But most criticism is edible, even if it is not enjoyable. Take it, eat it, and slowly digest it.

What happens during the digestion of real food? Your body breaks down and sorts everything you've eaten. Some usable parts of the digested food will be retained and incorporated into building the cells of your body. The unusable parts of the digested food will be rejected and eliminated from your body all together.

The same goes for the digestion of edible, critical judgments from other people. Your mind should slowly break down and sort everything that was said to you. Some usable parts of the criticism should be retained and incorporated in order to make you better. The unusable parts of the criticism should be rejected and eliminated from your mind, emotions, and life all together.

Having made these two important clarifiers, let me double down on this admonition: live above the judgments of others. May your mentality always be: *I can't stop you from judging me. But you can't stop me from living above your judgment.*

These two survival skills: 1) learning how to think, and 2) learning how to live above the judgments of others, will help keep you from being dominated in life. They are absolute essentials for walking the path of freedom and for feeling free in a world of slavery.

Now let me now give you some very specific preparation for living in this world of slavery. I'm going to share with you how to protect yourself from various types of *power-class* dominators (the religious, ruling, and rich classes) and *practical-class* dominators (parents and siblings) who will want control of your diamonds.

CHAPTER 14

You Were Not Born to be Dominated by the Religious Class

You were born free. You were not born to be the slave of the religious class.

They don't own you. Protect the diamonds of your identity and your inner peace from the religious class. *When* the religious class comes for them, look them in the eyes and tell them, "You can't have them. I was born to be free. I wasn't born to be dominated by you."

I encourage you to live your life open to the question of God's existence. But I highly encourage you to live your life closed to organized religion.

My parenting style is kind of obvious. My parenting of you five children is governed more by my weaknesses than by my strengths. It is directed more by my internal pain than by what has brought me pleasure in life.

If something is a weakness with me, I want it to be a strength with you. If something has hurt me, I don't want it to hurt you.

Nothing has hurt me more in life than religion. I don't want it to hurt you. Nothing has caused me more pain in life than religion. I want you to avoid this pain. Nothing has filled my heart with fear more than religion. I don't want you to be afraid of it. Nothing has perpetually poisoned and ruined my sense of inner peace and harmony more than religiously trained guilt. I never want you to feel and carry such a load of worthless guilt.

You were born free. You were not born to be the slave of the religious class. Never give the religious class the diamonds of your identity and inner peace. Come to your own conclusions about God, the meaning of this life, if there is an afterlife, etc. Never let a religion do your thinking for you. Never let a religion threaten you if you do not accept their conclusions.

Most of the religious world would hate the advice I just gave you. It's a threat to their dominance and to their survival.

Where does one start on the subject of living a life free from the religious class?

For starters, let me make a big concession. *If* there is a God…then he does have a right to tell us what to do. We are his servants and he should expect our loyalty and obedience. The diamonds of our identity and inner peace are gifts from him and to be used for him.

But the problem with this is obvious. It's a big "if." We just don't know *if* there is a God. No one does.

That is why it is called *faith*. If someone *knows* that there is a God, then no *faith* is required. If someone *knows* that there is a God, then this should be called *knowledge*, established fact based on hard evidence.

But instead, we call it *faith*. Because we don't *know*. Faith is the imaginary certainty we create out of our uncertainty. We live like something is true even though, if we are painfully honest, we don't *know* if it is *true*. And we do this for our own survival and sanity.

And that is not really a criticism. I get it. I really do.

I absolutely hate labels. But today I would consider myself *agnostic* when it comes to the existence of God. I just don't know.

That is not a copout. It is not that I am being mentally lazy. To the contrary, I'm just mentally exhausted from contemplating this question for over 40 years.

I do not deny the existence of God. But I do doubt it. Sometimes I look at the vast universe and our tiny planet and think, "How can there be a God?" And then sometimes I look at it all and think, "How can there *not* be a God?" Let me first talk about the three things that make me doubt the existence of God.

First, Astronomy makes me doubt the existence of God. Billions of stars, planets, and moons, in billions of galaxies that are billions of light years away from each other.

- Where did they come from?
- How did they form?
- How old are they?
- Is there a fine tuning and order to it all, or is it more chaotic than we care to admit?
- Can we observe the birth of a star?
- How was it born?
- Can we observe the death of a star?
- How did it die?
- Can we truly measure the accuracy of the distance between stars?
- Is there intelligent life "out there"?

Natural explanations and answers to these Astronomical questions seem more plausible than the supernatural explanation of Genesis 1 – the foundation for all monotheistic religions. In that account of the absolute origin of all things, in the beginning you simply have an eternally existent God and the blackness of nothing-ness.

Then God creates planet Earth and light. So now it is just God, Earth, darkness, and light.

No sun. No moon. No solar system. No other planets or dwarf planets. No other galaxies or solar systems.

Then, according to Genesis 1, on the fourth day of creation, God builds the entire universe around the Earth. He makes the sun of our solar system. He makes our moon.[5] Implicit in the phrase "he made the stars also" (Genesis 1:16) is that God also made on the fourth day: Mercury, Venus, Mars and its two moons, Jupiter and its 79 moons, Saturn and its 82 moons, Uranus and its 27 moons, Neptune with its 14 moons, and the dwarf planets Pluto and its 5 moons, Eris and its 1 moon, Haumea and its 2 moons, Makemake, and Ceres.

And of course, on this one day, he also made the billions of other galaxies, solar systems, planets, and moons.

I find this hard to believe. Earth suspended in the blackness of nothingness all by itself. Then the entire universe was built around it. Astronomy makes me doubt the existence of God.

Second, history makes me doubt the existence of God. When I look at history, it looks more like God is absent than present. That it really isn't "His-story." That, at best, he is an indifferent spectator of what is going on rather than an involved participant.

Many call this the "Problem of Evil." If there is a God, how can he allow so much pain and suffering on this planet? Why the brutal battle for survival? Why the food chain? Why dominance hierarchies? Why human sex trafficking and grooming gangs? Why cartels? Why constant war? Why racism? Why sexism? Why caste and class systems? Why slavery? Why genocide? Why rape? Why disease? Why hatred? Why hopelessness? Why starvation and thirst? Why all the cruelty and coercion?

[5] https://solarsystem.nasa.gov/moons/overview/ - Full credit for all this information goes to NASA's website.

In short, the whole gamut of the "How the World Works from A to Z" observations that I shared with you, all make me doubt the existence of God. History makes me doubt the existence of God. I say this without apology. If this is God's plan, it sucks.

Third, morality makes me doubt the existence of God.

Yes, I just said that.

Because most religions would point to the concepts of morality, so-called *conscience*, and innate feelings of right and wrong as maybe the chief evidence for the existence of God. They would argue, if there is no God, then where do you get your morality and your sense of "conscience" from?

But the question is not where do *I* get *my* morality from? The real question is: throughout history, where *has* humanity gotten its morality from?

You know what I presently believe. That morality comes from survivability. From both the perspectives of the dominator and the dominated.

But what about the monotheist (the Jew, Christian, or Muslim) and his argument that there is one, true God, and that morality comes from him? That God has spoken and plainly revealed to mankind how he wants us to behave.

Did he?

- When did God reveal his morality?
- To whom did he reveal it?
- And why to that person or people?
- Why not to everybody on Earth, at one time – so we're all on the same page?
- How many times did God reveal his morality in history?
- Did the morality he revealed at various times stay consistent?
- Did it ever change?
- Why did it change?
- Does God himself live by his own standards of morality?

If you want to know the cause of much of Earth's craziness, it can be found in the answers people create to these morality questions.

It sounds so good to say that God is the author of morality. But which God? Yahweh of Judaism? The Heavenly Father of Christianity? Allah of Islam? Are all these the same God?

To be sure, there's some obvious overlap in morality between these three religions. For instance, all three religions put a premium on charity to the poor.

But there are many differences in defining morality between the three monotheistic religions. They differ on dietary morality that God supposedly has revealed. That is, what foods and meats they believe God wants a person to eat or not eat. Jews and Muslims cannot eat pork chops or ham (Leviticus 11; Deuteronomy 14; Sura 2:173). Christians sure can (Acts 10:12-15; I Timothy 4:1-5).

The three differ on whether or not God allows a person to drink wine or beer. Jews can drink (Psalm 104:14-15; Ecclesiastes 9:7). Christians have historically been divided on the issue (Romans 14:21) even though Jesus himself clearly drank wine and was criticized for drinking wine (Matthew 11:19). Muslims seem to be divided as well on the issue (2:219; 4:43; 5:90).

But all three religions have this in common: they lose their minds when people violate and trouble their *conscience* of supposedly God-revealed standards of dietary morality.

And I have to also point out what is downright hilarious – if it wasn't so sad. Just pointing out mere dietary and drink differences between the Monotheistic religions exposes how morality drives humans mad.

The Christian observing the dietary habits of the pork and shrimp abstaining Jew might think, "Jeez, chill out. You're so strict. You're too restrictive. Go to Golden Coral and enjoy."

But then when the same teetotaling Christian observes that the Jew drinks wine and beer he will think, "You sinner. You're so lax on moral issues. You're too permissive."

Which is it?

- For the Christian, is the Jew too morally restrictive on diet or too morally permissive on drink?
- For the Jew, is the Christian too morally restrictive on drink or too morally permissive on diet?
- Which religion accurately reflects what God has revealed on diet and drink?

To be fair, this is not just a problem between rival religions. This is a universal human problem. Numerous examples could be given of bizarre moral conundrums between any and all rival people groups on Earth. Groups that condemn each other for being too morally restrictive in one area while being too morally permissive in another area.

Can you see why this world is crazy? And as a result, why morality makes me doubt the existence of God?

The three monotheistic religions also differ on marital morality that God has allegedly revealed. How many wives can a man have?

- Judaism and the nation of Israel was created from Jacob and his four wives (Genesis 46:8ff.). Israel's King David and his royal family was comprised of multiple wives (II Samuel 3:2-5; 12:8). The Torah doesn't forbid polygamy anywhere.
- Paul of Christianity says one (I Corinthians 7:2).
- Islam says up to four (4:3).

Can a person divorce? Is remarriage permissible and under what circumstances? Judaism and Islam allow for divorce and remarriage (Deuteronomy 24:1-4; Sura 2:231). Christianity, which would see itself as more loving and forgiving compared to the other two religions, has historically been brutally cruel and rigid on this issue (Matthew 19:1-12).

The three religions also differ on Sabbath or day of rest observances that God has revealed to them. Friday is special to Muslims (62:9-10). Saturday is special to Jews (Exodus 20:8). Sunday is special to Christians (Mark 16:9; Revelation 1:10).

And those are just some of the practical differences on moral issues. They also differ greatly on big picture stuff like salvation. Which, the bottom-line goal of salvation is being judged by God to be good, just, and moral – and therefore accepted by him on judgment day. And as a result, saved from his punishment of eternal fire and rewarded with eternal life.

Judaism, Christianity, and Islam have different ideas of how to "secure" this acceptance. Each has come up with varying combinations of obedience, forgiveness, sacrificial atonement, martyrdom, and grace. What someone must do to be "saved" varies between the three monotheistic religions.

And the bottom line for each: it's all *faith.* No one *knows* that God will accept them on judgment day. They can only do their best, believe, and hope.

The point I'm making is this: apparently God is NOT telling the monotheistic religions all the same standards of morality. The message is not consistent. And the differences are not insignificant. Throughout history, all three monotheistic religions have killed one another over these differences of morality.

And how do each of these monotheistic religions view one another today? They still condemn the others as being false. That the morality God revealed to them is the truth, and that the morality God revealed to the other two is false or outdated.

And such moral confusion is a far worse matter than the irrefutable fact that Judaism, Christianity, and Islam cannot agree with each other on the morality they believe "comes from God."

Each of these three religions cannot even agree *within their own religion* on countless matters of morality.

One of the strongest arguments leveled against Christianity is that there is no such thing as Christianity (singular). That there are only Christianities (plural). If there are some 34,000 denominations of Christianity, which one is the true one? Which one represents pure Christianity? Which one got it right concerning God's revealed morality?

During my 40 years in Christianity it was always a fiasco trying to figure out God's morality on ten thousand different issues. The words you could say or not say. Places you could go or not go. The entertainment you were allowed or were forbidden. The music you should not listen to and could listen to. The clothes you could wear or not wear. The facial hair you could have or not have. The authors you could read or not read. The other types of "Christians" you should separate from and the ones you could associate with. How much money should be given to the church. Bible versions you should use or not use. Holding a microphone vs. standing behind a microphone. Padded pews vs. folding chairs.

To name a few. You get what I'm saying.

And the debates over the intangible, theoretical doctrinal issues were endless. You could subdivide each of the "core doctrines" on God the Father, God the Son, God the Holy Spirit, angels, church authority, salvation, justification, sanctification, glorification, the end-times, the inspiration of the Bible, etc. into scores of debates over the tiniest details and nuances.

And Christianity always turns doctrinal differences into moral issues.

Did you catch that?

In Christianity, if you don't believe "right," you're not behaving right.

- If you do not believe Jesus is God, you go to hell – just like the serial killer.

- To the Roman Catholic, if you believe in justification by grace through *faith alone apart from works*, you go to hell – just like the serial rapist.
- To the Protestant, if you do NOT believe in justification by grace through *faith alone apart from works*, you go to hell – just like Hitler.

In Christianity, if you don't believe right, you will be punished as though you didn't behave right.

In short, for 40 years, I observed churches splitting left and right because they could never agree over matters of morality and doctrine. I witnessed chronic debate and dispute over who God is, the morality he supposedly has revealed, what pisses him off, and what makes him happy.

And Judaism and Islam have all the same issues. Maybe they have less denominations and sects than Christianity, but they are still divided. Shia and Sunni Muslims have infamously slaughtered one another throughout history because they believe the other group to be "wrong" and "worthy of punishment" for holding to some "heretical" position in matters of authority and morality.

Can you see why morality actually makes me doubt the existence of God? Can you see why I am encouraging you to never surrender the diamonds of your identity and inner peace to the religious class? It seems abundantly clear from the three monotheistic religions that God doesn't tell everybody the same thing.

When it comes to morality, religion creates more questions than it provides answers.

Are the three monotheistic religions really the origin of all morality? Can you not read Hammurabi's Code or other ancient law codes predating Moses and the 10 Commandments? Isn't it clear that humans had some sense of morality before Judaism, Christianity, and Islam?

And why was God's morality revealed so "late in the game" of human history? Even from the Genesis timeline, the Ten Commandments were given about 2500 years after Adam and Eve were kicked out of the Garden of Eden. Why not reveal to them the Ten Commandments right then and there? Why wait two and a half millennia?

Why is Heaven and Hell, these crucial matters of such "eternal" importance according to Christianity and Islam, revealed so late in human history? Why reveal these things 4000 years after creation? If there is an eternal hell to shun, shouldn't that have been revealed about 4000 years earlier? Shouldn't Adam and Eve, Noah, Abraham, Moses, and the entire nation of Israel been disclosed this vital information?

And why is God's all-important, universal morality for the entire human race always revealed to one guy in one, brief time period?

Why not to all people on earth? Frequently. Unmistakably.

Instead, we all have to believe that he revealed his morality *to someone else*. To one person who had to spread the message of God's revealed morality to the rest of the planet. It seems to me that God is a pretty inefficient communicator of his morality.

This makes God very impersonal. Why do Jews in the 21st century have to believe that God talked to Moses on a mountaintop 3500 years prior?

Surely the Jew must ask himself, "Why doesn't God talk *to me*? Instead, I have to believe that God talked *to him* – some guy 3500 years ago. Why doesn't God suspend the laws of nature and perform miracles *for me*? Instead, I have to believe that God performed miracles *for him* – some guy 3500 years ago."

21st century Christians can ask the same questions. "Why doesn't God talk *to me*? Instead, I have to believe that God talked to some guy – or even 12 disciples of this guy – 2000 years ago near Jerusalem, Israel. Why doesn't God suspend the laws of nature and perform miracles *for me*? Instead, I have to believe that God performed miracles for those guys 2000 years ago."

21st century Muslims can ask the same questions. "Why doesn't God talk *to me*? Instead, I have to believe that God talked through the angel Gabriel to some guy in an Arabian cave 1400 years ago."

Do you see the problem here? God doesn't talk to *us*. We have to believe that he talked to *somebody else* – thousands of years ago.

I can hear the immediate, explosive response from the religious class, "Oh, but he does talk to us today!"

Hmm.

Does he?

- When?
- How often?
- What does he say?
- Do you really think this is God speaking to you?
- Or is it Jesus?
- The Holy Spirit?
- An angel?
- The devil?
- An ancestor?

Or is it possible that it is *you* speaking to *you*?

Could it be that any internal dialogue you are experiencing is not a unique, supernatural phenomenon? Is it possible that what is going on inside you is merely the universal, natural process of how all human minds and nervous systems function? Have you considered that the still, small voice(s) occurring inside of you are nothing more than: 1) your creative imagination, 2) blending with your known information, and 3) forming a biased interpretation of all of your life circumstances?

Did you catch that?

Is it not possible that your "personal conversations with God" are nothing more than a survivability soup – a stirring together of the three ingredients of imagination, information, and interpretation? Is it not possible that your "inner spiritual life" is nothing more than just another child of survivability?

If God actually talks to you personally, and on a frequent basis, then why would you ever need advice from a holy man? Why would you ever grapple in decision-making, discerning God's will, and guidance for life?

"Ah, but he also speaks to me through my holy book!"

Does he?

Why does God need a holy book to talk to someone? Is that how he talked to Adam, Noah, Abraham, Isaac, Jacob, Moses, Jesus, Paul, and Mohammed? Why did God stop talking to people personally? Why did he start using holy books?

Concerning holy books, where did yours come from? Can you tell the story of your holy book's formation? Could you put on a homemade timeline your holy books' compositions, compiling, editing, canonizations through the voting process of men, etc.? How much of human history did not have your holy book? How many people in history could not read your holy book? Was the holy book really written for you?

"Ah, but he also speaks to me through the *conscience* he gave me!"

Does he?

Where does this "conscience" live inside your body? In the amygdala of your brain? In your gut? In your upper left abdominal region? Where is the "conscience" located in the human body?

Why does it seem like no two "consciences" on earth rule the exact same way? How can two people claim to be acting in "good conscience" when their moral positions are in complete opposition to one another? How do you explain 10,000 religions and 34,000 denominations of Christianity whose "consciences" cannot get on the same page? Do you really think there is one God and one Holy Spirit of God telling everybody the same thing through the "conscience"?

What is "conscience" then?

Another child of survivability. Everything I have said in this book about morality applies to "conscience." I have observed that a religious "conscience" is nothing more than programmed promptings or trained triggers. Promptings and triggers that you were not born with. Promptings and triggers that were programmed into a person by religious dominators. Promptings and triggers that were conditioned into a person through the same punishment and rewards methods you would use on a dog.

As a result, I have observed that having a "good conscience" is not the result of having done *right*. It is the result of gaining *relief*. Relief that you will not be hurt by a religious class dominator. Proving that a "good conscience" is predominantly about gaining relief from the fear of being hurt by a dominator is another book in itself.

Bottom line: I have doubts – serious doubts – that God talks to us. Not audibly and personally. Not internally and mystically. Not through a Holy Book. It is my present belief that what humans have interpreted as supernatural communication, is really nothing more than the natural circuitry of the human brain and nervous system.

But I will be humble and honest enough to admit, I could be wrong.

However, what is factual and undeniable is that humans have slaughtered each other for thousands of years over what they believe God spoke to the founder of their religion. Humans have justified slaughtering each other over matters of morality, "conscience," and holy books. Humans moralizing the dominance hierarchy.

Sound familiar?

Are you kind of getting why I don't think you should give the diamonds of your inner peace and your identity to the religious class? Or as to why I think you should think for yourself on the matters of God and morality?

Astronomy, history, and morality all make me doubt the existence of God.

Believe it or not, after everything I just said, I do not deny the possibility of God's existence. There might be a God.

I just don't know.

And there are some things that make me think God exists.

The fact of invisible energy and power makes me think God is a possibility. While I can see the results of gravity, I can't see gravity itself. I can't hold it in my hand. Where does gravity come from? Where does energy come from? Where did the force of energy come from that created the alleged Big Bang? Is energy eternal? What is the source of this invisible power?

Biology and genetic information (DNA) make me think God is a possibility. Many think this closes the door on God as a reality. I think it opens the door to God being a possibility. When it comes to life and – yes – the design of life, where did the genetic information come from? The information does reveal intelligence. Where did the information come from? Can non-living matter produce living organisms with a genetic code?

Hallie, *you* make me think that God might exist. When I think of your formation through the replication of cells, the beating of your heart for the first time, the development of your brain, eyes, ears, nose, teeth, digestive system, immune system, excretory system, etc. – it's overwhelming. When I think that you were attached to your mother by an umbilical cord that did not mix your blood with hers all the while nourishing you inside her womb, it's pretty remarkable. Having observed the incredible nuances involved with your mother's milk production and your nourishment through it – I find it hard to imagine an evolutionary process that slowly "got this right" over time.

Just the overall fact of my own existence and being alive makes me consider God. To think that non-life created life, that unintelligence created intelligence, that non-consciousness created consciousness, and that chaos created order is hard to comprehend. It's *very* hard to believe.

It seems something or someone has always existed. In a world of cause and effect, something or someone was the original "uncaused cause" that began it all. A living, intelligent, conscious God is a possibility.

The "Problem of Pleasure" makes me consider God's existence. I believe it was G.K. Chesterton who pointed this out. It is easy to point out the "Problem of Pain." That is, all of the pain and suffering in the world that make us doubt God's existence.

But we must also be humble and honest enough to point out the "Problem of Pleasure." That being, all of the beauty, love, and pleasure in the world that make us consider God's existence.

- The unbelievable pleasure of marriage that I have experienced with your mother.
- The pleasure of holding a newborn child in my arms.
- The pleasure of raising you five children through all the stages of life.
- The pleasure of listening to the remarkable language of music.
- The pleasure I feel observing mountains, meadows, wildlife, rushing rivers, and vast oceans.
- The pleasure of humor and laughter.
- The pleasure of eating and drinking.
- The pleasure of social community and camaraderie.
- The pleasure of feeling life's sweetest emotions.

And this "Problem of Pleasure" makes me consider God's existence. And if he exists, maybe he isn't so cruel and mean. Maybe he isn't such a "bad guy."

Having brutally criticized religion in this book, let me say two things to slightly balance the equation.

First, despite their shortcomings, the lifestyles of some religious groups are among the best on Earth. Judaism, Christianity, and Islam are actually all strong, historical critiques of human behavior. All of them have pointed out foolish human behaviors and choices. All of them have pointed out wise human behaviors and choices.

Living a good life is about making wise choices. Choices that have constructive consequences.

Living a good life is about avoiding foolish choices. Choices that have destructive consequences.

Take Judaism for instance. It is my observation that there are three macro-morality principles in the Jewish Old Testament: 1) No idolatry. Instead, love the Creator God. 2) No injustice. Instead, love your neighbor as yourself. 3) No immorality (sexual). Instead, form and love your family.

If we are brutally honest, this makes sense. Idolatry, injustice, and immorality are foolish and destructive choices. Loving God, loving others, and family are wise and constructive choices.

If the whole Earth functioned by a love God, love others, and family ethic, it would be an infinitely better place.

Yes, the Monotheistic critiques of human behavior should be critiqued themselves. Without question. But at the same time, we must be humble enough to happily concede that there is much wisdom to be gained from these religious traditions. And we are foolish to not learn from them.

Second, the stories of religion, in a very general sense, do have some credibility. Enough to make one consider God's existence.

Many attempt to prove that Jewish history has no evidence of being true. That the Torah (first five books of the Bible) is completely false. However, the Tanakh (the entire Old Testament) and its storyline is plausible just by a general observation of the world.

The story of the Old Testament is about the nation of Israel and the royal family who lead them (the house of David). The end of the Old Testament has Yahweh scattering Jews all over the world as punishment for their idolatry – the worship of false gods. A small remnant remained in or returned to their homeland after a period of exile.

Like it or not, this is congruent with what I see when observing the world. Jews are scattered all over the world. They have been incredibly prosperous. They have been incredibly persecuted.

Am I saying they are God's chosen people? No. But I'm not denying it either. For anyone doubting or denying God's existence this is an uncomfortable fact that we all must deal with.

Christendom is also a reality. Some today want to prove that Jesus didn't even exist. But there is a problem. Jesus has two billion followers on Twitter – so to speak. Yes, these followers disagree with and fight one another on points of doctrine and ethics. But the figure they build their systems around is a singular identity.

Where did two billion Christians come from? If you begin traveling backwards in time to uncover the first followers of Jesus, it is difficult to explain away the church fathers of the 2nd, 3rd, and 4th centuries. Going back even farther, it is difficult to explain away all of the New Testament letters of a historical figure named Paul from the mid-1st century. Even if Paul is a couple of decades removed from Jesus, who was he talking about? Did Paul really talk to and know the disciples who had traveled with Jesus, had learned from him, and had been commissioned to spread his message?

For one doubting or denying the existence of God, this uncomfortable fact remains: there are two billion Christians today. They came from somewhere. And you can trace them back to the mid-1st century. Maybe I can't "prove" the existence of the first seed that started a forest of two billion trees. But the forest exists none-the-less. With a standing forest, it's pretty hard to deny the existence of the first seed.

Similar arguments could be made for Islam. One can deny the experiences and revelations of Muhammad in a cave in Arabia. But one cannot deny that there are 1.5 billion Muslims in the world today.

Is there a God? Sometimes I look at the world and think, "How can there be a God?" Sometimes I look at the world and think, "How can there NOT be a God?" I just don't know.

But here's what I do know. The "Is there a God?" question continues to divide the world. It makes peace on Earth, and freedom on Earth impossible at this stage.

I really wish that God, if he exists, would take personal responsibility to get everybody on the same page. That he would personably speak in an unmistakable voice, to all peoples on Earth, at one time. No games. No mysteries. No prophets. No mediators. No holy books. No faith required.

Just clear, compassionate communication to a confused and crazy world.

Let's talk about you. Even though your father is presently agnostic, it is still accurate to say that you were born into a Christian family. One that comes from more of a Baptist Christian perspective. Your mother is a believer. Your grandparents are all believers, very devout ones. Most of your aunts and uncles are believers. And they are all good people – really good people. But they will push you very hard to be what they are.

Am I against this? No, if coercion and shaming is taken out of the equation. If you come to accept Jesus as Lord and Savior because you are convinced he is the truth – so be it. But do not let the forceful personalities of your grandparents and relatives coerce you into making the "choice" they want you to make.

You were born to be free, even free to believe. It will be your choice.

But let me be clear on why I am saying these things to you. Whether or not there is a God is one question. But whether or not I should submit to the domination of a certain interpretation of God, a religion, is another matter altogether.

Continue to wrestle with God and His existence. But do not be deceived by the slavery systems of the religious class. Religious class dominators who historically have invented an interpretation of God, and then threatened with murder anyone who questions what they have imagined and systematized.

Most who are born into and dominated by these religious slavery systems have no hope of ever being rescued. And I concede that many are happy within these systems. They have accepted their slavery. And they receive minimal punishment because they obey what their masters say. They experience what I call the "inner peace of a slave."

I will even go so far as to say that many religions have much to offer. They provide a moral structure to people's lives. They provide a social network. They provide deep meaning and purpose in people's lives.

I do not deny this at all. I simply deny large portions of the truthfulness of the claims within religion.

It is obvious, religion triggers me. Nothing has caused me more pain in this life than religion. I don't want religion to hurt you.

Therefore, I would encourage you to certainly live your life open to the possibility of God. But at the same time, I would highly encourage you to never surrender the diamonds of your identity and inner peace to a religion. You were born to be free. You were not born to be dominated by the religious class.

CHAPTER 15

You Were Not Born to be Dominated by the Ruling Class (Part 1)

You were born free. You were not born to be the slave of the ruling class.

They don't own you. You were not born to the slave of the government. Protect the diamonds of your identity and your inner peace from the ruling class. *When* the ruling class comes for them, look them in the eyes and tell them, "You can't have them. I was born to be free. I wasn't born to be dominated by you."

We live in a day when people are afraid of their government. Government has created a rule for almost every detail of our lives. With every rule the ruling class creates, they attach a threat of punishment to make us afraid of breaking that new rule. And the government will hurt us if they catch us disobeying them.

Fear. Fear. Fear. And more fear.

Fear is the nucleus in the replicating cell of society.

Between the religious class and the ruling class, it is no wonder mental health is such a problem in the world. Every step a person takes in this world is seemingly covered by another rule and another threat of being hurt. It is my strong belief that *most* anxiety on this planet is created by dominators – fear of punishing authorities.

Government is like the wild ivy vines that grow in the mountains of North Carolina. If the ivy vines are contained in a tiny area, like on a small hillside at the back of the house, it can be a beautiful touch in the landscaping of that property. Ivy in a small, contained, limited area can be nice. As a small, complementing piece to a much larger whole, ivy can be helpful. Ivy can save a lot of work in that given area.

But the homeowner must always keep the ivy accountable. Ivy needs to stay contained within its assigned realm by being constantly trimmed back to keep it from growing and spreading.

But ivy doesn't like being contained. Ivy doesn't want to be a small, contained, complementing piece. Ivy wants to be a large, uncontained centerpiece. And ivy is completely unaware of just how ugly it can make a home, or a forest look when it has been allowed to grow and spread without resistance.

If ivy vines are left alone, to grow as they will, they have no intention of ever stopping. If left uncontested, growing ivy will climb and cover whole houses. Growing ivy will zealously climb and wrap itself around every tree of the forest. Ivy will suffocate other living organisms in the quest for its own survival.

Government is just like wild ivy. When government is kept as a small, contained complementing piece to human existence, it can be very helpful. It can save a lot of work.

But government must always be kept accountable. Government needs to stay contained within its assigned realm by being constantly trimmed back to keep it from growing and spreading.

But government doesn't like being contained. Government doesn't want to be a small, contained, complementing piece. Government wants to be a large, uncontained centerpiece. And government is completely unaware of just how ugly it can make nations, states, counties, cities, and towns look when it has been allowed to grow and spread without resistance.

When government is left alone, to grow as it so wills, it has no intention of every stopping. If government is left uncontested, growing government will climb and cover whole civilizations, communities, economies, companies, families, and individuals. Growing government zealously climbs and wraps itself around every person in the *forest* of this world. Ruling class dominators gladly suffocate other human beings in the quest for their own survival. To gain and maintain their dominance.

The *Founding Fathers* of the United States understood this. That is why the Constitution contained the Bill of Rights – the rights to free speech, to carry weapons, privacy, etc. To contain the ivy of government. To keep government in a small, contained, complementing realm of life. To keep government from becoming a large, uncontained centerpiece in human existence. To keep the ivy of government trimmed back.

The *Founding Fathers* understood with great clarity that human thirst for power had historically ALWAYS behaved like wild ivy. Therefore, they overthrew their suffocating, overgrown British government and established a new American government. And the Constitution and the Bill of Rights within it were communicating, "This government is not allowed to grow, spread, climb, and suffocate the individuals living in this nation. This government is not for the enforcement of tyranny and domination. It is for the protection of human freedom."

The *Founding Fathers* knew the lessons of history. That dominators never lay down power. That dominators never diminish or lessen their power. That dominators are endlessly ambitious to grow, spread, and increase their power. That ruling class dominators are like wild ivy.

You were born into a world where the ivy of government has taken over every tree in the forest of our lives. The ivy of our American government has long ago grown over the "No trespassing" signs contained in the Constitution and Bill of Rights. Free speech is dying. The right to protect yourself with guns from a dominating government is dying. The right to privacy is dead. Excessive fines are the rule, not the exception.

Freedom is not dead, but it is dormant. The vision of the *Founding Fathers* that created the greatest leap in freedom for humanity is no longer being realized. Not surprisingly, people are generally unhappy.

The torch of freedom must be relit. People again need to be free and to feel free. To live their lives free to make their own choices in life. To live free and unafraid. To say with honor and conviction once again, "I own me. No one has the right to order me. No one has the right to oppress, threaten, and hurt me. No one has the right to coerce me into thinking, saying, doing, or being anything."

It is my firm conviction that the world would be instantly 50% better overnight if two things would take place: 1) remove all government coercion, and 2) aggressively trim back the ivy of government so that all that is left of the ruling class is government as a B.M.R.

B.M.R.?

The ivy of government should be radically trimmed back, so that it *only* serves as a **b**odyguard, a **m**ediator, and a **r**esource. That government is no longer a coercive bully, master, and ruler. Its leadership is stripped of all lordship and ownership. Government as only a B.M.R.

First, government should merely be a *bodyguard* that protects free peoples from hurting each other. Government is not there to coerce people into doing things. It is there *to stop* people from raping, murdering, stealing, kidnapping, and assaulting each other. Government should help protect people and their property from being hurt.

Government should have the same mentality as a presidential bodyguard. A presidential bodyguard does not try control speech. He's not focused on trying to zealously micromanage every word that comes out of every individual in every crowd. He doesn't try to shut down every heckler in the crowd. A presidential bodyguard has a clear priority and focus – the literal, physical safety of the President.

Government should simply be a bodyguard that protects against violent crime. It has a clear priority – the literal, physical safety of every person and their property. To protect people from being the victim of violent crime. Government is NOT to be a moralizing, micromanaging bully.

Second, government should be a *mediator*. If I were to give the role of government one word, it would be the word *mediator*. Government should exist to mediate territory and resource disputes between free peoples.

I've seen people get triggered over two feet when it comes to property lines and boundaries. Bad blood can be created in an instant when people get territorial. It is good to have government to impartially mediate between free peoples.

Government can also mediate our travel from place to place so that we do not kill each other in transit. Although the travel and traffic laws need to be reformed – especially the punishment for profit schemes that have been set up – the principles should stay in place. Government should be a mediator, not a master. But government should never be allowed to force its mediation on free peoples not wanting their mediation.

Third, government should be a *resource*. But as a resource, it should be optional. Government should provide optional resources, not oppressive requirements. Government should never use coercion to force their solutions upon free people.

For example, if government wants to make itself available as a resource to build private homes, great. But government should not be allowed to tell people what they can and cannot do with their homes. They should not be allowed to tell people who they can and cannot use to work on their home. Government should not be allowed to force codes and requirements on every light socket, 2 x 4, stairwell, septic system, H-Vac Unit, electric wire, bathroom, etc.

Government as an optional resource to tap into for private home construction? Fine. Government forcing their mediation, codes, inspectors, etc. on "free" people? Never. This is overgrown government ivy.

And the ivy of government is hideously overgrown when it comes to the economy, education, healthcare, housing, etc. In matters such as these, government can be an optional resource for people to voluntarily tap into if they should so choose. But government should never force these things on "free" people under threats of fining and cages.

The world would be 50% better overnight by: 1) removing all government coercion, and 2) aggressively trimming back the ivy of government so that all that is left of the ruling class is a B.M.R. Government as merely a bodyguard, a mediator, and a resource. Government never again as a bully, master, and ruler that terrorizes people born free, and who desire to live free, and to feel free.

For the first 40 years of my life, I never thought much about government and ruling classes. The first four decades of my life were spent obsessing over keeping God's endless rules. As a Baptist, I was too busy working feverishly to avoid being saved by good works (Did you catch the irony of that statement?). I was perpetually distracted with avoiding eternal hell and telling others about "the wonderful Christian life that I had found."

After leaving Christianity, I thought life would be way better. That I had been delivered from some evil, coercive, fear-based, mind-control cult that wanted to dominate every detail of my life.

My apologies to Christianity. An infinitely more evil, coercive, fear-based, mind-control cult was waiting for me.

The government.

I know Christopher Hitchens wrote a book entitled, *God is not Great: How Religion Poisons Everything*. But it's not merely religion that poisons everything. Coercion poisons everything – no matter who is doing the coercing. Being forced to do things, against your will, under unrelenting fear and threat of punishment poisons everything.

Government coercion poisons *everything*.

After hoping to find relief from religious coercion, I found that a worse coercion was waiting for me. Government coercion. I quickly discovered that I could do nothing – as an adult – without trying to get "permission" from daddy and mommy government.

After leaving ministry, no one was really interested in hiring an ex-Bible professor and pastor with two masters' degrees. So I went back to my roots as a farm-boy. I decided to start a lawn care business.

This seemed simple enough. Mow people's grass.

First, I bought what I needed. I purchased a used Dodge Ram truck, a 6 x 12 trailer, a Husqvarna zero turn mower, a push mower, a weed eater, and a blower.

Good to go right?

Enter the ivy of government.

1. The government ruling class forced me go to the DMV to register my truck.
2. The government ruling class forced me to pay for an inspection in order to get my truck registered.
3. The government ruling class forced me to buy insurance to get my truck registered.
4. The government ruling class forced me to pay sales tax on the purchase of the used truck.
5. The government ruling class forced me to pay for a license plate for the truck.
6. The government ruling class forced me to also pay property tax on my truck.

7. The government ruling class forced me to pay for a business license for lawn care. I needed their permission to "legally" survive and feed my family.
8. The government ruling class forced me to pay for business insurance to obtain the business license.
9. The government ruling class forced me to also pay them for a license plate to put on my trailer. That is, for my non-motorized accessory to an already licensed vehicle.
10. The government ruling class also forced me to pay annual property taxes on my mower, blower, and weed eaters. I'm not joking. Items to which I already paid hundreds of dollars in sales tax.
11. The government ruling class forced me to pay state and federal income tax on the income from my lawns.

Just to mow people's grass to feed my family. Invasive, suffocating, annoying government ivy.

And each of these eleven things – the government ruling class forces me to do every year. And I should mention that the government ruling class is not yet forcing me to pay a sales tax on my lawn services. My ruling class dominators are so good to me.

I'm not sure if there is an afterlife or not. What I do know is that we all have been given this one life. And this one life we've been given is too short to live underneath the domination of human government. Having a Mommy was great when I was 6. I don't need one at 46.

If you want to better the world overnight by 50%, remove coercion and radically trim back the ivy of government.

Hallie, learn to live with government. Not under it. They don't own you. They don't have the right order you around and to control all the details of your life. They don't have the right to oppress and hurt you. Never be afraid of your government. Push back. Resist their domination. They are not interested in your freedom. They will never give it to you. You must claim freedom for yourself.

This is the heritage of the country you were born into. America was founded on the spirit of freedom and willful disobedience to ruling class dominators. America was founded on the spirit of liberty and stubborn resistance to government.

The *Founding Fathers* of America resisted the domination of their ruling class. They resisted, disobeyed, and rejected the authority of 1) their mother country England, 2) their king – George III, and 3) their law-making body called Parliament.

Wow.

Imagine our state, North Carolina, saying, "We're fed up with the United States federal government. We are tired of them invading and suffocating our lives like wild ivy. We don't want to live under their rules anymore. We want to rule ourselves. We declare complete independence from Washington D.C., the rest of the country, from the President, from Congress, from their economy, and from their military protection. *We free ourselves* from any obligation to ever obey them again. We will never again live under their laws; we will forever live above their laws and apart from them."

The *Founding Fathers* thought like this. The *Founding Fathers* did this.

These days, I frequently hear a question being asked with the identifiable, Pharisaical stench of self-righteous moral indignation: "What, do you think your above the law? Hmm?"

According the *Declaration of Independence*, the founding document of the United States of America, the answer to that question is "Yes!"

Read these first two paragraphs of the *Declaration of Independence*. As you read these two paragraphs, answer the following two questions: 1) By what authority did the *Founding Fathers* reject England's authority? 2) Why did the *Founding Fathers* see themselves as being above the laws of Parliament and King George III ("God's ordained authority")? I have used bold and brackets to make emphasis and commentary.

The unanimous **Declaration** of the thirteen united States of America, When in the Course of human events, it becomes necessary for one people **to dissolve the political bands which have connected them with another**, and to assume among the powers of the earth, the separate and equal station to which the Laws of Nature and of Nature's God **entitle them**, a decent respect to the opinions of mankind requires that they should **declare the causes which impel them to the separation**.

We hold these **truths** [notice that this word is plural – look for the five truths that will be set-apart by the word "that"] to be self-evident, **that** all men are created equal, **that** they are endowed by their Creator with certain unalienable Rights, **that** among these are Life, Liberty and the pursuit of Happiness.--**That** to secure these rights, Governments are instituted among Men, deriving their just powers from the consent of the governed, --**That** whenever any Form of Government becomes destructive of these ends, it is the Right of the People to alter or to abolish it, and to institute new Government....

Again, why did the *Founding Fathers* see themselves above the authority their government? And why did they see themselves as being "above the law" and "God's ordained authority"?

The *Founding Fathers* rejected their government's authority and laws by holding on to five "self-evident" truths that Thomas Jefferson articulated in writing. Were you able to pinpoint these five truths distinguished by the word "that"? Here they are.

1. **that** all men are created equal,

Humans are not to be broken down into two unequal categories – the dominators and the dominated, the ruling class and the ruled class, the elite and the enslaved. All men are created equal.

2. **that** the Creator of all men has given them rights that are unalienable

The Creator of mankind has given men unalienable rights, something an individual possesses that can never be taken away from them. More on the word "unalienable" in a little bit.

3. **that** among these are.... "Among these" clearly implies that there are many unalienable rights besides the three that are stated. But Jefferson lists these three:

- **life** = self-ownership.
  - I own me. I am self-owned, not government owned.

- **liberty** = self-authority.
  - I rule me. I make my own choices and decisions. Self-authority and autonomy. Not government authority and sovereignty.

- **and the pursuit of happiness** = self-directed destiny.
  - I direct me. I design my own life. My life is self-designed, not government designed.

4. **that** governments are created by humans to protect these unalienable rights, and that the authority of these governments come from the willing consent and agreement of the governed.

To be honest, this fourth self-evident truth is "pie-in-the-sky" idealism – which I actually like. I love what Jefferson was saying.

But it's not reality. It never works this way. It's like saying the ruled class gets to tell the ruling class what to do. The dominated tell the dominators what to do. Government is to live in subjection to their governed.

Uh huh, right. That's how it works.

However, I'm still glad he wrote it. Humanity needed this ideal to be trending towards. This was the idealistic dream that made America the greatest nation in human history. America alone made human dominance hierarchies look much less like animal dominance hierarchies. America represents vastly less coercion and cruelty. While still remaining very coercive and cruel.

America was an incremental step towards greater freedom for humans. America traded in a King and a Parliament, for a President and a Congress.

An improvement.

But humanity still has a long way to go. The founding of America was not the apex or pinnacle of human freedom. It provided the foundation and ground floor for freedom. America was founded on the idealistic dream that government exists to protect the natural human desire for freedom. That government exists to protect a person and their property. That government exists merely as a just mediator between free peoples, keeping them from hurting one another. That government wants to leave people alone to own, order, and organize their own lives.

5. **that** when a government loses its way as a protector and turns into a persecutor, it should be overthrown.

The Founding Fathers overthrew their ruling class dominators. *The Founding Fathers* overthrew their government.

The *Founding Fathers* seized the diamonds of their identity and their inner peace back from the British Empire. They thought for themselves. They lived above the judgments of their dominators. They were not afraid of being called "traitors," "rebels," "treasonous," etc. They realized that these words were simply manipulation techniques from their dominators. Dominators who were moralizing their dominance. Dominators who wanted to maintain their power and dominance.

These five self-evident truths that Jefferson articulated are powerful and timeless.

But we live in a world that is nothing more than one, big battle for survival. We live in a world that is nothing more than one, big dominance hierarchy battle. Are these five "self-evident" truths really true?

I don't know.

But I want them to be true. It does reflect the desire of my heart. Jefferson put into words the greatest statement of freedom in the history of Earth.

Yes, but wasn't it hypocritical for rich, white, slave owning men to say these things – those at the top of the dominance hierarchy in the 13 colonies? Did the *Founding Fathers* see themselves as the equals of the poor, the black slaves, the women, and the children? Did Benjamin Franklin, George Washington, Thomas Jefferson, John Adams, etc. believe that "All men are created equal" should be applied broadly and universally, or applied only in a narrow, limited sense?

All legitimate questions. All fair questions.

Despite hypocritical human messengers, the message was what humanity longed to hear. That we want to be free. That we are self-owned, not state owned. That we are free to think for ourselves and make our own decisions. That we don't have to live our lives afraid of ruling class dominators. That we can have self-directed and self-designed lives, not government-directed and government-designed lives.

Flawed, imperfect *Founding Fathers* stated nearly perfect words. That we were born to be free. That we were born to live free. That no human lord, law, or legion is above individual human liberty. That no one is like a dominate male lion – claiming the right to rule others just because he has the might.

On what authority did the *Founding Fathers* reject the authority of the British Empire?

On the authority of freedom.

That freedom is above force. That liberty is above law. The human beings have been given "unalienable" rights from their Creator.

That word, *unalienable,* is not a word we often use. But powerful when you break down the word into its three parts.

- *un* = no
- *alien* = outside force
- *able* = is able

Now put it all together. All men have been given rights by their creator *that no outside force is able to take away.*

No ruling class dominator. No government.

And in its immediate context, not even 1) a King, 2) laws created by a law-making body called Parliament, or 3) the whole of the British Empire. None of these ruling class dominators can take away the unalienable rights of an individual.

"No one is above the law!"

Really? The *Founding Fathers* were.

When someone smugly asks you, "Do you think your above the law? Hmm?"

You can boldly look them in the eyes and state, "According to the *Declaration of Independence*, the answer is 'Yes!'"

And then you can ask some of these follow-up questions to the one loyal to ruling class dominators:

- Do you think that law is above liberty?
- Or do you think that liberty is above law?
- Do you think you or any government is above my liberty?
- Do you think I was born on this earth to be dominated by you?
- Do you think I was born on this earth to be dominated by a ruling class?

- Was America founded on the spirit of submission to government domination?
- Or was America founded on the spirit of resistance to government domination?
- Did the *Founding Fathers* and the Revolutionary generation gain their freedom through obedience or disobedience to their government?
- Hmm?

And you could accurately follow with "I'm for freedom, you must be for force. I'm for choice, you must be for coercion. I'm for voluntary cooperation, you must be for involuntary submission. I'm for liberation. You must be for domination."

The *Founding Fathers* put into words and actions something that most people in the world desire – either secretly or openly. That we want to live our lives free. That we have no desire to hurt anybody. We just want to be left alone to live our lives in peace.

Unfortunately, nearly 250 years after the immortal words of the *Declaration of Independence*, the whole world continues to be one, big battle for survival. It continues to be one, big dominance hierarchy battle.

And in the 21st century, the ruling class – the government – has turned into the apex predator on Earth. The ruling class is now supreme above the religious class.

I know most people would be uncomfortable with the previous chapter on living your life free from religion. Most people would also be *extremely* uncomfortable with this chapter on living your life free from government.

Why?

Because government has in its possession, the two diamonds of almost every person on Earth. Almost every person on Earth is living under the domination of a ruling class. Almost every person on Earth has a mind programmed to be afraid of and loyal to government.

Anyone reading this is likely to experience an internal contradiction. Part of them will feel joy because of their inner desire to be free from the invasive, suffocating ivy of government. While at the same time, another part of them will break out in a cold sweat because of fear of being punished by the government. Most people in the world have a mind controlled by the extreme fear and dread of their ruling class dominators. Because their inner peace is almost entirely conditioned and controlled by the government.

Many people will defend their ruling class dominators.

- "How can you say these things?"
- "Government keeps everything from descending into chaos."
- "Government is responsible for life being as good as it is."
- "Government protects me from the bad guys."
- "Government provides for those who can't provide for themselves."
- "We all depend on the government for our survival."
- "Government people are the salt of the earth. They are public servants."

I understand these statements. And in a chapter that is not so much anti-government, as it is anti-coercion and pro-freedom, let me attempt to strike a balance.

It is not uncommon for us to go to extremes when it comes to our thinking. Our thinking many times will swing back and forth like a pendulum until it settles into a middle resting place.

When I was my most zealous as a Christian, my Baptist Christianity could do no wrong. It was 100% the truth. It reflected 100% morality and goodness.

When I first left Christianity, my pendulum swung all the way to the other side. I hated Christianity. I hated everything about it. It was complete garbage. It was 100% falsehood. It reflected 100% immorality and evil.

But over time, my pendulum has come to a middle resting place concerning my Baptist Christian upbringing. I can see that it is a mix. On the one hand, I can plainly point out how it has hurt me. And I won't let it off the hook. Much of this book is driven by the pain Christianity has caused me. I make no attempt to hide this fact.

On the other hand, I can also now happily admit how my Baptist Christian upbringing has helped me. The Baptists were the children of the Radical Reformation. They were a freedom movement. They rejected the domination of the Pope and of Roman Catholicism. They rejected the domination of the more militant, authoritarian Protestant Reformers like John Calvin. I'm grateful for the Anabaptists, and ultimately the Baptists, because they were an incremental step toward a freer humanity.

And even though I now reject many of the Baptists' man-made rules, doctrines, and beliefs, I retain much of its "morality" and behavioral values. Living like my parents did (your grandparents) is a wise way to live. Living a clean, compassionate life is a smart way to live. Living a life of constructive behavior is clearly superior than living a life of destructive behavior. My pendulum thinking on the religious class is beginning to find a more balanced, middle resting place.

As is my pendulum thinking on the ruling class. The government.

In recent years, my pendulum was all the way over to one side. I completely despised and hated all ruling classes and human governments. I loved the idea of just being an all-out peace-loving Anarchist (not the angry mob kind).

I loved the idea of having no ruling class. That people simply operated by the non-aggression principle. That society is completely voluntary. And some of the videos that I would watch on these themes would have an Anarchist standing alone in the middle of the woods telling me why government sucks at every level. And I loved every minute of these videos.

But more recently, my pendulum has come back middle when it comes to government. Going to China in 2018 had a big impact on me. I took two of your brothers and we went on a whirlwind tour of five major cities in Eastern China, including Beijing and Shanghai. The population of each of these five cities ranged from 6 to 20 million people. A massive amount of humanity.

I took many things from this trip. I'll only mention two. First, it is easy to do a video on Anarchy while standing alone in the middle of a forest. I'm not sure you could shoot the same video and deliver the same message while standing in the middle of Beijing with 15 million people around.

It is simply unrealistic to believe that 15 million people will all self-organize and live peacefully together without a mediating government. That 15 million people will all peacefully resolve their territory, property, and resource disputes. That violence will not break out. That retribution for harm and offense will always be measured and just. That 15 million people coexisting without mediation will avoid a rapid descent into jungle law that returns to looking like wolf packs and lion prides.

Second, my China trip made me a little more understanding of the former "one child" law in China. America and China are similar in geographical size. But China has four times the number of people.

Imagine taking the 330 million people in America and then doubling our population to 660 million people. Then doubling it again to be 1.32 billion people. We would then be like China. That's a lot of people to mediate. That's a lot of people to feed. If America had 1.32 billion people on our current land mass, we would probably have a 1 or 2 child law as well. While I do not like the thought of someone telling me how many children I can and cannot have, I get it.

My trip to China pulled my pendulum back towards the middle. Some of the shine came off my Anarchist ideas.

Don't get me wrong. I still despise any government believing it has the right to own, order, and dominant me. And to be clear, I still believe that TRUE Anarchy should not be associated with a dystopian nightmare.

True Anarchy should instead be associated with a utopian dream. True Anarchy is the dream that we no longer have a dominance hierarchy or a ruling class. True Anarchy is the dream that all humans live together in peace and harmony. True Anarchy is the dream that love, and not fear, holds everything together. True Anarchy is the dream that any remaining human leadership structures have been eternally stripped of all lordship. True Anarchy is the dream that no one owns me, rules me, represents me, orders me, oppresses me, intimidates me, or dominates me.

The TRUE Anarchist is sounding an important note that needs to be sounded. That people want to be free. That people don't want to be owned. That people don't want to be threatened with a cage. That people do not want their life designed for them. That government coercion is evil. That people want to be left alone to live their life in peace.

I love the TRUE Anarchist. Humanity should be trending toward true Anarchy – as a good thing.

However.

There is the ideal. And there is the real. There is the idealistic. There is the realistic.

The reality: we still live in a brutal world of nearly 8 billion people. Humans in the 21st century are still organizing themselves like animals. Humans left to themselves to resolve their own territory and resource disputes will still inevitably turn to Hatfield vs. McCoy type of violence to resolve their differences.

History is unequivocally clear on this. Humans have slaughtered one another throughout the ages. Humans have more frequently chosen killing over kindness. Greed over generosity. Hatred over love. Subjugation over serving.

Yet, I readily admit that governments have contributed to all this as much as they have resolved and controlled it. Therefore, I still hate government.

But I get why we have it. I really do.

Let me revisit a couple of statements I've already made. *Everybody is, what he or she is, because they had to become that – in order to survive.* If you want to know why the Earth seems to be on complete government lock-down right now, it's because it had to become that – in order to survive. And I'm referring to the perpetual threat of violence, not the present threat of a virus.

Also, remember that *survivability has many children*. The burden to survive has produced many, many children. The dominance hierarchy. Morality. "Conscience." Religion. Government.

Where do you think human government came from? The father of human government is the dominance hierarchy. The grandfather of human government is survivability.

Government truly is the lesser of two evils. The first evil is the brutal, animalistic dominance hierarchies of history. Thousands of years when humans resolved their own territory and resources disputes like wolves and lions. The second, and only slightly lesser evil, is a coercive government to *supposedly* mediate these territory and resource disputes and theoretically create a thriving and prosperous society.

Government is something that you have to learn to coexist with. It will be part of your life for the entirety of your life. Government makes external freedom in this world impossible.

But there is a way to at least feel free and to experience internal freedom from ruling class dominators.

How?

First, you must reclaim the diamonds of your identity and your inner peace. Never again judge yourself as a "good person" or a "bad person" based on the ability to keep the rules that government has written *for you.*

Never feel "bad" or "guilty" for breaking rules of the government. They do not own you. They do not have the right to order you. They do not have the right to oppress and hurt you.

Never let the government dominate you. Never let government force you into thinking, saying, doing, feeling, or becoming something.

Never again be afraid of government. When government invades your life, liberate your soul to refuse them, resist them, push back against them, and if necessary, fight them. We'll talk more about this in our chapter "How to Feel Free in a World of Slavery."

Second, you must be able to recognize the lies about government and ruling class dominators. I will now dedicate an entire chapter to recognizing six of these lies.

CHAPTER 16

You Were Not Born to be Dominated by the Ruling Class (Part 2)

I am about to swear – a lot. If family members or people from my religious background ever read this and are offended – so be it. They're going to have to get over it. Because I won't be apologizing. Ever.

We live in a bullshitting ass-kissing world.

Those in ruling class power are full of shit. They bullshit and lie to their dominated. Not as an exception, but as a rule.

And the people living under fear of their power are ass-kissers. They say and do whatever keeps them from being hurt by ruling class dominators.

We will never have a free future as long as this continues. This bullshitting ass-kissing world will never move us forward as a species. This bullshitting ass-kissing world will never heal the planet.

Bullshitting phrases such as "in the interest of national security" have to die – forever. This is a bullshitting phrase that simply means, "If you knew the real story and not just the "official story," you would never obey us. If you knew what we decide and do behind closed doors, you would never submit to our rule. Therefore, we have to constantly bullshit you."

Ass-kissing phrases such as "politically correct" have to die – forever. This is an ass-kissing phrase that simply means, "I only say what ruling class dominators allow me to say. I don't want to get in trouble. I don't want to get fined , fired, or jailed."

The longest part of this book is dedicated to freeing your mind from ruling class dominators. That's because they are the biggest reality in our world of slavery. We don't even know if God exists. Therefore, it's actually a notch "easier" to dismiss the false authority of religious class dominators.

But government does exist. And they monitor every step we take in this world. And they have established a bullshitting ass-kissing world. One where we believe their bullshit. One where we dishonor and sell our souls to kiss their ass.

No more.

No more bullshitting. No more ass-kissing.

Jesus famously said that when an individual finally understands the truth, it will set him free (John 8:32). Therefore, it must also be true that slavery, being bound, is the result of believing lies.

Slavery comes from bullshitting and ass-kissing. Freedom and liberation will NOT come UNTIL we reject bullshitting and ass-kissing.

In this second chapter on freeing yourself from ruling class domination, I want to expose the bullshitting and ass-kissing connected with the cult-like belief in human government. Since America is usually perceived as being the world leader in freedom, I will highlight six lies Americans believe about our government and ruling classes.

Lie #1: America is a free country.

Truth: Bullshit. America is not a free country. No one lives in a free country.

Almost everything connected with ruling class dominators is bullshitting and ass-kissing. Government rhetoric seems true but isn't. It's all an intentional deception.

Perhaps the biggest pile of bullshit that ruling class dominators feed us is the lie of "living in a free country."

The irrefutable truth is this: *no one lives in a free country.* There is no such thing as living in a free country. While someone may live in a "freer" country, no one lives in a free country. The entire planet is now controlled by ruling class dominators.

To prove you do not live in a free country, and that the government controls 100% of you, simply disobey. See what happens.

For example, if you do not give the government 20+% of your income, they will assume control over 100% of your life and its mobility. The Government of your "free country" will throw you into one of their designated cages – by force.

True, or not true?

Still believe you live in a free country?

We are not free. We are completely slaves, forced to play in and pay for a game designed *for us*.

What happens if you disobey, resist, and refuse to obey just one of the government's tiniest rules? Even in this scenario, the government will assume control over 100% of your life and place you in a cage.

True, or not true?

Therefore, you are not free.

Let me be specific. Let's say that I refuse to pay a parking ticket. What if I refuse to pay their fine because I disagreed with the placement of the parking prohibition to begin with? What if a few months later they come to arrest me, and I refuse to go with them? What if I resist them when they attempt to place their hands on me? What if I fight their force with force?

Would they kill me over an unpaid parking ticket?

Yes.

And they would moralize killing me by saying they killed me, not for the unpaid parking ticket, but for resisting arrest.

We are not free. We are dominated slaves constantly controlled by fear, force, and the threat of violence.

In every "free" nation on Earth, ruling classes will kidnap, criminalize, imprison, and even kill anyone resisting their dominance. And the narrative that these ruling class dominators will widely broadcast will be this: 1) government is the good guy, 2) the one resisting government domination is the bad guy.

And what is our defense against government coercion? Courts, judges, and lawyers? In other words, if I have a problem with one oppressive ruling class dominator, the solution is to go and appeal to another ruling class dominator for protection. I see.

Still believe you live in a free country?

Government always moralizes their dominance. More bullshit to blind the masses to this critical truth: *the act of resisting domination is NOT the evil; the act of domination itself IS the evil.* Disobedience to domination is NOT the crime. Domination is the crime. Rebellion against government is NOT the evil. Government bullying (tyranny) that provokes such rebellion IS the evil.

There is no such thing as a free country. This includes America.

Because our tiny ruling class, the *Founding Fathers*, were “freed” from Britain’s ruling class did not make the people of America free. The regular, everyday person was still forced to live under the new government that was set up. And if they resisted their new government’s domination, they would be punished accordingly. Just like they were under the domination of their British government.

Free? Please. There is no such thing as a free country.

Lie #2: America is special because it believes in the “rule of law.”

Truth: Bullshit. There is no such thing as the “rule of law.” There is only the rule of lawmakers.

“Rule of law” sounds so good doesn’t it? Almost ethereal. It almost sounds as if there are perfect, universally just laws that mystically and spontaneously spring out of the Earth and rule us all by themselves. Laws that are so universal, timeless, and infallible that they will never have need of being amended, improved, or removed.

Uh huh.

There is no such thing as the rule of law. All laws, ALL OF THEM, are created by lawmakers.

If by “rule of law,” is meant that laws are in place to protect those lower on the dominance hierarchy from being oppressed by the cruel, emotional whims of a mob and/or those higher on the dominance hierarchy – fine.

But even those laws are created by lawmakers. There is no such thing as “the rule of law.” More bullshit to dupe people into submitting to domination. There is only the rule of lawmakers. There are only the laws created by a tiny, elite ruling class.

On one July 4th in recent years, I found myself a little depressed. Rather than celebrating freedom, I was awakened to a painful reality. That nearly

250 years ago, people were not really freed from a tyrannical monarchy. All that happened was a slight upgrade to an oligarchy (rule by a few).

That is, America traded in an oligarchy for a slightly upgraded oligarchy. The *Founding Fathers* rejected the King. And they replaced him with a President – one they could vote on. America could now choose who their most powerful dominator would be.

And the *Founding Fathers* rejected a law-making body called Parliament. And they replaced them with a law-making body called Congress. In short, we traded in a King and Parliament for a President and Congress.

America has always been an oligarchy – a tiny few who rule a massive many. Calling America a *democracy*, or even a *republic*, is just plain bullshit. We're an upgraded oligarchy. We've always been an oligarchy. And at any point in our history, if you resisted the domination of the oligarchy, they would assume control over 100% of your life.

Still don't believe that America is an oligarchy?

- What percentage of the American population makes the federal laws?
- And why do we have to obey them?
- Why do we have to submit to their domination?
- Why do we have to submit to their methods of hurting us for non-compliance?
- Do we have any opportunity to disagree or refuse consent without punishment?
- No? Then we all live under the domination of an oligarchy.

Let's do the math on the percentage of our population that makes the national (federal) laws.

America has a population of 330,000,000 people (330 million). How many individuals from this massive number create the federal laws?

- 435 in the House of Representatives

- 100 Senators
- 9 Supreme Court Justices
- 1 President
- 1 Attorney General

That makes 546 federal law makers. I know I'm leaving some powerful people out, so let's round the number up to 600. Why do 330,000,000 people have to obey an oligarchy of 600 people?

Hmm. 600 divided by 330,000,000 = .0002% of our population who makes the rules for the rest of us. Rounding up, that is 2 ten thousandths of 1% of our population that creates the "rule of law" for the other 99.9998% of us.

And these are just "elected" federal officials.

A tiny, miniscule amount of our population *that we don't elect*, create hundreds and thousands of laws that impact our daily lives. Our ruling class dominators have created Federal Government bodies such as the Environmental Protection Agency (EPA) and the Food and Drug Administration (FDA).

Agencies such as these also create legions of laws that we are expected to obey, or they will assume the authority to hurt us. We will be punished if we get caught disagreeing and disobeying what this tiny group of people have decided *for us*. An oligarchy we never voted on, consented to, or agreed with.

America is special because it believes in the "rule of law"?

Let's also not forget the common practice of "Executive Orders." One person, the President or Governor, exercises an "Executive Privilege" (like a Monarch) to decide some detail in the lives of 330,000,000 people. And we will be punished if we get caught disagreeing and disobeying what this one human being decided for all of us.

America is special because it believes in the "rule of law"?

And the math isn't a whole lot better at the state, county, and city levels. It is still an oligarchy. Way less than 1% of the population creates the "rule of law" for well over 99% of the population – commanding what they can and cannot do. While using force and coercion to accomplish their will. Even these "local authorities" will punish their dominated through stealing money/property and by assuming 100% control over a person's life – placing them in a cage.

America is special because it believes in the "rule of law"?

There is no such thing as the "rule of law." There is only the rule of lawmakers. There is only the rule of an oligarchy. An oligarchy that has no right to dominate your life. But beware, they do have the might.

Lie #3: America's ruling class are your representatives.

Truth: Bullshit. America's ruling class are your rulers. You do not have a choice in obeying what they decide and decree. They are not your equals. They are your dominating superiors. And they will punish you for non-compliance.

Talk about bullshitting and ass-kissing. The whole concept of "representative government," carries a hideous presumption. That we want to be represented. That we want to be dominated by a government ruling class. That we all agree with, and willingly consent to, any laws the ruling class creates. That we will submit to any punishment they create for disobedience to their will.

The cry of the 13 original colonies was "No taxation without representation." In other words, you have no right to tax us if you don't give us a representative voice in Parliament.

I have a different cry. Something that would look great on a bumper sticker. How about "No taxation, NOR representation."

I don't want to be represented. I want to rule myself. I want to own myself. I want to control my own life. I want to represent myself. I don't want to hurt anybody. I just want to be left alone, to live my life in peace.

That government officials are our "representatives" is a bullshitting ass-kissing tactic to dupe people into submitting to domination. Submission to representation is submission to domination. It is choosing force over freedom. It is choosing political lordship over personal liberty.

"Representative" government is a joke. For starters, the majority of our supposedly free, democratic nation *does not even vote* but are somehow still obligated and "legally bound" to obey. In the 2016 election, about 139 million people voted in the Presidential election.[6] Which means that the better part of 200 million people did not vote. Many were not old enough to vote. Some were not qualified to vote for various reasons. Many were not interested in voting.

And of those who did vote, about 63 million voted for Donald Trump.[7] Therefore, about 19% of our country chose who would "represent" 100% of the population. And all 100% of the population will be subject to punishment for non-compliance to any Executive Orders signed by our "representative" Donald Trump. Our "representative" that 81% of the country never voted for, consented to, or agreed to. But the 81% will be subject to punishment for non-compliance as though they did vote for him.

Does this sound like a representative or a ruler?

I'm not picking on Donald Trump, Barack Obama or any other previous President in love with Executive Orders. I'm not interested in debating the wisdom or foolishness of the Electoral College.

In fact, I'd rather discuss the bigger picture of the whole "majority rule" voting method. That 51% gets to control the other 49%. That the glaring

---

[6] https://en.wikipedia.org/wiki/Voter_turnout_in_the_United_States_presidential_elections

[7] https://en.wikipedia.org/wiki/2016_United_States_presidential_election

problem with "majority rule" *is that it means the minority is ruled.* That the minority lives under the domination of the majority.

Is that the true path to freedom? Is that the best way to secure liberty and justice for all? Or is "representative government" just more bullshitting and ass-kissing? A system that is greatly in need of an upgrade.

For the 1/3 of the country who does vote, usually about 49% of them are disappointed on election day because their "representatives" did not win. How are these people "represented" for the next 2 to 4 years?

- Why should they be responsible to obey any laws that were created without their vote, agreement, and consent? Their wishes were not even "represented."
- How can you punish people who are not represented? "No taxation without representation" right?

Ruling class dominators are exactly that. Rulers. They are not representatives.

And how about the other 51% of the 1/3 of our population who voted? Those whose "representatives" won on election day. Are they really justified in being excited? Are they really "represented"?

- What happens when their winning candidate goes on to vote "yes" on law bills they disagree with?
- Or if their winning candidate votes "no" on law bills they do agree with?
- If they simply call their representative on the phone, will the representative be sure to vote how they want them to?
- And what happens when someone else from your county or state also calls the representative? And this other person asks him/her to vote the opposite of how you want them to? Which constituent will the representative represent?

- Is your representative really going to vote "your conscience" on every bill, or "their own conscience"?

Please. Enough bullshitting and ass-kissing. Government officials are rulers, not representatives. You are not represented. You are ruled over. You don't rule your representative. Your representative is simply a tiny part of a larger ruling class that dominates you.

Lie #4: Your vote matters. You have a voice.

Truth: Bullshit. Your vote doesn't matter. You don't have a voice.

As I write, it is a Presidential election year. And early this year there seems to have been massive voter fraud at the 2020 Iowa Caucus. I'm not going to get into the details. But stories of similar voting fraud are not uncommon.

One reason that your vote may not matter, is that vying for the dominate position causes people to do dishonest things. They will do anything to insure that their team wins. Power corrupts. Who knows how many elections have been stolen throughout American history.

But that's not the point I'm going to make here. Even if every election in U.S. history was done with 100% honesty, it still doesn't matter. It is nothing more than bullshitting ass-kissing methods of deceiving people into believing that they are free, that their vote matters, and that they have a voice.

Let me ask you, how much do you think your vote will really matter? How much of a voice do you really have?

Right now, in the first 17 years of your life, you have no vote. You have no voice. You are not represented at all. You don't have a choice. But you will be required to obey laws you never had a voice in, never agreed with, and never consented to. And you will be punished if you resist. You will be required to live under the domination of the ruling class.

One day, when you are 18, your vote and your voice will supposedly matter. And your 1 vote out of 750,000 people in our particular voting district means that your "voice" will make up .0000013%, of our voting district.

Did you catch that? You will have .0000013% of a voice in who your "representative" will be. Your State Representative who will have 1 vote out of 435 in the House of Representatives. Your representative who will have .0023% of a voice on any law bill he/she gets to vote on.

Impressive isn't it?

Again, if your representative candidate didn't win the election, your vote did not count. Your vote did not matter. Your voice was not heard. You are not represented. But the ruling class will still require you to obey the laws they decide against your will, apart from your agreement and consent, and without you being represented.

At any given time in our country, half the nation feels like this. No wonder everyone is so angry these days.

Let me give you another brutal dose of reality. If your candidates do win, they probably don't even know you exist. If you make a point to know your "representatives," to keep them informed of how you want them to vote, will they obey you?

- Will they really vote the way "you want them to"?
- Will they vote "your conscience" on every bill?
- Or will they vote "their own conscience" on every bill?

Do you really think you have a voice?

And let's be realistic, your .0000013% of a voice in just our tiny voting district, ends with your *one vote* made *on one single day*. After your election day vote, your "booming voice" is silenced.

Oh, we can make phone calls. We can send emails. But our "representatives" will go on to vote on scores, maybe hundreds of laws each year apart from our counsel and consent.

- We will NOT get to vote.
- We will NOT have a voice.
- We will NOT be given a chance to agree or disagree.
- We will NOT be given a chance to willingly give or refuse our consent.
- We will NEVER be given veto power.

This is ruling class domination over a dominated people. Dominators who fool people into believing they are free, that their vote matters, and that they have a voice because they checked a box on a ballot.

Bullshitting and ass-kissing.

If I were to break down how much of a "voice" you have in the Senate, and at the state, country, and city levels – the numbers are still humbling and disheartening. You will quickly realize that your one life and "voice" is about as identifiable, distinguishable, and important in the vast sea of ruling class power, as is a single shrimp at the bottom of the 187 quintillion gallons of water in the Pacific Ocean. In a world of ruling class dominators, you will feel small, insignificant, and able to be swallowed up and snuffed out in a moment – never to be remembered.

The point I am making is this: your vote doesn't matter. You don't have a voice. You are not represented. You are ruled. Ruling class dominators believe they have the right to control your life and punish you for disobedience. All without your agreement and consent.

I don't say this to depress you. I say this to liberate you.

- Why should you listen to ruling class dominators?
- You were born to be free.
- Ruling class dominators have no rights over you.
- They don't own you.
- They have no right to order you.
- They have no right to oppress, threaten, and hurt you.

Never give the ruling class the diamonds of your identity and your inner peace.

The whole system of ruling class domination disguised as "representative government" is a joke. America loves attempting to topple governments like Iraq, Egypt, Libya, Syria, Venezuela, etc. in the name of spreading "freedom."

And the supposed symbol of freedom is setting up "democratic elections" and "representative governments." Elections where the people in these disrupted countries will have as much of a "voice" in their "new" country as we have in ours.

People in these countries will excitedly choose who their "democratically elected" dominators will be. Dominators who will use similar coercive force against them just like the tyrants who were toppled. These newly "liberated" people will also believe the lies that their vote matters, that they have a voice, that they are represented.

Bullshitting and ass-kissing.

The mass of regular people in these countries are not free.

- They are still being ruled.
- Their new "Democratically elected" dominators will still use fear, coercion, confiscations, cages, and killing to maintain dominance.
- Their new ruling class dominators will still assume control of the details and destinies of their lives.
- The people of these nations will be dominated apart from their agreement, without their consent, under threat of punishment, with no opportunity to refuse.

As long as there are ruling class dominators, your vote doesn't matter. You don't have a voice. You are not represented. You are ruled.

Lie #5 – You must obey the law.

Truth: Bullshit. You do not have to obey the law.

Yes, I just said that. Wipe the sweat off of your forehead and off the back of your neck.

I'm not sure there is a bigger lie that we believe in this world than the lie, "You must obey the law" or stated even more commonly, "You must keep or play by the rules."

"You must obey the law."

Why?

"Because!"

Because why?

"Because it's the right thing to do!"

Says who?

"Says our authorities!"

What makes them my authority? What if I don't recognize their authority?

"You have to! Your supposed to! You're a terrible person if you don't! You'll get punished if you don't! They have the power to punish you if you don't!"

Now were getting somewhere.

Ah, our two diamonds and the dominators who want them.

One of the biggest and most deceptive bullshitting ass-kissing tricks that dominators use on weak-minded people is their lie, "You must obey the law." As though "the law" is the very essence of moral perfection. That you must identity as "good" or "bad" and "feel good" or "feel bad" based on your obedience to "laws" others have made for you.

Laws you would never agree to if given a free choice. In other words, if you ever want to "be good" and "feel good," you must surrender your two diamonds to "lawmakers."

A few things. First, why are they called "laws"? Doesn't a law represent something that is bordering on a universal constant? Laws such as the law of gravity and the law of entropy?

You cannot write such laws. They just are. You cannot debate such laws. They just are. You cannot repeal gravity. You cannot remove entropy. They are laws that are universal constants.

Human "laws" are anything but a universal constant. They are simply random rules based on the wants and wishes of alpha humans dominating a given territory.

They are anything but laws. They should NEVER AGAIN be called "laws." Calling them "laws" is lying. It is simply more bullshitting deceit from dominators trying to gain and maintain dominance.

Compare the "laws" of various nations. Be sure to factor in the differing ideologies, worldviews, and religions influencing each individual nation. Factor in each individual nation's views on diet, the many topics connected with sexuality, money, taxation, employment, wages, marriage, women, children, abortion, education, health care, immigration, religion, violent crime, the death penalty, etc.

Are the "laws" of all nations on Earth universal and constant?

- Are the "laws" in Saudi Arabia identical to the "laws" in America?
- Are the "laws" in America identical to the "laws" in China?
- Do the "laws" of China perfectly mirror the "laws" in England?
- Do the "laws" of England reflect all the "laws" of Iran?
- Are the "laws" of Iran exactly like the "laws" of Nigeria?

Of course not. Not even close. And in some cases, on the complete opposite ends of an alleged moral spectrum. Some nations will beat or kill a woman breaking a "law" connected with failure to wear a head covering. In stark contrast, some nations protect pornography by "law." Some nations celebrate same-sex unions. While other nations kill them for breaking a "law" prohibiting such behavior.

How can the "laws" of all the nations of Earth differ so widely?

Because their "laws" are not laws. Anything that can be established, amended, repealed, and removed on any given day by an oligarchy should never be called "laws."

They are rules. They are called "laws" because it's a great bullshitting manipulation technique to maintain dominance. It's a great method of bullying the identities and inner peace of those living under domination. Calling rules "laws" make them sound weightier and more effective at creating conditioned guilt triggers within a person. Thus, making the weak-minded masses more controllable. More bullshitting and government mandated ass-kissing.

And it's not only the "laws" that differ between nations. Consider how "laws" change over time within a single nation. Are the "laws" today in America, in 2020, the same as they were in 1820? How about 1920?

Think of Prohibition. How can alcohol be legal, then illegal, then legal once again? Sound like a "law," a universal constant? Or does it sound more like an arbitrary rule dependent on who happens to be the ruling class dominator at the time?

How about "laws" regulating slavery up until the mid-1860's. "Laws" on the buying, selling, trading of other human beings. "Laws" forbidding the assistance of runaway slaves. "Laws" mandating the return of runaway slaves.

How can slavery be protected by "law" at one point, and then prohibited by "law" at a different point? Sound like true "laws" that are universal constants? Or does it sound more like arbitrary rules dependent on who happens to be the dominator of the day?

How about the Jim Crow "laws"? How can segregation between blacks and whites be protected by "law" in one era, and then prohibited by "law" in another era? Sound like true "laws," universal constants? Or does it sound more like arbitrary rules dependent on who happens to be the dominator of the day?

How about the voting rights of women, the poor (non-landowners), and blacks through the centuries? How can these groups of people be prohibited from voting by "law" for most of American history, and then protected by "law" to vote in modern history? Sound like true "laws," universal constants? Or does it sound more like arbitrary rules dependent on who happens to be the dominator of the day?

How about "laws" on marriage, divorce, adultery, fornication, homosexuality, pornography, etc. through the nearly 250 years of this nation's history? Have they been universally constant from beginning to end? Or have the "laws" on these issues radically been altered through the centuries – particularly since 1960? Sound like true "laws," universal constants? Or does it sound more like arbitrary rules dependent on who happens to be the dominator of the day?

All these examples expose that ruling class "laws" are not laws. They are not universal constants.

They are rules. Temporary rules about slavery, segregation, voting, and sexuality. These are anything but fixed, permanent laws.

And let's go beyond comparing past American "laws" with present American "laws." How about comparing present American "laws" with present American "laws." In 2020, how can a person go to jail for breaking a Marijuana possession "law" in North Carolina, when someone else enjoys it recreationally in Colorado without fear of punishment? In 2020, how can come someone possess and feel protected by an AR-15 gun in Indiana, when someone else in California would be severely punished for being caught with one?

And such "law" comparisons go beyond state to state. "Law" comparisons can also go county to county, city to city, and town to town.

"You must obey the law!" No. You don't. Because ruling class "laws" do not exist. It's all bullshitting and government required ass-kissing.

Laws are universal constants like gravity and entropy. Human rules that are constantly made, changed, debated, amended, repealed, and removed are not laws. They are rules.

Second, we must break free from feeling guilty for breaking "laws" made for us by the government. I'm not talking about the "Duh" rules about not murdering, raping, and robbing. I'm talking about almost everything else.

As I stated earlier in the book, I have become convinced that guilt is all about fear. Guilt is not about failure to do right. Guilt is about relief. We don't want to get hurt. We want to feel relief that we will not be punished by dominators. Guilt is the fear of punishment. And for the one brainwashed through domination, guilt is the mental programming to feel like one "deserves" to be punished.

Reclaim your two diamonds. Reject such guilt. Recognize that such guilt is bogus and false. Recognize that guilt is just fear of being hurt by punishing authorities. Which drives us to feel relief from such fear.

Think of other countries. Do you feel guilty for breaking one of Saudi Arabia's rules? You don't wear a hijab, a head covering. Do you feel guilty about that?

Of course not. Why? Because those dominators are not within striking distance to punish you. If you lived within Saudi Arabia, do you think you would have deep fear, perhaps even guilt, for not wearing a hijab? Yes. Why? Because you are within striking distance of being hurt by dominators.

I have five children. I have never felt guilty for breaking China's one child "law" (now two). Why? Because Chinese dominators are not within striking distance to hurt me.

I enjoy a good beer or wine now and then. I have never felt guilty about breaking Iran's Prohibition "laws." Why? Because Iranian dominators are not within striking distance to hurt me.

We homeschool your oldest brother and he's thriving. I have never felt guilty for breaking Germany's "laws" forbidding homeschooling. Why? Because German dominators are not within striking distance to punish me and take him from us.

Thankfully, we do not yet live under such "laws." But millions do.

"Laws" that are not close to us do not fill our hearts with fear and guilt. Why? Because "laws" are not really about right and wrong. They are about whose weak and whose strong. "Laws" are about how dominators in a certain territory maintain their dominance. "Laws" are about fear. "Laws" are about enforcing a way of life on dominated peoples. "Laws" are about fear, force, and the threat of punishment.

And feelings of "guilt" from breaking "laws" is really nothing more than fear of being punished by dominators. "Guilt" is nothing more than the effective mind-control of dominators controlling the diamonds of your identity and inner peace.

If we do not feel guilty for breaking Saudi Arabia's, China's, Iran's, and Germany's "laws," why do we feel guilty for breaking American laws?

Because American ruling class dominators are within striking distance. They have the power to hurt us. They don't have the right to hurt us, but they do have the might.

We should never again feel "guilty" for reclaiming the diamonds of our identity and inner peace. Never again dial your moral compass to see yourself as "good" or "bad" or to "feel good" or "feel bad" based on your ability to keep "laws" American ruling class dominators have made FOR YOU.

Third, I can almost hear an objection that goes like, "But living in a given country, state, country, county, city, town, etc. is an unspoken agreement to keep all their 'laws.'"

Really?

- Who is my master?
- Who owns me?
- Who owns America?
- Who owns North Carolina?
- Who owns our county and city?
- When did I give such consent to live under domination?
- When did I make such an agreement?
- When and where did I sign such a covenant or contract?
- Am I really free?
- Am I free to refuse obedience to "laws" I disagree with?
- And in such cases, may I live free from fear of punishment?

Some may further object with, "What is your problem?! Do you have a problem with rules?"

Not really. I have no problem living by the non-aggression principle. That is, never using my freedom to commit offensive acts of aggression against another person or their property. I have no problem choosing voluntary cooperation with common sense rules. I have no problem driving on the correct side of the road at a respectable speed.

But…

- I do have a problem with threats.
- I do have a problem with bullshitting and mandatory ass-kissing.
- I do have a problem with being lied to.
- I do have a problem with being told that I live in a "free" country when every detail of my family life – my children's healthcare, their education, etc. is governed by fear, coercion, and threats.
- I do have a problem with every detail of my house, my car, my income, my business, etc. being governed by fear, coercion, and threats.

Problem with common sense rules? Not really.

Problem with government coercion? Oh yeah. Problem with perpetual threats of fining, confiscating, and caging? Oh yeah. Problem with ruling class dominators who moralize their dominance over the details and destiny of my life? Oh yeah.

2020 has been the year of *quid pro quo*. This is a Latin phrase that means "this for that" and refers to an even exchange of goods or services.[8] But in the political sense and context it has been frequently used in 2020 , *quid pro quo* refers to a ruling class dominator saying in effect, "I won't give you what you need, until you give me what I want."

President Donald Trump was indicted (impeached) by the House of Representatives for allegedly using *quid pro quo* against the nation of Ukraine. Supposedly Trump threatened to withhold military aid from them ("I won't give you what you need") if they did not investigate Joe and Hunter Biden's dealings in a Ukrainian energy company ("until you give me what I want").

Joe Biden is currently the Presidential nominee for the Democratic Party. It is said that Biden also used *quid pro quo* during his time as Vice President under Barack Obama. That Joe Biden also had threatened to withhold aid to Ukraine ("I won't give you what you need") if they did not stop a certain prosecutor from investigating Hunter Biden's involvement with the Ukrainian energy company ("until you give me what I want").

I have no intention of attempting to unpack either of those *quid pro quo* cases. I reference them to make an illustrative point. In 2020, the term *quid pro quo* was used in a negative sense. That is, how dare any ruling class dominator withhold what someone needs to survive, until the needy one obeys against their will. How dare a President or Vice President withhold what one nation needs until he got what he wanted. How dare he leverage and manipulate people to his will.

---

[8] https://simple.wikipedia.org/wiki/Quid_pro_quo

Again, I'm not saying if Donald Trump and Joe Biden are guilty or innocent. I'm trying to point out the natural, moral outrage people feel by a negative *quid pro quo* scenario. The idea that "You can't have what you need to survive…until you give me what I want."

Forget Donald Trump. All governments ARE GUILTY – despicably guilty – of *quid pro quo* against the people they "serve."

As a rule, governments withhold what people need to live, move, and survive until the people submit to their rules.

- "Sign here giving your 'willing' consent, or you don't get your house."
- "Sign here giving your 'willing' consent, or you don't get your license."
- "Get your car inspected, or you can't register it."
- "Get car insurance, or you can't register your car."
- "Sign here giving your 'willing' consent, or you cannot receive medical treatment."
- "Wear your facemask, or we will not sell you food."
- "Sign here giving your 'willing' consent, or you cannot receive…"
- "Republicans, concede to us Democrats on these 15 issues that serve our political agenda ('Give us what we want'), and then we will pass the multi-trillion dollar financial relief bill due to the COVID-19 lockdowns ('then we will give you what you need'). It was immoral and illegal when Donald Trump (allegedly) used *quid pro quo* on Ukraine. But it's moral and legal when we use *quid pro quo* on the American people."

Quid pro quo. "We won't give you what you need…until you give us what we want."

How does such a bullshitting, dishonest setup respect true consent? How does such a dishonest setup respect true agreement?

In 2020, when is the individual allowed to refuse without fear of punishment? And why sign anything? You will be punished for non-conformity whether you signed or not?

I like the analogy of *Captain America: Civil War*. The ruling classes of the world chose to bring the superhero group known as *the Avengers* under their domination. According the governments around the world, they were creating too much co-lateral damage as they were saving the world.

So the governments of the world created the Sokovia Accords which each of the Avengers were to look through and agree with by signing. Iron-man, War Machine, Vision, and Black Widow signed the agreement. This placed them under the punishing authority and accountability of the governments of the world via the Sokovia Accords.

But Steve Rogers, Captain America, did not sign. He refused. He would not agree. He did not give his consent.

Because Captain America did not give his consent, he was not under the punishing authority of the Sokovia Accords. Right?

Wrong. World governments, especially the American government, hunted him for years trying to catch and imprison him for violating the Sokovia Accords.

The Sokovia Accords which he never signed. Which he never agreed to. Which he never consented to.

Captain America didn't sign. So why is he being treated as though he did? And if that is the case, why sign in the first place?

All the ruling class dominators do this. They make rules. And they term it "passing laws." "Laws" you never signed, agreed to, consented to, etc. But you are "legally bound" as though you did.

And all paperwork you ever do sign to make you "legally responsible" is *quid pro quo*. You will be withheld something you desperately need for survival (i.e. insurance, driver's license, healthcare, etc.) unless you sign. And if you don't sign, you will be punished as though you did.

"You must obey the law!"

No, you don't.

The world needs to be liberated from ruling class dominators. The world needs to stop being afraid their governments. In the meantime, out of self-preservation, the common person needs to obey enough "laws" to avoid punishment.

But any "laws" we do break, we should never feel guilty about it. Such guilt is nothing more than the fear of being punished. It's about getting relief, not about doing right. It's nothing more than ruling class dominator mind-control and the moralization of their dominance.

Governments do not own you. They have no right to order you. They have no right to oppress and hurt you.

Feel free to break the laws made for you by the government. And never feel a moments impulse of guilt for doing do. Resisting government domination is not evil.

- Government domination is the evil.
- Government coercion is the evil.
- Government invasion into the lives of peaceful people is the evil.
- Raping the wills of people who want to live free and to feel free is the evil.

Again, I'm not referring to committing acts of violent aggression against other human beings and their property.

I'm referring to everything else. Especially the endless government regulation of all the details of your life. I'm talking about government coercion. Forcing people to think, believe, say, do, and become things against our will, out of fear of being punished.

Enough.

Lie #6: Government officials are public servants that provide invaluable services.

Truth: Bullshit. Government officials are public masters that force their will and services upon you.

You guessed it, more bullshitting and ass-kissing. Dominators are mind manipulators who love to spin terminology to assist in their deceptive illusions. Calling the *ruling class,* the *serving class*, is near the top of the twisted list. Closely followed by ruling class dominators calling their mandates, *services*.

Government officials are not public servants. They are public masters. We live under their domination. They tell us what we can and cannot do. We are not allowed to tell them what they can and cannot do. The ruling class believes they have the right to hurt us for disobedience. They are not our equals; they are our superiors. The ruling class has claimed for themselves the self-assumed power to invent "laws" and punishments regardless of the public will. They do not have the right to do this, just the might.

"Public servant"? Please. They should NEVER AGAIN be called this. They should always be referred to as "public masters."

Even police officers and soldiers, should not be referred to as servants of the public. Police officers and soldiers are servants of power. They take orders from the ruling class, not from the public. True, or not true?

Yes, police officers and soldiers do many things to serve and protect humanity. And their best work is to protect the public from violent crime. And they risk their lives doing so. In these instances, their bravery should be honored and respected.

But there needs to be an awakening among the police and military when it comes to obeying the ruling class on all matters. These men and women in uniform must become mindful, conscious individuals. They must all graduate today and forever from the mindless, robotic "I don't make the laws, I just enforce them."

Such a statement is terribly self-incriminating. It is saying, "I don't think for myself. I don't judge right and wrong for myself. I just hypnotically carry out the orders of my ruling class dominators – whether way down deep I think it's right or wrong."

Most police officers and soldiers have also been brainwashed into moralizing their dominance. Most of them will prioritize enforcing the tyranny of power above protecting the freedom of the public.

Historically, the police and military have been mentally programmed to believe it is their "duty" to obey their ruling class dominators above all else. Therefore, they were justified and right in oppressing, caging, and slaughtering their fellow humans.

There are too few *real* police officers and soldiers who can judge right and wrong for themselves.

- Those who have been awakened and made aware of this reality: "I'm not honorable for keeping a promise to do dishonorable things."
- Those who will gladly live with the "lesser guilt" of disobeying any promises they were coerced into making to their government, if they have been ordered by their ruling class dominators to carry the "greater guilt" of oppressing, caging, and killing men, women, and children.

Those who are part of police forces and military branches also need to reclaim the diamonds of their identity and their inner peace from ruling class dominators. I am growing persuaded that many former policeman, soldiers, judges, and lawyers HAD to get out of their professions. They knew they were in the anti-freedom/pro-coercion business of dominating their fellow human beings.

Not only is the term "public servants" a bullshitting lie, but so is the term "public services." Government "services" are usually ruling class "mandates." Decrees and mandates that must be obeyed or we will be punished.

They should NEVER AGAIN be called "services." They should always be referred to as "mandates."

If someone forces their services upon you, it is not a service. It is intimidation and an invasion.

If an uninvited carpet cleaner shows up at your door with a loaded Glock pistol and forces you to pay him to clean your carpet, that is not a service. It's an invasion.

If government uses fear and force to make you receive their services of education, health care, police protection, and law-making, then they are not services. They are an invasion. They are moralized domination.

Forced services do not deserve your respect. Dominators designing your life for you, does not deserve your respect.

Government forcing their services upon us, does not give them sovereignty over us. Forcing us to receive their "generosity" to us, does not give them domination rights over us.

If government officials would respect our right to freely choose in all things, without the threat of punishment, they would be more likely to receive our respect.

I can hear the objection. "Will you not teach your daughter to respect authority?"

No. I will not.

I will teach you to respect ALL people as equals. "Respect authority" is bullshitting and mandatory ass-kissing for "Submit to domination."

Something I will never teach you to do.

Why "respect authority"? Because they put themselves in harm's way? Fine.

But there is nothing I resent more than someone who throws "generosity" in my face attempting to justify their claim of dominance over me. The attitude of, "Look what I've given you. Now I get to dominate you. Look what I've done for you. Now you have no choice but to obey me. Look what I've given, now I'm your judge and you're subject to my punishment. I'm your superior. You are indebted. Therefore, you are my slave."

I can hear another objection. "Aren't you teaching your daughter to reject accountability?"

No. I'm teaching you to reject authority. Accountability can be fine. Accountability is implicitly about equality and persuasion. Imagine me holding both of my hands up at eye level, at an equal height. That's what accountability looks like.

Authority is not fine. Authority is explicitly about superiority and punishment. Imagine me holding one hand up at eye level with the other hand directly under it in a submissive position. That's what authority looks like.

Reject authority. Be cautiously open to accountability.

Hallie, you were born free. You were not born to be the slave of the ruling class. You were not born to the slave of the government. Protect the diamonds of your identity and your inner peace from the ruling class. *When* the ruling class comes for them, look them in the eyes and tell them, "You can't have them. I was born to be free. I wasn't born to be dominated by you."

CHAPTER 17

You Were Not Born to be Dominated by the Rich Class

Admittedly, this will not be my most profound chapter. My thoughts are not as developed on critiquing the rich class as they are the other power classes – especially the religious class. I am currently in the process of learning how the rich class dominates every level of existence on our globe.

Give me another half decade, and I will be able to put more meat on these bones. I have many thoughts for "how to fix" this broken world created by rich class dominators. But these proposed solutions are still embryonic and not developed enough to publish in a book.

Those humbling admissions being made, I will do my best to give you a starter kit for rejecting the self-assumed authority of rich class dominators.

Hallie, you were born free. You were not born to be the slave of the rich class.

They don't own you. Protect the diamonds of your identity and your inner peace from the rich class. *When* the rich class comes for them, look them in the eyes and tell them, "You can't have them. I was born to be free. I wasn't born to be dominated by you."

Arguably the most famous message in world history, the *Sermon on the Mount*, began with the words, "Blessed are the poor in spirit: for theirs is the kingdom of heaven."

"Poor in spirit" – what an interesting phrase. People who are rich or poor do carry with them a "spirit." There is a frequency, energy, or aura that radiates from an individual that signals to others if they are rich or poor.

Rich people undoubtedly have a *spirit* about them. Rich people usually possess an unmistakable attitude and demeanor of superiority. They are high and mighty. They are socially confident. Their posture is straight and strong. Their shoulders are square and pinned back. Their head is held high with their nose tilted slightly upward. Their eyes morph back and forth between signaling confidence and conceit. Their clothes, their shoes, their rings, their necklaces, their wrist watches, their sports cars, their gated mansions, etc. all have the smell of success upon them.

Such people are materially rich. And they want everyone to know it. In their minds, they are superior. In their minds, they are judge. Anyone lesser is the judged.

The "poor in spirit" are also a reality in this world. Everything that I just described about the rich, is the opposite when describing the poor. There is an attitude of inferiority. They are not socially confident. Their posture is hunched and timid. Their head hangs low. Their eyes look down and defeated. Their clothes, shoes, absence of jewelry, junky cars, shabby homes, etc., all have the smell of poverty upon them.

And how do the poor feel in the presence of the rich? How do the poor feel about themselves when they sense that their clothes are not as nice, their experience is not as broad, their education is not as extensive, their net worth is a tiniest fraction of the rich man's, and that their entire house could fit in one bay of the rich man's garage?

They feel bad. That their identity is "I'm a poor person, that's who I am." That their inner peace is disrupted by feelings of shame and inferiority. That they can only find inner peace by pleasing the rich man and finding some means of approval from his judgmental gaze.

"Poor in spirit."

When I was growing up, I admittedly surrendered the diamonds of my identity and inner peace to the rich class. I grew up identifying myself as a "poor farm boy." I grew up feeling poor and inferior because I viewed myself this way.

Was my family poor? Yes, and no. My dad, your Grandpa Gowerstreet, was a self-employed Farmer. He was extremely hardworking. He was a self-starter who was self-motivated in all that he did. Besides a couple of Christmas mornings, I have almost no memory of him ever sleeping in. As a farmer, he primarily planted and harvested wheat, soybeans, and corn on nearly 400 acres. He also worked with his two oldest brothers helping them with their over 1000 acres.

To supplement the income he brought in from grain farming, my father also had about 20 to 25 crossbred beef cows which had calves each Spring. We would use some of the calves for 4-H, and the rest we would fatten up and sell as yearlings at the local auction. In the later years of his life, Dad also worked as an insurance agent in our county in rural Indiana.

Mom was a homemaker for the entirety of my upbringing. She did not bring in more income for our family. But her presence in our home – made it home. The amount of work she put into raising five children cannot be measured by monetary value. That's not just a sweet sentiment. It's the truth.

From the income Dad gathered from farming, beef cattle, and insurance, we were always provided for. We never missed a meal – not one. And you could even say from an asset's standpoint, Dad was even "rich." At the time of his death in 2002, he owned nearly 400 acres free and clear. Land that was worth two million dollars. In a way, your Grandpa Gowerstreet was a self-made millionaire.

However, growing up we were always cash poor. We never had the nicest clothes. We never had the coolest shoes. We never drove very nice cars. Our cars were usually older, used station wagons that were easy to be ashamed of. Our house was very nice, but not extravagant. We rarely vacationed and traveled outside of our state. We never looked rich. And I'm sure we were never viewed as rich.

I remember in my childhood having friends over to our house. And when we were playing basketball in our big red barn, things got heated in competition. And one of my friends, trying to get the dominant, high ground position, fired at me, "Well, at least I'm not poor!"

Ouch. I'm not sure if that comment originated within him, or if it came from his parents. But in that moment, I gave him at least a cut of the diamonds of my identity and my inner peace. His labeling judgment hovered over me. And I lived under that judgment for many years.

Now in my mid-forties, I look back and scoff at this incident with the contempt it deserves. But as a child, I did not have a perspective on the idiotic rich, poor, and middle-class paradigms that humans have created. As a result, my identity and my inner peace were shaken over rich class snobbery.

Hallie, never give the diamonds of your identity and your inner peace to dominators in the form of the rich class. Never.

But the world is what it is. You were born into a world dominated by wealthy people. They dominate how societies and communities are designed. They own the media outlets. They control public opinion. They own the ruling class politicians. They pay for their campaigns in exchange for favors. Therefore, they dominate the rules that the rest of us are forced to live by.

In many ways, the rich class holds our survival in their own hands. They have created a world where you need money to survive. To get money, you have to work for the rich and borrow from the rich. A world of slavery. A world where you live under the domination of the rich class. You were born into a world of Rothschilds and Rockefellers. Of Soros' and Slims. Of

Koch's, Gates', Bezos', and Zuckerberg's. Of Amazon, Google, and Facebook. Of multi-billionaire bigshots.

But they don't own you. They have no right to order you. They have no right to oppress you. They have no right to tell you want you must think, believe, say, feel, do, and become. You have every right to disagree with them. You have every right to disobey them. You have every right to "censor" them.

Rich class dominators. Being rich doesn't make them wise. Being rich doesn't make them good. Being rich doesn't confer upon them domination rights over the masses or individuals. They are merely the temporary human alphas in 21st century dominance hierarchy battles. They were born naked and with nothing like you were. And one day they will die and take none of their wealth and possessions with them.

I must prepare you for this world. The rich class has created a world that attempts to force you to measure your personal worth by this standard: *how rich are you?* How much money do you have in the bank? How many "things" do you possess? What is your net worth? How much value do you bring to the marketplace?

If someone is richer than you, they will assume the position of your dominator. In their minds, they have "earned" the right to be judge. If they so choose, they can be mean and nasty, because they believe themselves to be better than you.

We've been over this. People will constantly be judging themselves to be superior or inferior to you, based on the conclusions they have come to concerning some of these following money and materialism questions:

- What does your father do for a living?
- What does your mother do for a living?
- What neighborhood do you live in?
- How big and how nice is your house?
- How nice is the car your parents drive and drop you off with?

- How nice are your shoes and clothes? What brands do you wear?
- What size T.V. do you have?
- Do you have the latest smartphone?
- Do you play video games?
- Where does your family vacation? Have you been to Disney World?
- Does your family go to Florida for Spring break?

If someone feels "richer" than you, they will act superior to you. If someone feels "poorer" than you, they will act inferior to you. I'm not saying this is right. I'm saying this is the way it is. Money is mastery. Dough is domination. Possessions are power.

What a world. It is why humans still treat each other like animals. It is why we still organize ourselves like animals. We just moralize it all and wear a pious mask. But in the end, it's still all about dominance, territory, resources, hierarchy, intimidation, judgment, killing, and hypocrisy. It's still all about the have vs. the have nots in a grand battle for survival.

You were born into a world that is dominated by the rich class. And the lives of those living under their domination suffer as a result. We live in a real-life Monopoly game. We are slaves to our shelter, our transportation, and our education. We are debt slaves to rich class dominators.

Rather than societal order, societal chaos results. The family, the very foundation stone of a stable society is massively undermined and weakened.

Let me give you the example of an imaginary couple that reflects the reality of the world created by rich class domination. I'll give these two the names of Sam and Jen.

To play in this Monopoly game set-up by rich class dominators, the newly married couple of Sam and Jen begin their wonderful lives together carrying a mountain of college debt. This greatly hinders their ability to buy a house. Therefore, Sam and Jen become rent debtors. Each month they shell out lot of money to pay for a temporary shelter. Money they will never see again.

Once Sam and Jen are finally able to get a loan to buy a house, this only puts them under another slave debt. This usually requires both Sam and Jen to work – even when a child is born. Soon after bringing a beautiful child into this world, Jen will need someone to watch the child so both parents can participate in this Monopoly game created for them by rich class dominators.

Because both Sam and Jen are working, their children will spend the majority of their waking hours in the first 18 years of their life away from their Mom and Dad. Daycares and Public schools become central in the character formation of their children. Their children are indoctrinated with the morals and values that rich and ruling class dominators want them adopt. Sam and Jen are reduced to the supplemental role in their children's formation as people.

And let me say something in passing. I marvel and am mystified that so many mock the concept of homeschooling, while never mocking this concept of coercive government *clone schooling.* My acronym for government C.L.O.N.E. schooling is as follows. It's when children born free have their two diamonds stolen and are taught: :

C = Conformity

L = Labeling

O = Obedience

N = No Skills

E = Enslavement

Clone schooling. Rich and ruling class indoctrination centers.

And while their kids are being clone schooled, Sam and Jen will spend the majority of their adult lives working to afford a lifestyle. A lifestyle that makes Sam and Jen look more acceptable on the dominance hierarchy. There's a certain house they need to have. There are certain types of cars they need to drive. There are certain types of clothing lines they need to be dressed in. There are certain types of vacation destinations they need to be able to claim in conversation.

Money is the center of Sam and Jen's one human existence.

Hallie, my counsel to you concerning the Monopoly game setup by rich class dominators is incomplete at this point. At present, I'm *very* conflicted.

Part of me would encourage you to reject the Monopoly game outright. As an adult, move to another country that isn't driven to this extent by money, covetousness, consumerism, materialism, etc.

When I was an Assistant Pastor in greater Chicago, I was moved by a testimony from a missionary woman from West Africa. In her family's slide presentation at our church, you could see pictures of her children holding snakes and sleeping with monkeys. Images which I'm sure made wimpy American parents a little queasy and uneasy.

When this lady gave a few words on their mission work, she made a remarkable statement. "In the end, the snakes and monkeys are not nearly as dangerous to our children as the materialism of America."

Agreed. Part of me would counsel you to reject the greed, materialism, consumerism, competition, and the "American Dream" of this nation. It's actually the American nightmare for most people. Don't take the one life you've been given for sure, and waste it on playing the Monopoly game of American rich class dominators.

Another part of me wonders if the answer is to stay in America, but become part of a small, rural intentional community. A peaceful commune that is about voluntary cooperation and shared existence. But without all the coercion of systemic socialism. One that doesn't stifle individuality and creativity. One that values family instead of diminishes it. One that is egalitarian and rejects authoritarianism.

One of my lawn customers in recent years, I'll call her Renee, told me of her experience living in an intentional community in Ohio. And it was every bit as idyllic as you could imagine. Something like ten families possessing

100 acres. Each family owned 5 acres of their own. And 50 acres was for everybody to share and to work together on. Renee's now adult son later told her that she did not prepare him for real life. And this was not a deep criticism. It was just saying that his childhood was so peaceful, he was not prepared for the dog-eat-dog Monopoly game that awaited him in the "real world."

Still another part of me thinks that you should play the Monopoly game, win the game, and get out of the game. That you should dedicate ages 8 to 22 to becoming a multi-millionaire by age 30. That you find a way to win the game. Then get out of the game and do what you want with the rest of your life. That you no longer work for a living. But that you create for a living. That you do what you love for a living. That you live for a living. For the rest of your life.

However, a very small part of me thinks maybe you should just accept the world that rich class dominators have created for us, as it is. That it's not all that bad. Conform. Get with the program. Borrow money. Go to college. Get a job. Work for a living. Get married. Get a 30-year mortgage. Spend the majority of your life paying off debts to the rich. Teach your children to do the same. At least it's more predictable and established.

And then there's still another part of me that would challenge you to fight the Monopoly approach of this world. That the vast majority of the world needs to pick up the Monopoly game that's been setup by rich class dominators, throw it in the trash, and then burn it to ash. That you should spearhead breakaway societies that have moved way beyond the Capitalism, Communism, Socialism paradigms.

- Societies that have love instead of fear as the nucleus of their society.
- Start ahead, resource-based societies instead of start behind, money and debt-based societies.
- Voluntary societies that value the quality of care for every individual in the community instead of the quantity of one's cash.

- Societies that have overthrown money as a destructive master and reduced it to a constructive servant.

And all done without threats and coercion.

Which is why Capitalism and Communism always fail. Neither has figured out how to shed the DOMINANCE HEIRARCHY approach of fear, force, and the threat of punishment. Neither has created a system of DOMESTIC HARMONY. Neither has been able to put freedom and love together to heal the world.

Maybe you can help to develop a 22nd century societal system that is a massive upgrade over these two outdated 19th century models of organizing people. It is time for humans to think outside of these two boxes. A revolutionary societal structure that removes rich class domination and truly moves humanity closer to liberty and justice FOR ALL. One that exposes and yanks out the root of all evil – the love of money.

Arguably the biggest dominator and enslaver on the planet is money. The tool of rich class domination. It is the human use of money that solidifies all the evils of the dominance hierarchy outlined in this book.

Nothing exasperates me more than the fact that rich class dominators have created a world where our very survival is dependent upon money. That the quality of your life experiences is dependent upon how much money you have.

Money in and of itself seems benign. Money is merely a medium of exchange for goods and services. It doesn’t matter if the money medium is digital numbers on a screen. It doesn't matter if the money is gold and silver. It doesn't matter if the money is printed paper. It doesn't matter if the money is acorns and walnuts.

Everything that now is, didn’t use to be. Including money. Humans simply invented the entire concept of money, what would be used as money, what would be the value of the money, and here we are today. Money, as a third-party tool used in human interaction and exchange, seems so innocent.

But nothing could be more guilty of hurting our one human experience than money. Money is the embodiment and solidification of the dominance hierarchy. Money creates a Grand Canyon divide between the human experiences of the 1% who have much, and the 99% who have little or considerably less.

Money morality creates a very immoral world. People kill for money. People steal for money. People kidnap for money. People enslave for money. And that's just the governments.

Money is the source of perpetual conflict. Wars are started over money and resources. Marriages break up because of money more than anything else. Nothing brings out man's baser qualities of greed, selfishness, deception, hatred, and lust for power more than money. If you want to find the root cause of any problem in the world, you only really need to just "follow the money."

Although I no longer identify by the name Christian, I think I understand the Christian message better now, than when I was a Bible professor or pastor. I am growing persuaded that Jesus' primary mission was not personal sin redemption for each individual, but wholesale societal reform.

The good news of the gospel Jesus initially brought was the kingdom of God on Earth. What a country organized and governed by God would look like.

- To remove money as the nucleus in the replicating cell of human society. And to replace it with mercy.
- To replace the economy with empathy.
- To replace domination with liberation.
- To replace subjugation over others with humble service to others.
- To replace competition with communion.
- To replace hatred with harmony.
- To replace greed with generosity.
- To replace retribution with reconciliation.

- To replace revenge with release (forgiveness).
- To replace order with wholeness.

In Matthew 6, Jesus explicitly stated that a root problem in this broken world was money. I don't think Jesus was trying to be clever when he stated that there are only two gods in the world: God and money.

And Jesus said these two are not reconcilable. He said you can only choose one of these gods. Choosing money results in darkness, a rotting out of the entire human soul. Choosing God's righteousness, justice, and way of living results in light, a purification of the entire human soul.

Worshipping the money god results in the subjugation and the enslavement of your fellow human. Worshipping the real God results in love and the building up of your fellow human.

In Matthew 19, when a rich class dominator came to Jesus and asked what he had to do to enter this kingdom of God, Jesus gave him a simple answer. He needed to love God and to love others. To which this rich class dominator claimed, "I've done this. What else do I need to do?" Jesus said to the rich class dominator, "Go and sell everything you own. Then take the money, give it to the poor. Then you can come and follow me and live the lifestyle I am living."

This rich class dominator totally rejected Jesus' proposal. He chose the money god's lifestyle over the real God's lifestyle.

And this story of Jesus' interaction with the rich class dominator did not seem to be an exception to the rule. In the book of Acts, Jesus' new church had its members selling all of their possessions, giving it to the church, and then redistributing the money to those in their new faith community who were in greater need.

Maybe this is what Christianity was intended to be. Not popes, cardinals, doctrines, creeds, dogmas, sacraments, Sunday school, choirs, and other nonsense. Practical love, not pious liturgy. Christianity was to be a light to the world. To model how humans could live peacefully together in community. An example for the rest of the world to desire and imitate.

Isn't this what 20th century Socialism/Communism was supposed to accomplish? Weren't they supposed to solve the rich class dominator problem of the world? Why didn't it work? Why was the result a pile of 100 million bodies?

Because 20th century Socialism/Communism still acted like wolves and lions. They used authoritarian fear, force, and violence to bring about their egalitarian utopia. That fear and extreme order is the way to hold a community together. That coercion is the cure. That force and coercion will heal the world.

At some point – MAYBE NOW – humans have to get way beyond the coercion of Socialism/Communism and Capitalism.

Many argue that humans should graduate from old outdated religious systems of thought like Judaism, Christianity, and Islam. Maybe we should also begin arguing the same for 19th century political systems of thought.

Almost a quarter of the way through the 21st century, should we keep asking "Is it Capitalism or Communism?"

Maybe it's NEITHER.

Hallie, maybe you can begin thinking of a societal system that uses freedom and love to fix the world. One that doesn't require a massive overdose of fear and coercion.

If you had the power and influence to change the world, what would you do? What would your *utopia* look like?

If you want a starter kit that generates ideas for what your better world would look like, simply use "How the World Works from A to Z." This represents why the world is on edge. Why we are being crushed under the burden of existence. Why the world is crazy. How fear and coercion rule us all.

Use these 26 points to imagine an opposite and infinitely better world. One that represents a world at ease. One that makes life a blessing for all humanity. One that removes the burden of existence. A sane world. One where freedom and love heal us all.

Like I said at the beginning of this chapter, my *utopia* is in embryonic form. I'm just starting to muse on the form I would suggest. A world that incorporates the creativity and ingenuity of Capitalism and the equalitarian ideals of Communism.

And without the threats and coercion from both of those systems.

Maybe in a half decade or so I will make an attempt at spelling that out to you in book form.

In the meantime, I've given you some things to start thinking about. And for starters, know that rich class dominators do not own you. You were born free. You were not born to be dominated by the rich class.

CHAPTER 18

You Were Not Born to be Dominated by Your Parents

You were born free. You were not born to be the slave of your parents.

We don't own you. Protect the diamonds of your identity and your inner peace from even us. If there is a time that you sense we are coming for them, look us in the eyes and remind us, "I love you. But you can't have them. I was born to be free. I wasn't born to be dominated by you."

This is one of the hardest chapters for me to write. Not because your mother and I have any desire to "own," "dominate," and "enslave" you. But because we know that there is no way to avoid the inevitable hypocrisy that will come with this chapter.

I have observed in recent years, that beneath this Earth's atmosphere, there is only one law as constant as gravity.

Hypocrisy.

It's in all of us. I have observed the law of hypocrisy in everybody I meet. And I have been awakened to see the rampant hypocrisy in my own thinking and behavior.

I detest when you children yell at each other with harshness. Yet I know that you learned that from me. Especially when I'm yelling at you, telling you not to yell.

I hate when you call each other names. But you learned that from me.

I have scolded you on occasion for getting into candy you shouldn't be. Yet, I exercise tyrannical and dictatorial domination over your stash of yearly Halloween Candy. There are so many things that you do that I refuse to tolerate and overlook. And then I hypocritically expect you to tolerate and overlook these *exact same deeds* when they are being done by me.

And here I am now, writing you an entire book on freedom. That you were born to be free. That freedom is good, and that force is bad. That choice is virtuous, and that coercion is vile. That voluntary cooperation is borderline "the only way." And that involuntary submission is borderline "pure evil."

And writing this book creates an inevitable hypocrisy. Because I know I will force you to clean your plate. Whether you like it or not. There will be times I will coerce you into cleaning your room. Whether you like it or not. There will be times I will pull rank on you and demand involuntary submission when it comes to you exercising kindness to your brothers.

This is why freedom can be a very elusive subject to discuss. Yes, we will be making a lot of your choices for you in the first 12 years of your life. But we can promise you, it's out of love, not a desire to dominate. I can honestly say that we are NOT trying to design your life, as much as we are just trying to give you the tools to design your own life with.

And your mother and I are not just interested in the skills you acquire, or what you can do. We are far more interested in who you become as a person – the substance of your personal character. Perhaps our highest goal is to teach you the three important virtues of character, wisdom, and love. I like to define character this way: *character is the self-control to do what is right in any situation.*

But let's face it. Sometimes you won't always know what is right to do in certain situations. Therefore, you need wisdom. *Wisdom is the ability to judge what is right to do in any situation.*

And there will even be times when you lack wisdom to instruct you in some extremely difficult situation. Therefore, you need love. *Love is always right to do in any situation.*

Never forget:

Character: the self-control to do what is right in any situation.

Wisdom: the ability to judge what is right to do in any situation.

Love: what is always right to do in any situation.

What is the role of your mother and I in your upbringing?

We do NOT see ourselves as your dominators. But we will hypocritically act like it at times. Just know that we see ourselves as your *temporary* guardians and mentors that will constantly be teaching you character, wisdom, and love.

Please know that we are your biggest fans who are NOT raising you to be our subordinates or equals. To the contrary, we want you to be a thousand times better than us in every way. We are your advocates, not your adversaries.

Struggling to believe this? Just know that our "rule" over you, is temporary. We are raising you to release you, to set you free. We don't own you. It is your life. And at some point, probably around age 18, almost every decision in life will be under your control, not ours.

Most of history has not agreed with this perspective of parenting. Why? Go back and read the chapters on the dominance hierarchy. Parents, particularly fathers, have been very dominating figures in the lives of their sons and daughters. Parent's firmly held the diamonds of a child's identity and inner peace. Sometimes for the entirety of their lives.

Historically, parents dominated the details and destinies of their children's lives. All the while the religious, ruling, and rich classes dominated the details and destinies of the parent's lives.

Let me give one example of this. Most of history was marked by arranged marriages. The choice of who you married, was not your choice. The choice of who you married was your parent's decision. And where your parents fell in their societal dominance hierarchies was all important. You would marry someone of your same faith. You would marry someone of your same social status. The rich would marry the rich. The poor would marry the poor.

That is why some of the great stories of literature show the societal chaos that resulted from interclass, interreligious, and interracial marriages. Like Jane Austin's novels. Her novel *Pride and Prejudice* highlighted two individuals, Mr. Darcy and Miss Elizabeth. Darcy and Elizabeth are iconic figures that seized the diamonds of their own identity and their own inner peace and broke societal rules of love and marriage.

Love will do that. Love is powerful. Love is the one force in this universe that empowers people to break the rules and "laws" of dominators. No one obeys their way to freedom.

Let me say that again.

No one obeys their way to freedom. No one. Disobedience to a dominator is the absolute requirement for breaking free from the dominator. Love is the most powerful force in this world. And it has the power to give people enough leverage and courage to disobey, and to break free.

But the point at hand is this. Historically, parenting was/is more about programming and controlling one's children, rather than connecting with them. If freedom is fundamentally about choice, children have historically had very little freedom. And nothing illustrates this more clearly than the choice of a marital partner.

However, I have to be fair. Arranged marriages actually worked pretty well. Today, when we think we have found the superior way to find a mate through dating and experimentation, half of all marriages fail, usually in short order. The psychology behind all of this is something that can be saved for another time.

But let's talk about you. Who you marry will ultimately be your choice. If you marry, will be your choice. What you want to do with your life, will be your choice. The things you will want to study and pursue, will be your choice. Where you want to live one day, will be your choice.

Your mother and I will be as involved or uninvolved as you like. Right now, we will try to do our best to prepare you for life. We will do our best to teach you the character, wisdom, and love to make good choices.

Hallie, this chapter is near and dear to my heart. Because I believe in many ways, my life was designed for me by my mother. How I lived for the first 40 years of my life was greatly dominated by her vision for my life.

At this point, let me make some important clarifiers. First, I do not despise my mother for this. I get what she was trying to do.

Second, I really did/do have a fantastic mom. My mother was/is exceptionally loving, affirming, and supportive. And I'm not just saying this. I feel like I'm not half the parent to you, that my parents were to me. They were outstanding parents in so many ways. I am exceedingly grateful for my parents.

Third, my mother was not a micro-manager. One of the reasons I absolutely hate coercion, is because so little of it was used against me growing up. One of the reasons I am so obsessed with freedom, is because I had so much of it growing up.

Fourth, my mother and father gave me the most idyllic upbringing imaginable. Growing up in a tiny farm community in the middle of nowhere was a peaceful paradise.

In fact, to feel free in a world of slavery, this is a key ingredient in the recipe: deurbanize. Get out of the concrete jungle of the large cities.

Live in a small, rural community. Breathe the fresh air. Connect with nature. Enjoy the space.

I've lived in greater Chicago for a decade. I've lived in a mid-size county in Florida of 300,000 people for a decade. I've lived in small towns.

My small Indiana community was the best. Small rural towns are the best for the freest lifestyle. My parents gave me an amazing upbringing in so many ways.

Having made these extremely necessary clarifiers, I must also honestly say that there is something my mother did, that created a huge problem for me in the first four decades of my life. That being, I had to live under the constant pressure of being her "miracle baby."

Before your uncle Lynn and I – the youngest two children in my family – were born, mom prayed concerning each of us while we were in her womb, "Lord, may this child serve you all the days of his life." Near the end of Mom's pregnancy with me, she became extremely ill and was admitted to the hospital.

While at the hospital, Mom was given medication to assist with her symptoms. When a new nurse came in later to check on her, she picked up the clipboard to look through the paperwork.

Obviously puzzled, the nurse said to my mother, "So where is this baby?" To which mom replied, "What?" The nurse said, "The chart here says that you're pregnant, where are you hiding this baby?"

Mysteriously, my mother's baby bump (me) had vanished, and sunk back into her body. What had likely happened, is that she was given the wrong medication.

This launched a litany of tests to determine if there was any kind of heart-beat and evidence of fetal life. After these tests, a panel of 10 doctors gave their opinion as to the results of the tests. Nine doctors said that the baby (me) was dead. One doctor said that he didn't know for sure, but that the baby was probably dead.

Needless to say, my mother was crushed. She began to grieve and to sob. Later that night, while mom was in complete despair, a nurse attempted to comfort her. She said, “Mrs. Gowerstreet, would it be of any comfort if I checked again for a heartbeat?”

Mom agreed. The nurse listened closely for a heartbeat and said that she thought she might have detected a heartbeat.

The nurse was right. Because about a month later, I was born.

This only fueled my mother's belief that she had given birth to a special “miracle baby” that would be the answer to her prayers. A child that would “faithfully serve the Lord all the days of his life.”

Throughout her years of raising me, Mom had this desire *for me*. In my teen years, when I showed a propensity for public speaking, and when I found some modest success in various activities in my small high school, our pastor's wife also believed that God was calling me to ministry. She too began praying for me.

Then after a dramatic “conversion experience” at age 16, I started becoming more zealous in my faith. I became a real spiritual leader in my high school. At a “See You at the Pole” Christian prayer event, I took the lead. Afterward, one of my teachers remarked on what I great job I did. And that I had a real ability in that area of leadership. More confirmation *from others* of who I was, and what I should be.

After high school I would attend Stewart Christian College. In the opening preaching revival, the high-powered Evangelist said, “You've always heard the question, ‘Why should I be a preacher?’ I have a different question for you, ‘Why shouldn't you be a preacher?’”

And the Evangelist, with an extremely forceful personality, anticipated the initial objection of, “Well, I’ve never been called.” So the Evangelist’s response to this was, “Why not just volunteer? Go that way (give your life to Christian ministry) and see if God stops you.”

So, at 18 years old, I volunteered. Long story short, this eventually led to me being a Bible professor for six years, and a pastor for nine years.

And there were some great times. I had great friends. I had a wonderful social network. I loved teaching and the massive amounts of approval I received from my teaching gift. I loved caring for people and walking with them through the darkest moments of their lives.

For those 15 years in Christian ministry, I know my mother was very proud of me. I was a living answer to her prayers. Her miracle baby was serving God.

But I'm no longer in ministry. And while I have a hundred good things to say about Christianity, I no longer identify as a Christian. I know I have deeply hurt my mother. And very few things in life are as painful as knowing you have wounded someone who loves you more than life itself. It is excruciating.

But after leaving ministry, my other siblings provided some insight. I wasn't the only child to feel like they were living under the domination of mother's expectations. One of my older brothers, who had been an incredible auto mechanic, told me of the sting he felt from mother's disapproval for having left that area of employment. That being a mechanic was his "calling."

My sister told me of the burden mom placed on her growing up to marry a pastor or someone in ministry. We all felt the pressure to live the lives mother wanted us to live.

These things have caused me to reflect on my entire life. That to some degree, I had in principle always lived the life that mom designed for me. That I had never been "called" to ministry. Jesus had never appeared to me. Jesus had never spoken to me – audibly or internally – that I was supposed to be his messenger in his ministry.

All these "choices" that I made concerning faith and ministry were all done in high pressure atmospheres. "Choices" I made in front of people standing over me while they held my two diamonds.

But now, the diamonds of my identity and inner peace are back in my hands. Today, I have to create my own identity and determine my own inner peace.

And it's okay. It's okay not to be a pastor anymore. It's okay not to be a Christian anymore. It's okay not to be afraid of death and hell anymore. It's okay to create a new identity. It's okay to reinvent myself.

As silly as this sounds, the children's movie *Bolt* will always be special to me. A few months after leaving ministry, our family was in Virginia visiting my best friend from college. You know him as Uncle Frank. He too, had just resigned from Christian ministry, and was wondering what the next step of his life would be.

So here we both were, about 20 years removed from college. We both had spent the last 20 years in Christian education and ministry. And we both were depressed and wondering, "Now what?"

One day during our stay at Uncle Frank's house, all of the children were in the living room watching the movie *Bolt*. About half-way through the movie, Frank and I decided to sit down and watch the movie too.

The point in the movie was when the Bolt the dog had been awakened to the painful reality that he was not a superhero. He was just a regular dog.

Bolt had been taken by a television company as a very small puppy and had been placed in a very controlled environment. His mind was programmed to believe he had superpowers. That he had unbelievable speed, a supersonic bark, etc. He had been led to believe that the perfect lightning bolt marking on his body was the identifying mark of his specialness – instead of the work of make-up artists.

Bolt had been programmed as a slave to perform for another's profit. He had been dominated. And to maintain this dominance, his dominators kept him ignorant. They carefully avoided any exposure to the outside world and any information that might tip him off to the fact that his reality, was not real.

For the entirety of his conscious existence, Bolt never knew that the whole thing was fake. He thought it was real. The diamonds of his identity and the programming of his inner peace had been taken from him in his infancy. His diamonds were in the firm grasp of his dominators.

But then it happened. Bolt was exposed to the outside world. He was awakened to the fact that his whole life was one of brainwashing. It was painful for him to realize he didn't have supernatural strength and invincibility; he could bleed. That he actually had extreme limits to his ability to jump and run. That he didn't have some supersonic bark, he just had a normal dog voice.

Bolt was crushed and overwhelmed by being so painfully normal. Until he was reminded by Mittens, his new cat friend, "It's okay to be a regular dog."

The moment Mittens said these things to Bolt, Uncle Frank turned to me in that moment, and said, "That's a word for us." To which I replied, "I was thinking the same exact thing!"

You see, for 20 years we were in "the ministry." We were pastors. We were the voice of God to the people of God. We were supermen able to leap tall buildings in a single bound. We were on-call 24/7. We preached. We taught. We counseled. We comforted. We influenced decisions that would affect families and generations of families. We were special.

But now we were both out of ministry. Our superpowers were gone. Our identity was ruined. Our inner peace was troubled and disturbed. Our lives seemed over.

But then we heard, "It's okay to be a regular dog." Feel the wind in your face. Chase a stick. Pee on a fire hydrant. It's great being a regular dog.

At the writing of this book, it's been 7 years since Uncle Frank and I's "Bolt moment." To this day, we still on occasion remind each other, "It's okay to be a regular dog."

It's okay to live a regular life, one different than one designed for you by a dominator. Even when the dominators are wonderful, loving, and well-intentioned parents. Parents who truly do want you to go in a direction that they believe will bring you well-being and happiness. Parents who sincerely want what is best for you.

We're human. Your mother and I will be opinionated about who your romantic interests are. We will have our takes and views about your hobbies, your methods as a parent, where you live, what you pursue, etc.

Just roll with it. You can't stop us from judging you. But we can't stop you from living above our judgments. Digest what we are saying. Sometimes we might be right. Sometimes we might be wrong. Most times we will be partially right and partially wrong – you will have to sort out to what degree we are both.

Make sure that you do not give your mother and I the power to define your identity and determine your inner peace.

We know you love us, but in those moments remind us that it is your life. Remind us that these are your choices. And we will do our best to honor that. You were born to be free. You were not born to be dominated by your parents.

CHAPTER 19

You Were Not Born to be Dominated by Your Siblings

You were born free. You were not born to be the slave of your siblings.

They don't own you. Protect the diamonds of your identity and your inner peace from them. When your siblings come for them, look them in the eyes and remind them, "I love you. But you can't have them. I was born to be free. I wasn't born to be dominated by you."

Diamond stealing dominators can be found in the very house you live in. As we discussed last chapter, dominators can take the form of your parents. As we will discuss in this chapter, dominators can take the form of your siblings.

You are the "baby" of five children. I am the "baby" of five children. We are both at the bottom of our respective birth order dominance hierarchies. Watching how your brother's treat you, and one another, has been enlightening. It has given me a front row seat in understanding my own childhood.

My oldest brother Gene is 13 years older than me. Al was next, and he is 11 years older than me. Then came Leigh, 7 years older than me. Fourth was Lynn, 4 ½ years older than me. I was born last, the bottom of our family hierarchy.

Growing up, I'm sure Gene and Al bullied me on occasion, but I have very few memories of this. It was rare.

Why? They were over a decade older than me, and I was never a threat to their dominance.

Ditto for Leigh. She might have mothered and bullied me some. But again, I have very few memories of this.

Lynn was another matter. You can imagine that as the third boy, he got plenty of bullying from the two older, more dominant brothers and a load of mothering from big sister. I'm sure he was sick and tired of being bossed around by the older three children. So when I was born, his desire to dominant someone found an outlet.

You are in a similar position as I was. Ray is 11 years older than you. Lands is 10 years older than you. Joe Jr. is 6 years older. Max is 2 and ½ years older.

When I watch you children, my confirmation biases about dominance hierarchies are constantly realized. Every day, I see you all vying for dominance over one another.

- One of you wants to be the judge so that the other is the judged.
- One of you wants to blame so that you are not blamed.
- One of you wants control so that the other does what you want.
- The bigger, stronger, more experienced, more learned, and more spirited child loves to dominate the smaller, weaker, less experienced, more ignorant, and weaker spirited younger sibling.

Every day.

And I have been observing this for years. The first time 15-month-old Ray was introduced to his little brother Lands, his first response was to put his little hand on Lands' head and shove it away.

Ah, the dominance hierarchy.

To be sure, Ray has been very good to Lands through the years. But as a young child, he wanted to dominate Lands like we dominated him.

Lands, our Down's and Autistic child is our "normal" child. He is what we all should be. He doesn't live like there is a dominance hierarchy. He is love incarnate. I have never once seen him bully another human being. He doesn't even attempt to bully other people. The whole "How the World Works from A to Z," doesn't apply to him. He has never tried to dominate his younger siblings. He is the anomaly.

Let's talk about Joe Jr., our middle child. Joe Jr. is the most natural alpha in the family. It just seems to be in his DNA. He tries to dominate us all, regardless of age, size, and experience. However, he struggles to dominate Ray at this point in life because of the 6-year difference between them.

And let's face it, Ray is physically imposing. He's a monster. Nevertheless, despite these age and size differences, there are plenty of battles for dominance between Ray and Joe Jr.

Then Max came along. We all "resent him" because he seemingly won the genetic lottery for good looks. Max definitely epitomizes everything about the dominance hierarchy. He hates the attempts of Ray and Joe Jr. to dominate him. He scratches, screams, and claws to keep them from dominating him.

But he loves trying to dominate you. He is the essence of the law of the dominance hierarchy – hypocrisy. He hates being dominated. He loves to dominate.

At this early stage in both of your developments, we have to correct Max every day for mistreating you. He is constantly pushing your buttons, frustrating you, invading your space, parenting you, and loves acting like a scary monster to frighten you. Which is carbon copy of what Ray does to him – on an almost daily basis.

This is a nasty cycle. Ray pushes Max's buttons, frustrates him, provokes him to anger, acts like a scary monster and frightens him. With the result being that Max is crying, screaming, and running to your mother or I for protection. The worst part of all this seemingly benign behavior, is that Ray has a look of satisfaction and a sadistic smile on his face. He has found inner peace through the disrupting of Max's inner peace. He has found happiness in making Max unhappy.

In these moments, Ray possesses the demeanor of a dominator. The look of "I'm stronger and smarter than him. I succeeded in making him afraid of me. I manipulated him. I controlled his actions and attitude. I exercised power over him."

As much as Max hates Ray's attempts (and success) in dominating him, you would think his mindset would be: "I hate being treated this way…I resolve never to let another person feel this way."

Nope.

He wants to dominate someone else the way he has been dominated.

Ah, and you came into his life. He loves you for multiple reasons. One reason is that he has a candidate to dominate. Someone he can bully.

And I have seen it on the same exact day. On the same day that Ray intentionally pushed his buttons, Max will turn right around and do the same thing to you. He will push your buttons until you come crying and screaming to us.

And Max will have the same exact look of satisfaction and sadistic smile on his face, that Ray had when tormenting him. Max finds his inner peace through the disruption of yours. Max finds happiness in making you unhappy. Max now possesses the demeanor of a dominator.

I told Max just this week to train himself to find his happiness in making you happy. And not to allow himself to feel happy when intentionally trying to make you unhappy.

Everybody is, what he or she is, because they had to become that – in order to survive. Remember that about Max. Why does he try to dominate you constantly? Because he has two parents with forceful personalities that dominate him. Two of his three older brothers attempt to dominate him on an hourly basis. He is sick and tired of people trying to dominate him. He wants to dominate someone else.

When you were born, Max now had immediate access to one person in his life that he was bigger than. Someone he was more experienced than. Someone he was more knowledgeable than. Someone he could manipulate, dominant, and control.

Don't get me wrong, Max loves you. But he is human. He wants to dominate you. He has been pushed around by his two older brothers, and he's not afraid when we are not looking to push you around and down. He's not afraid to be your third parent telling what you can and cannot do. Sometimes he's accurate. Sometimes his motives are pure and he's trying to protect you from harm. Sometimes his motives are not pure, and he simply wants the high ground over you.

This is normal. This is even cute sometimes. But it can be a source of great conflict as you get older.

I have built this entire book around the concept of diamonds – the diamonds of your identity and your inner peace. And that dominators who want possession of your diamonds take many forms. And it is easy to look at the large-scale dominators like the religious, ruling, and rich classes – the *power* classes. But what should not be overlooked are the everyday dominators – the *practical* classes. Those who you live with. Those you grow up with. Those you love. Those you fight with.

I believe there can be a lot of damage done within an individual as a result of dominance hierarchy battles within a family. Battles for dominance with brothers and sisters. All trying to be the dominator, not the dominated. All trying to be judge, not the judged. All wanting ridicule rights over the other person. All wanting to control the identity of a sibling through labeling and name calling. All wanting to disrupt the inner peace of a sibling through intimidation and manipulation.

Families are a complex conversation. On the one hand, nothing is better in this world than home and family. It is a safe space. It is the one place on Earth that I can "let my hair down" and be at ease.

Everywhere else and to everybody else on Earth I have to constantly be on edge. I have to wear a mask. I have to show everybody what a good person I am. My better self must always be on display and I can never let my guard down. I can never let people to see my baser, darker side. I have to pretend it doesn't exist.

And it's hard work. If I allow other people even the briefest glimpse into my baser self, I'm in trouble. Anyone observing and documenting that I am not perfect, will be glad to discredit me. They will certainly make a mental note of my outburst of emotion, momentary harsh tone, and questionable speech. They will build a monument to this moment and define the entirety of my character by this moment.

And they will use this moment as an opening for dominance over me. In their mind, they are now my judge. And they will bring up this "evidence" as leverage for any future rejection they want to formally bring my way. They will have all the "proof" they need to justify no longer loving and accepting me.

Such is life.

But family is different. Our homes are often the one place on Earth where both our better selves and our baser selves are on full display. Both our angels and our demons live there.

When we enter our homes, we are able to hang our societal actor's masks on the coat rack by the front door. At home, the real, unguarded you comes out. At home and among family, the best and worst versions of ourselves come out. At home, you are loved for both of these versions. You are loved for the totality of who you are. In theory, family is the place where you don't have to perform to be loved. You are loved because you are family.

But.

The freedom to be ourselves in the home, will result in our dark side showing itself on occasion. We find more liberty in the home to express our baser thoughts and emotions. And damage is done. Sometimes, a lot of damage.

Home and family can also create substantial heartache. Parents can say and do things to children that they would never say and do to a stranger. Brothers and sisters can say and do things to one another that they would never say and do someone they just met. In the home, we often unleash our dark side upon one another.

Why? Because we are counting on still being loved and accepted after acting like the world's biggest jerk.

While we find relief within family for being loved in our best and worst of moments, damage is still done to those we've treated like crap. The harsh name-calling, bullying, meanness, anger, and hell we unleashed upon our loved ones does affect them.

There are some family fights that may result in forgiving, but not in forgetting. What was said in those explosive moments burns deep within the emotional memories of those targeted in the outburst. And even though someone sincerely apologizes and declares, "I didn't mean it," it is still hard not to live under the judgmental words spoken in those regrettable moments.

Now in my mid-forties, I have a lot more perspective on my family growing up, and our family now. When I watch how Joe Jr., a hyper brilliant alpha personality attempts to control Max at every turn, and then how Max attempts to control your whole life, it helps me understand my own upbringing.

I'm not only like you, in that, I'm the baby of five children. But I'm also like Max, in that I am the fourth boy. And there is a very strong dominating male personality just above me in the birth order dominance hierarchy.

More than I realized, my brother Lynn dominated me very much growing up. In all points? Of course not. But he had no problem being a jerk to me. All the time? No. Is he forgiven? Certainly.

But forgiving is not always forgetting. Because forgetting words spoken with deep ridicule or explosive emotion cannot be forgotten. And these words still attempt to dominant.

I remember Lynn ridiculing and calling me names growing up. Just to be mean. When I was in Elementary school, he would say, "Joe butt, buck toothed baby." And he would say it again and again. Why? To dominate me like he had been dominated. To be the judge, not the judged. To control my identity through name calling and labeling. To find his inner peace by disrupting mine.

And what could I do about it? He was four and a half years older. He was bigger, stronger, and smarter.

It our teenage years, he was a rage monster. He would cuss with vehemence and in a certain cadence. Something I picked up from him. To this day, when I lose poise, I can launch into a profanity laced tirade and I use the same cussing cadence I heard him use growing up.

And some of his profanity was directed at me. I will not write what he said. But it was targeted right at me, and he never apologized for it. When Lynn cussed me out in our teenage years, what could I do about it? When he ordered me around, there was little I could do about it. He was still bigger, stronger, and smarter than I was.

My oldest two brothers would also occasionally order me around as well. But they were so much older and higher up the dominance hierarchy, there was very little confrontation. They were my clear superiors.

But down the line, Lynn clearly lived out the unwritten rule of the dominance hierarchy. I have the right to disrespect you, but you better respect me. I can hurt you, but you cannot hurt me. Your accountable to me, but I'm not accountable to you.

But I'm grateful for Lynn. Having a brilliant older brother made me smarter. Having a creative, innovative older brother made me more creative and innovative. Having a strong, athletic older brother helped me become more athletic. I owe much to him.

And while I am highlighting a few bad moments, we had legions of good moments together. And Lynn's best and worst qualities have shaped a part of who I am. He was the brother closest in age to me, and the one right next to me on the birth order dominance hierarchy.

But sibling rivalries do not end in childhood. They will also be a potential problem in adulthood. The desire for one sibling to dominate another in adulthood still happens.

Even in adulthood you will have to guard the diamonds of your identity and inner peace from your siblings.

- They will judge everything about you as an adult.
- They will constantly compare themselves to you.
- Your wealth, your possessions, your family, etc. can also turn into a "I'm better than you" competition, if you are not careful.
- Your adult siblings will attempt to dominate you in some of these things.
- They will judge you because they are insecure, and they want you living under their judgment.

When your mother and I got engaged, we each had an older unmarried sibling who just couldn't handle it. They were extremely frustrated that their "less dominant" sibling was passing them up in some area of life. Both of our siblings verbalized their critical judgment of our engagement. Not for our sakes, but for their own.

In at least one area of life, our two siblings were losing their spot on the dominance hierarchy. They were falling behind. They were exasperated. And the truth is, their identity and their inner peace were in great turmoil. In a last-ditch effort to maintain dominance, they wanted to make us suffer. They wanted to cause our inner peace to be shaken by their disapproval.

This taught your mother and I a very valuable lesson in life. Never give anyone, especially your siblings, your two diamonds. Your mother and I refused to give to our temporarily jealous older siblings power over our identity and inner peace.

We moved forward. We moved beyond our siblings. And actually, do you know what living above, not under, the judgment of our siblings accomplished? It motivated both of our siblings into action in their own romantic lives.

Hallie, I will do my best to make sure your siblings treat you with respect. But I won't be there for every moment of every day. I won't be there when some ugly words are spoken in private. I won't be there when some deeply personal name-calling may take place. I won't be there when your siblings attempt to steal your two diamonds.

Can you run to me when such things happen? Sure. But the better option is that you make a powerful choice. The choice to refuse surrendering the diamonds of your identity and inner peace to your brothers. Refusing to let them dominant and manipulate you.

If your brothers mistreat you, that does NOT define who you are. It defines who they currently are in that moment. If your brothers achieve inner peace by disrupting yours, that is present character deficiency in them, not you. It reveals that they presently are internally troubled, insecure, and want to feel the false security that comes by bullying and intimidation.

And all this is true in reverse. Your brothers were not born to be dominated by you. Their identity and inner peace should not be placed under your power. You are responsible to treat them with honor, respect, and love. You are responsible to build your brothers, not destroy them.

But this is painting a worst-case scenario. In all honesty, I really do like the chances that all of you siblings will have solid relationships with one another throughout life.

However, if something goes sour between you and one of your siblings, first look in the mirror. Honestly assess and ask yourself, "What could I have done different? To what degree am I to blame in this dispute?" If you are in the wrong, humble yourself. Mend the fence. Reconcile with your sibling.

But if you honestly believe that you are not being self-deceived when you say, "I really don't think I've done anything wrong. I think they just want me to live under their judgment. They are just jealous and resentful." Then simply move forward and do not allow your identity and inner peace to be hindered in the slightest by your sibling.

Love them. But do not pander to their manipulation techniques to bring you down to their level. Live above their judgment, not under it.

Your life is your life. Your brother's lives are their lives. You were born to be free. You were not born to be dominated by your siblings.

CHAPTER 20

How to *Feel* Free in a World of Slavery

This is a world of slavery. The whole planet is on lockdown by dominators. And I was using this terminology in the writing of this book before the global lockdown due to COVID-19.

Now it's *really* on lockdown.

And even though we all want a sense of inner freedom, to feel free, we don't. Because we're not.

But many of us fantasize about being and *feeling* free. One of our favorite family movies is *Swiss Family Robinson*. It captures our imagination because it would be incredible to have an island all to ourselves – free from dominators.

When I hear of exoplanets, planets that could potentially sustain life like our Earth, I would love to leave this world and go to our own planet. Dominators and slavery make you want to desert this crazy world.

But right now, there's no escape. We have to learn how to live in this bizarre place. One where ruling class dominators have used COVID-19 as justification for making this whole Earth a prison. These government dominators are operating on the huge assumption that we want them to dominate us, "represent" us, and make choices for us. That their supposed concern for public safety magically grants them public sovereignty over every detail of our lives.

Remember the concept of "moralized dominance"? The government handling of COVID-19 at every level looks and sounds like the subtle evil of moralized dominance to me. Ruling class dominators acting like their motive is the good of people. When their real motive is greed and power. "Let us help you…or we'll hurt you."

Remember the two tests for freedom?

1. Is the choice mine to make?
2. Is coercion being used against me?

Ruling class dominators are removing choices and using coercion at an alarming rate.

And it's time to take our lives back. Government dominators are not going to give them back.

But ruling class dominators are not the only reason this is a world of slavery. Let's not forget the religious class dominators who also want control over the entire planet.

Remember, there's never just one player on the global Monopoly board.

- Islam will not rest until it's won its struggle to bring the entire world under the submission of Allah and Sharia law.
- Christianity envisions a day when every knee shall bow, and every tongue shall confess that Jesus Christ is Lord of all (Philippians 2:9-11).
- Israel imagines a day where it is the pre-eminent nation on Earth (Isaiah 53).
- On the flip side, Atheists dream of a day when we live on a planet liberated from the idea of God entirely.

And rich class dominators may be more responsible than anyone else for making this present world one of slavery. They have caused their money god to become the most destructive, oppressive, tyrannical god in world history.

- Multibillion-dollar corporations are more important than the individual soul.
- Maintaining the military industrial complex is more important than peace between the peoples of Earth.
- The pharmaceutical industry is more important to maintain and keep running then the wholeness, health, and sanity of all of the peoples on Earth.
- Keeping up the multi-trillion-dollar gas and oil industry is more important than saving the health of our planet and its people.
- Burdening humanity with the perpetual anxiety of debt is more important than their mental health.
- Drowning humans in an ocean of materialism and consumerism is more important than people living in simplicity, humility, unity, and community.

In 2020, Earth really is a world of slavery. How do you feel free in a place that has no interest in you being free or feeling free?

How do you ever feel free in a world of slavery?

I don't know.

I doubt that feeling *entirely* free is even possible. But I am growing convinced you can feel *extremely* free.

Here is what I have learned so far on my journey. Here are seven ways to at least feel *extremely* free in a world of slavery.

First, you must get your two diamonds back. You must reclaim full possession and ownership over the diamonds of your identity and inner peace. And then never give them back to a religion. Never give them back to a government. Never give them back to the wealthy.

Never give them back to anyone. Declare that, "For the rest of my life, no dominator has the right to identify me as 'good' or 'bad.' For the rest of my life, no dominator has the right to control my inner peace to make me feel 'good' or 'bad.'"

You were born free. You were not born to be dominated.

Take your right hand and reclaim the diamond of your identity. From this moment on, YOU define your identity. Renounce the identities forced upon you by the power classes – the religious, ruling, and rich classes. Renounce the identities bullied upon you by the practical classes – those dominating you in your everyday life.

You are who YOU say you are. You are NOT who THEY say you are. Reclaim your honor, your integrity, and your identity.

Then take your left hand and reclaim the diamond of your inner peace. From this moment on, YOU determine your inner peace. From this moment on, never again feel like you are a "good person" or "bad person" based upon your ability to keep the rules dominators have made *for you* apart from your agreement, consent, and *free* choice.

You were not born with feelings of guilt. You were programmed, burdened, controlled, and cursed with them by dominators. Never again let their false guilt ride you.

Do a reversal and begin riding the false guilt of dominators. Ride their guilt until you break its back and kill it. Throw off the burden and curse of the bogus guilt they've programmed you with. Dominators and their systems no longer judge you. You judge them.

We sometimes call you "Captain Marvel" for multiple reasons. I know you like that movie. And Carol Danvers, who is Captain Marvel, really is a perfect illustration of someone who took back her two diamonds from the dominators who stole them.

In the movie *Captain Marvel*, Carol Danvers was a female Air Force pilot who was closely trained by Dr. Wendy Lawson. Someone Carol greatly respected and admired.

What Carol didn't know is that Dr. Lawson was from another world. She was actually Mar-Vell, a Kree from the planet of Hala. And she was working with an energy core powered by the Tesseract – one of the six Infinity stones so central to the Marvel Cinematic Universe. This energy core was helping Dr. Lawson create light speed technology.

But Dr. Lawson was viewed as a traitor to the Kree. She was not supportive of their mission to destroy all Skrulls, their sworn enemies. Lawson wanted to use the energy core to end wars, not win them. She was a liberator, not a dominator. She wanted peace, not power.

And this infuriated the Kree. Therefore, the Kree wanted to find Lawson and steal the energy core and her research.

One day, the Kree came looking for Dr. Lawson. Carol was given the task of helping Lawson fly to her satellite laboratory. In route, and out of nowhere came a Kree plane which shot them out of the sky.

Lawson was greatly hurt and revealed to Carol her true identity. Lawson knew the Kree were coming for the energy core and she wanted to destroy it before they could get their hands on it.

As Lawson raised her gun to destroy the energy core, she was shot by Yon-Rogg, an elite Kree soldier. Ultimately, Carol picked up Lawson's gun and shot the energy core to keep Yon-Rogg and the Kree from getting it.

When Carol shot the energy core, it exploded. It's power shot through her body and bonded with it. It also knocked her out in the process.

When Yon-Rogg observed that an unconscious Carol had absorbed the energy, he knew she would be unbelievably powerful. She could be an awesome weapon programmed to kill Skrulls.

At this point, it could be said that Yon-Rogg and the Kree took full possession of Carol's two diamonds. And they would use them to make Carol their slave.

Her new Kree dominators:

- Stole her from Earth and took her to Hala.
- Changed her identity to be known as "Vers."
- Convinced her mind that she was Kree, that blue blood was flowing through her veins.
- Gave her false memories. In her mind, instead of Yon-Rogg being the one coming to assassinate Dr. Lawson, they placed an image of a Skrull general, Talos, coming to kill her. They placed this false memory trigger to mentally program Carol to fear and hate Skrulls.
- Placed an implant on the back of her head. This implant would send electrical shocks and feedback to program her thinking. To condition her to only feel inner peace when obeying and agreeing with the Kree.
- Brainwashed her to feel that all of her powers were from them. And that they, her dominating masters, could take these powers away anytime they wanted. That she was utterly helpless without her Kree dominators.

In short, the Kree stole the diamonds of identity and inner peace from Carol Danvers. And they moralized their dominance over them. The Kree used these two diamonds to program Carol to be their slave – a pawn in their destructive agenda.

But the beauty of *Captain Marvel* is the process of Carol freeing herself from Kree domination. Her awakening to who she really was – her true identity. Her enlightenment to her true self – her inner peace.

In the climactic moment of the film, the Supreme Intelligence, the Artificial Intelligence Ruler of the Kree, condescendingly told Carol that she was merely "Vers, and we made you who you are. What we've given you, can be taken away."

In other words, "We still own you. Your two diamonds are still in our possession."

To which Captain Marvel looked at the Supreme Intelligence and said in essence, "My name is Carol. I'm taking back the diamond of my identity. I reject your rule. My powers never came from you. I'm taking back the diamond of my inner peace."

Carol then reached behind her head and tore off the mind-control implant. And in the face of her Kree dominator, she threw it to the ground in utter contempt.

Carol had broken free. She had reclaimed the two diamonds of her identity and inner peace.

We all must have this moment in life. We must reclaim full sovereignty and control over the diamonds of our identity and inner peace. We must live above our dominators.

Yes, you will have to learn how to live WITH dominators and their rules. But you should never again live UNDER dominators and their rules. Think for yourself. Judge right and wrong for yourself. Live as externally free as humanly possible. Live as internally free as humanly possible.

But be prepared for war. Reclaiming your two diamonds is a declaration of independence from dominators. Declaring independence from a dominator is the start of a war, not the end of it. Dominators are always about gaining and maintaining power. And they moralize their dominance. Dominators never lay down power. Dominators never decrease their power.

Resisting, disobeying, and deserting a dominator means war. The Declaration of Independence from Britain on July 4, 1776 was not a final step in transitioning 13 British Colonies into the newly identified 13 American States.

It was a first step. And it began a long war with their dominator who desperately wanted to maintain dominance over them.

Fight the good fight of freedom. There is not a more worthy fight on Earth.

Also, once you have reclaimed your two diamonds, you will have to patiently reprogram your mind and nervous system to support you in your war for inner freedom. All your triggers and promptings have been made to obey the dominator for so long, you will feel "bad" for disobeying the dominator.

Retrain your triggers and promptings to obey you, not the dominator. Reprogram your mind on this central truth: "Resisting domination is not the evil; domination itself is the evil."

To help you in your fight for inner freedom, be sure to frequently revisit your two-year-old self. Get in the imaginary time machine and go back to the time your mind was free from the fear of dominators.

- Revisit the time when you had no awareness of the existence of dominators, their mental programming, their rules, their threats to hurt you for disobedience, their control through guilt, and their methods of shame-based conformity.
- Revisit the time that dominators did not have the diamonds of your identity and your inner peace in their possession.
- Know that there was a time, be it ever so briefly, that you held in your own hands the diamonds of your identity and your inner peace.

To feel free in a world of slavery, you must resolve to get your two diamonds back – whatever it takes.

Do it right now.

Reclaim the diamonds of your identity and inner peace.

No one has the right to dominate you.

No one.

No religion.

No government.

No rich person.

No boss.

No parent.

No sibling.

No bully.

No predator.

When someone tries to dominate you, stand up straight. Square your shoulders back. Look them in the eyes. And ask them with strength and conviction,

- Do you own me?
- No? Then what right do you have to order and oppress me?
- Do you think that I was born into this world to be dominated by you?
- Do you think that I was born into this world so you could make choices for me?
- Do you think that I was born into this world to live in fear of you and your threats?"

Down deep, even dominators know that their claims of authority are fraudulent. Take back your two diamonds and do it right now.

Second, to feel free in a world of slavery, you must learn the difference between cooperation and submission. Learn how to cooperate and work with others. Reject the idea of submission to others.

Remember, dominators always moralize their dominance. They pretend to be the "good guy" in every situation. They pretend to be just, fair, nice, and reasonable. As a result, dominators tell one of their biggest lies when they consciously make NO distinction between cooperation and submission.

There is a great example of this in yet another Marvel movie, the first *Thor* movie. There was a time where the government agency S.H.I.E.L.D. invaded Jane Foster's research lab and stole all of her life's research and work. And this government agency did so apart from her foreknowledge, agreement, and consent. When S.H.I.E.L.D. was done stealing all of her intellectual property, Agent Coulson looked at Jane Foster and said with a maddeningly pleasant face, "Thank you for your cooperation."

Spoken like a true dominator. Dominators never make a distinction between cooperation and submission. They make them one and the same. Dominators are willful liars. They know how to moralize their dominance and make it sound "good" and respectable.

When dominators use the word *cooperation*, they really mean *submission*. Dominators will say, "Thank you for your cooperation." But you were never given a chance to disagree, refuse consent, and freely walk away. By "Thank you for your cooperation," dominators really mean, "You were smart to submit to our will, because we would've hurt you."

Cooperation and submission are clearly two different words. Cooperation begins with the prefix "co" implying equality and egalitarianism. Cooperation implies willful, voluntary choice. Cooperation implies evenness and a side-by-side mutual, voluntary respect.

Submission is completely different. Submission begins with the prefix "sub" implying a ranking beneath another, inequality, and authoritarianism. Submission means that one higher individual is dominating a choice and a situation. While the lower person is conceding power to the superior individual. And in almost every case, if the inferior person refuses to submit to the superior person, the stronger person will hurt them to whatever degree is needed to bring the weaker person back into a state of submission.

Jane Foster did not cooperate with Agent Colson. She submitted. She would never have given permission to the government to take her intellectual property. She would have never agreed or consented to the scenario she found herself in. If she physically fought back, she would have been restrained at the very least. Or she could have been killed, at the very most. She did not voluntarily cooperate. She involuntarily submitted to superior force. Standing down is submission, not cooperation.

Dominators are deceivers. They willfully manipulate terminology at every turn. When they use the word cooperation, they know that they mean submission. The power classes in particular are not really into cooperation. They are into submission.

If you want to feel free in a world of slavery, live a life of willing cooperation with like-minded people. Work with people, not under them. Life is better working with a team. Life is better learning how to be part of a group that can get along and accomplish incredible things together.

But understand that there is a difference between cooperation and submission. If you want to feel free in this world, only put yourself in scenarios of willing cooperation.

If you want to feel free in a world of slavery, begin systematically removing yourself from people and groups demanding your unquestioned loyalty and submission. Learn the difference between voluntary cooperation and involuntary submission.

Embrace a life of voluntary cooperation. Reject a life of involuntary submission.

Third, to feel free in a world of slavery, learn the difference between leadership and lordship. There's nothing wrong with following a leader. There is nothing wrong with following a leader or mentor with superior life experience, skill, wisdom, insight, and character. We should seek out worthy mentors. We should follow good leaders.

The problem is leadership that becomes lordship. A leader who is a dominator. A leader who functions as master and lord.

There is a distinction between leadership and lordship.

- Leadership is into providing a pattern and example. Lordship is into power and enslavement.
- Leadership is empowering. Lordship is disempowering.
- Leadership Is obsessed with transformation. Lordship is obsessed with conformity.
- Leadership is *a hand* that reaches down and lifts up to its own level. Lordship is a *foot* that stomps down and intentionally keeps inferiors from reaching its level.

One day I remember playing at a local lake playground with you kids. This particular playground had a climbing tower with four levels. There was a hole in the middle of each level that you had to climb through to ascend upward to the next level.

Watching children on a climbing tower is a tremendous window into human nature. It is a clear illustration of the difference between leadership and lordship. That leadership is a hand that lifts up and lordship is a foot that stomps down.

Many older children love to quickly ascend up the tower to the highest level. Then you can see the look of dominance, smugness, and superiority over the smaller children who are on the lower levels.

You may even see some older children discouraging anyone from joining them at their level. They may even simulate stomping the younger children down to keep them at a lower level. This is what lordship looks like.

But I remember using the climbing tower as an example of leadership for your brother Joe Jr. I told him that a leader would not mock those at lower levels. Instead a true leader ascends to the highest levels, then turns around and extends a hand. A hand to lift others up to the level you've already achieved.

This is what leadership looks like. Leadership is a hand that lifts up. Lordship is a foot that stomps down.

You must be able to discern the difference between leadership and lordship. If you ever find yourself in a community, a business, in a church, or any other scenario where you sense that you are being lorded over, remove yourself from that situation.

If you want to feel free in a world of slavery, look for true leaders to follow, not false lords to fear.

Fourth, to feel free in a world of slavery, learn the difference between self-respect and self-preservation. I challenge you to choose a life of self-respect over self-preservation.

Self-respect is the same thing as the old-fashioned word *honor*. And honor is really just the sum total of both of your diamonds, your identity and your inner peace, all rolled up into one. Honor is refusing to surrender your two diamonds to anyone – especially dominators.

Honor is currently dormant. It needs to be revived. The old guard of humanity made statements such as Patrick Henry's "Give me liberty or give me death!" The phrase on my favorite New Hampshire sweatshirt states the immortal words, "Live free or die."

This is the mindset of people living by honor. Honor is worth fighting for. Honor is worth dying for. And this world is never going to get any better until men and women of honor return to grace us with their presence.

It will be people of honor who stand up to the religious class. All the while the religious class will be calling them "infidels," "apostates," and "evil." Spoken like true dominators attempting to moralize and maintain their dominance.

It will be men and women of honor who stand up to the governments of this planet. All the while the governments will be calling them "rebels," "terrorists," "dissidents," "criminals," and "evil." Spoken like true dominators attempting to moralize and maintain their dominance.

It will be men and women of honor who shun the rich class and the world they have created. All the while the rich class will have their newspapers and media outlets run hit pieces on how "evil" and "dishonorable" those resisting their rule are. Spoken like true dominators attempting to moralize and maintain their dominance.

This world needs men and women of self-respect and honor to rise up. I want you to live a life that is long, happy, and healthy. I hope you live for over a hundred years.

But you may not. And I would rather see you live a short life filled with self-respect and honor, than a long one that simply bowed the knee to the power classes.

Don't get me wrong, there is a place for self-preservation. Because when you want to begin a freedom movement, there is a timing to it all. If someone like your father, whom no one knows, resisted government domination, they would simply lock me away forever in their cage or kill me. And few would really know or care. No freedom movement would start from an anonymous nobody.

There is a better method. Jesus is actually the model for this. He launched a freedom movement through four steps all beginning with the letter "m." The four steps are as follows: 1) a message, 2) a multitude, 3) martyrdom, and 4) a movement.

First, Jesus began with a revolutionary *message* of a liberation and a lighter yoke for humanity. Second, this empowering message drew a *multitude* – legions of overburdened people showed up eager to hear his message. Third, the religious and ruling classes ultimately executed him and made him a *martyr* for his revolutionary message. Fourth, the power classes were already too late, Jesus had launched a *movement.*

My point is that Jesus had a timing for all that he did. Yes, he lived and died with self-respect and honor. But he only did this when the timing was right.

Before the timing of his death was right, Jesus frequently chose self-preservation. He would flee from the power classes. He would avoid arrest for the better part of three years. But when his message was well circulated, and the multitude had been enlightened, he forfeited self-preservation and willingly gave himself as a martyr.

There have been many individuals in history who followed a similar pattern. What do people like the Apostle Peter, the Apostle Paul, Joan of Arc, Thomas More, Michael Servetus, Gandhi, Dietrich Bonhoeffer, Joseph Smith, Malcolm X, Martin Luther King Jr. among others have in common?

They all were resisting religious or ruling class dominators. They were spearheading people groups to live freer lives. There were times when they chose self-preservation. But they also chose to put themselves at risk and in harm's way. They chose a dangerous life. Many of the individuals I named chose to preach a more pro-freedom and anti-domination message.

And it cost them their lives.

But we remember them all. Why? They chose self-respect over self-preservation. They chose courage over fear.

People who live exclusively by self-preservation are dominated. They will never feel free.

People who live by self-respect and honor are the freest people on the planet. They fear no dominator. They do not fear death. They do not believe the lie that disobeying dominators is evil. They know that it's the act of domination itself that *is the evil.* I challenge you to live a life of self-respect and honor.

Fifth, to feel free in a world of slavery, learn the difference between the peace of a free man and the peace of a slave. The inner peace that a free man feels, is vastly different than the inner peace that a slave feels.

Both the free man and the slave can achieve the effect of inner peace. But the cause and catalyst in the achievement of their inner peace is completely different.

Let's first talk about the inner peace that can be felt by a slave. I remember first being enlightened to this whole concept of the peace of a slave vs. the peace of a free man when studying the Old Testament. In particular the Assyrian conquests of the nation of Israel like you find in II Kings 17.

Assyria subjugated Israel and made it a vassal state within its larger empire. It required Israel to pay an annual tribute tax. As long as Israel submitted to Assyrian domination and paid the tribute, there was "peace" between the two. There was no conflict. There was no war.

For years, Israel settled into the peace of a slave. The peace of a slave comes from conceding to dominators. If you obey the dominator, they won't hurt you. And there is a relief in avoiding punishment. There is a peace in knowing you won't get hurt. But down deep, you know you're a slave.

But eventually, a King named Hoshea began refusing to pay the tribute tax to Assyria.

And what do dominators do to maintain dominance?

Whatever it takes. Assyria immediately mobilized its military, laid siege by surrounding the walls of Samaria for three years, destroyed Israel, and relocated them around that portion of the world.

The peace of a slave lasts as long as submission to the dominator lasts. Do what the dominator says, and you won't get punished. You will experience the inner peace of a slave.

And there is a massive appeal to this. It's nice not getting beat up. It's sometimes just pays to do what the dominator says. And as long as you bow to the bully, the bully will probably be pretty good to you. He will even claim to be good to you. He will point out how much he's done for you.

The formula for false inner peace is simple. Obey the dominator, and there will be "peace" between you and the dominator. And you will be less afraid of the dominator and his punishments. Therefore, you will achieve the false inner peace of the slave.

But even after achieving this false sense of inner peace, this fact remains: you are not free. You are a slave living under domination. The peace of a slave. The peace that comes by conceding and accepting defeat at the hands of the dominator.

But there is other type of inner peace. It is the inner peace of a free man. The peace that comes by conquering and winning freedom and independence from a dominator.

Attempting to achieve the inner peace of a free man means terrible conflict. As long as the American colonies obeyed Parliament and King George III, there was "peace" in the colonies. But the moment the colonies declared their independence from their British dominators, their ruling class begin sending troops over 3000 miles across the Atlantic to bring the colonies back into submission.

The British ruling class had to maintain their dominance.

This began a brutal and bloody seven-year war. One side fighting to maintain dominance. The other side fighting to free themselves from dominators. For the latter group, they chose the difficult path of fighting to achieve the inner peace of a free man. Rather than the easier path of settling for the inner peace of a submitted slave.

In the middle of the Revolutionary War, it is likely that the 13 states had times of significant doubt about choosing the more difficult path. Surely, they had times where they reasoned within themselves, "Why did we ever resist Britain's domination? We were at peace just doing what they said? Maybe the peace of a slave is actually better. At least we're alive."

But they never settled for the peace of a slave. They kept fighting. They kept battling their dominators. And one day, their dominators finally surrendered at Yorktown, Virginia. And then two years later, the Treaty of Paris made it official. The 13 United States of America had liberated themselves from their British ruling class dominators.

Surely these men and women achieved a far different caliber of inner peace. The peace of a free man. One who has fought their dominator – and won.

How do you feel free in a world of slavery? You must be willing to renounce the easy path of settling for the peace of slave. You must choose the hard path of resisting dominators.

And it will be a hard path.

- You must know that dominators will come fast and furious to bring you back into submission.
- You must embrace the fight.
- You must temporarily forfeit inner peace – perhaps for years.
- You must embrace danger.
- You must embrace your mortality.
- You must embrace the possibility of failure and losing to the dominator.
- You must embrace that losing means the dominator gets to tell the story of the battle, moralize their victory, and demonize you as the loser.

There are some special individuals in this world who reject the peace of a slave. They will only settle for the peace of a free man. And they are willing to die trying to achieve it.

And if they do win their independence from their dominators? The inner peace that they will feel, and the inner satisfaction that they have gained, cannot even be put into words.

Do you want to feel free in a world of slavery? Choose the peace of a free man over the peace of a slave.

Sixth, to feel free in a world of slavery, you must learn the subtle difference between being a *conscious* person and being a person with a *conscience*.

Being *conscious*, in the context I am using it, fundamentally means being intelligently aware and moved to action. It involves original thinking and observance.

Being a *conscious* individual refers to the mind, emotions, and inner circuitry of the free person who is aware and awake. At the core of their being, the *conscious* person is motivated and guided by love, wisdom, and compassion. The *conscious* person is critical to group transformation. The *conscious* person is a danger to dominators.

By comparison, having a *conscience* simply means "with knowledge" or "having a knowledge of." Having a *conscience* usually refers to someone's moral memory of feeling guilty or good about their obedience or disobedience to the rules and values programmed into their sub-conscious by dominators. It involves unoriginal thinking and obedience.

Being a person of *conscience* refers to the mind, emotions, and inner circuitry of a dominated person who is afraid and asleep. At the core of their being, the person of conscience is guided by fear, guilt, and self-preservation. The person of conscience is critical to group conformity. The person of *conscience* is a delight to dominators.

We live in a day where people frequently talk about having a "good," "clean," or "clear" *conscience*. I personally believe all such talk is bogus.

Watching the two-year-old you confirms my bias. You are not yet a person with much of a *conscience*. But dominators are waiting in the wings to give you one. That way you will be guided by fear, guilt, and self-preservation. That way you will think their thinking is your thinking. That way you will be less of a threat to group cohesion and conformity.

Most people in this world have been programed and domesticated by dominators to become people of *conscience*. And their so-called *conscience* is nothing more than punishment promptings (guilt feelings) programmed into them by powerful dominators.

An individual who is a person of *conscience* is actually a person who is pretty selfish. They're trying not to feel guilty because they're concerned about being hurt by their dominator.

Their *conscience* is not a matter of doing right. Their *conscience* is a matter of gaining relief from the fear of being hurt. They want to avoid punishment from God, government, or guardian dominators.

Being a person with a *conscience* is synonymous with being a slave. Most of us live lives of incessant guilt because our dominators have programmed us with tens of thousands of rules – written and unwritten. And every single one of their rules carries with it a fear triggering threat. If you break the dominators rule, here's how the dominator will hurt you.

Being a person with a *conscience* has nothing to do with being a good person. It's all about being a weak, obedient person. A person who obeys the dominator and avoids being hurt. The person with a *conscience* is a person who has fully surrendered their two diamonds to dominators.

Being a *conscious* person is a different matter altogether. The *conscious* person is aware and awake. The *conscious* person is not afraid and asleep. The *conscious* person is not intimidated by dominators.

The *conscious* person does not let dominators do his thinking for him. The *conscious* person judges right and wrong for themselves. The *conscious* person is a person of action that values people over the policies of dominators. The *conscious* person is a person of action who sees a need and then meets it.

The difference between being a *conscious* person and a person of *conscience* is the same difference between Jesus and the Pharisees. The Pharisees were people of *conscience*. They were all about making and keeping rules. And the Pharisees were proud of their systems of micro-morality and hyper-conscientiousness as a path to dominance over their fellow Jews.

Dominance which the Pharisees loved to moralize. In fact, their chief weapon of choice to dominate their fellow human beings *was morality*. They happily condemned, marginalized, ostracized, and demonized any person who could not measure up to* the impossible standards of moral perfection they had created.

And the Pharisees were totally unaware and asleep to just how immoral their morality was. The Pharisees were people of *conscience.*

The Pharisees were not *conscious* people – like Jesus.

- While the Pharisees were conscientious with rules concerning clean hands, Jesus was conscious of communing with other people (Matthew 15). The Pharisees were into moralized social distancing. Jesus was into closing the distance.
- While the Pharisees had a contamination complex and were conscientious about not being touched by sinful people, Jesus was conscious of restoring dignity to broken lives (Luke 7).
- While the Pharisees were hyper-conscientious of Sabbath observance, Jesus was conscious of healing people bound with decades long illnesses (Luke 13).
- The Pharisees were all about controlling people and conscientiously keeping the rules (Matthew 23). Jesus was all about consciously connecting with people, loving them, healing them, and building them.
- The Pharisees were all about domination. Jesus was all about liberation (Luke 4:18-19).

I love the story of the Good Samaritan that Jesus tells. It perfectly illustrates the difference between a *conscious* person impelled by love and a person with a *conscience* compelled by fear.

In this famous story, a Jewish man was walking down the road when bandits ambushed him. These dominators beat him severely, robbed him, and left him for dead.

Eventually, a Jewish priest on his way for service at the Jerusalem temple walked by and saw his bleeding and dying countryman. But this priest was no doubt a person with a *conscience*. If he touched the bloody and possibly dead man, he would be impure and ceremonially unclean in his service for God. His *conscience* wouldn't let him touch that bloody body. He had important work for God to do. It would have bothered his *conscience* to touch the bloody or possibly dead man.

Mysteriously, it didn't bother his *conscience* to leave the man to die.

A little while later along came a Levite. He also saw his bloody and dying fellow Jew. Levites were kind of like assistant priests. This Levite responded the same way as his boss. He too was a person with a *conscience*. And his *conscience* wouldn't let him touch that bloody body because he needed to be pure and clean in the service for God.

Mysteriously, it didn't bother the Levite's *conscience* to leave the man to die.

Then along came the Samaritan. He too saw the Jewish man dying. Someone who was his natural enemy. Someone he had racial conflict with. Someone he had religious conflict with. Someone from the people who persecuted his people.

If the Samaritan would have simply spit upon the dying Jew and walked away, it would not have been surprising. If he would have claimed that his *conscience* wouldn't allow him to help a Jewish enemy, it would have been understandable.

But this Samaritan was not a person with a *conscience*. This Samaritan was a *conscious* person. His heart and mind were governed by love, not laws passed down from dominators. This Samaritan was a *conscious* person aware of human need. He was moved by human need.

And he ministered to human need. The Samaritan immediately halted his journey. He quickly stopped the bleeding and attended to the injuries of the Jewish man. He then put the Jewish man on his own donkey and took him to an inn. There he probably stayed up all night with the Jewish man until his health stabilized. He then worked out an agreement with the inn owners to cover all of the expenses for the Jewish man's stay.

If you want to feel free in this world of slavery, you must become a *conscious* person like the Samaritan. A *conscious* person is motivated by love, not fear. A *conscious* person is liberated from ridiculous, divisive rules made by self-serving dominators.

You must reject being a person of *conscience* like the Priest and the Levite. Their hearts and minds were slaves to their religious class dominators. Thinking they were doing right in the name of God, they committed the ultimate wrongs against their fellow humans.

Free your mind. Free your heart. Free your life. Love. There is no one beyond the need for love. And those hardest for us to love are usually the ones who need it the most. A person with a culturally conditioned *conscience* can't love this way. But a *conscious* person can.

Seventh, to feel free in a world of slavery, you must learn to disobey. I'm going to say this without apology and with very little clarification. The absolute requirement to living a life that is *extremely* free is disobedience.

No one ever obeyed their way to freedom.

No one.

Humanity needs to be emboldened to disobey. Dominators are the ones who moralize and preach order, obedience, loyalty, and duty. That's how they maintain dominance.

If people begin to disobey dominators, they lose their power. They lose their dominance.

The Christian church would not be nearly as free as it is today if Martin Luther hadn't chosen to disobey Roman Catholicism and disavow the Pope.

America would not have become the greatest country in world history if it hadn't chosen to disobey the British Empire.

African Americans would not be nearly as free as they are today, if Rosa Parks hadn't chosen to disobey rules on a segregated bus in Montgomery, Alabama.

India would not know as much freedom as it does today if Gandhi hadn't chosen to disobey the British Empire.

The heroes that we all admire are not the obedient. They are the disobedient. Those who look into the face of powerful dominators and say "No!" Those who resist and reject domination.

Have you ever noticed who you are rooting for when watching a movie? Do you find yourself rooting for the dominator and those obeying him? Or do you find yourself rooting for the ones disobeying, resisting, and fighting back against the dominator?

- In *Star Wars,* who are you rooting for, the Emperor or the Jedi?
- In *Hunger Games*, who are you rooting for, President Snow or Katniss Everdeen?
- In *Lord of the Rings*, who are you rooting for, Sauron or Frodo?
- In *Avengers: Endgame*, who are you rooting for, Thanos or Ironman?

In the movie theatre, we root for the disobedient. We want them to defeat the dominator.

But in real life, we are terrified to be the disobedient. We are afraid of being hurt by the dominator. We are afraid to speak against or fight back against dominators.

But we will never be free and feel free until we gain the courage to disobey and fight back against dominators. And yes, we may die trying. But even that act of final defiance means that you died in freedom.

One of my favorite lines in any movie is from *Braveheart*. It was the moment where the Scots were facing a huge British army. The Scots began to despair and started complaining to William Wallace. They stated, "You've brought us to our deaths." To which Wallace replied, "Then if we die, we die as free men!" If the Scots would die in this battle, at least they would die in disobedience to British domination.

Freedom is a muscle. When is the last time you exercised it? Never forget:

- It doesn't take a strong person to obey.
- It doesn't take a strong person to submit to domination.
- It doesn't take a strong person to join a mob.
- It doesn't take a strong person to agree with "experts" and "authority."

All of these reflect weakness, not strength.

It takes a strong person to disobey. It takes a strong person to resist domination. It takes a strong person to stand alone against a mob. It takes a strong person to disagree with "experts" and expose their false authority.

All of these reflect strength, not weakness.

But you must choose to exercise the muscle of freedom. The more you exercise it, the stronger it gets. The more you passively stand down and shut up, the weaker it gets.

True freedom is not given back, it's taken back.

This advice to disobey dominators makes people extremely uncomfortable. Very few people on Earth would be comfortable with me giving my daughter the green light to disobey. They believe disobedience to dominators is evil. They do NOT believe that the domination itself is the evil.

Evidently, most people believe they were born to be dominated. That they do not own themselves. Apparently, they value force over freedom, coercion over choice, fear over love, domination over liberation, conformity over transformation, and order over wholeness.

No one ever obeyed their way to freedom.

Name one person or one people group who obeyed their way to freedom. The absolute requirement for freedom and living a free life is disobedience to the dominator.

Obeying a dominator will bring you deliverance from being hurt by the dominator. But obedience will never deliver you from the dominator and his dominance over you. In fact, obeying the dominator only tightens the chains of their domination. Deliverance from domination only comes through disagreement and disobedience.

Do we really admire those who are obedient to dominators? Do we admire the police and military of Adolph Hitler who obeyed orders to slaughter six million Jews? They were just doing their jobs. They were just doing their duty. They don't make the rules, they just enforce them. Obedience to orders was the right thing to do wasn't it? Or is their actually such things as immoral obedience and moral disobedience?

Can you really call such men "honorable"? Those who faithfully obey the commands of their moralizing dominators to do dishonorable things?

Do we really admire the U.S. Army soldiers who slaughtered hundreds of Cheyenne and Arapaho men, women, and children in the Colorado Territory in the Sand Creek Massacre of 1864? They did their duty. They obeyed orders. They fulfilled the will of their moralizing dominators. Obedience was the right thing to do wasn't it?

How many atrocities have been committed in the name of moralized obedience? How many tens of millions have been slaughtered out of obedience to religious class dominators? How many tens of millions have been slaughtered out of obedience to ruling class dominators?

How many hundreds of millions have died throughout history in the name of obedience to a dominator's will?

The whole wide world needs to be liberated to disobey.

- You don't have to be a Muslim. You can disobey.
- You don't have to be a Christian. You can disobey.

- You don't have to keep all the laws of the ruling class and government. You can disobey.
- You don't have to live the life that the rich class has designed. You can disobey.
- You don't have to stay in an abusive situation. You can disobey.

No one ever obeyed their way to freedom.

No one.

To be free and to feel free, you must disobey. If you want to feel free in a world of slavery, the absolute requirement is disobedience. We must all learn to say "No!" to dominators.

And when it comes to disobeying the government, we should stop referring to this as "civil disobedience." This is just another weak, hollow, sanitized, moralized word that even dominators are comfortable with.

We should begin using phrases like,

- "Saying 'No!' to dominators"
- "Disobedience to dominators"
- "liberation from domination"
- "enforcing freedom."

To be clear, disobedience to dominators will mean conflict. And there are three levels to interacting with dominators: 1) those who comply with them, 2) those who compromise with them, and 3) those who confront them.

First, are the level one people who simply comply with dominators. Such people give two "yes" replies to dominators. That is, their attitude is "Yes, you can dominate me," and "Yes, you can hurt me and I won't resist." This is most of humanity.

Second, are the level two people who compromise with dominators. These rare individuals hedge their bets. They comply with most of the dominator's domination. But these people have the boldness to occasionally resist.

If these second level people find a rule they don't want to obey, they are willing to compromise and give a "no" and a "yes" to the dominators. That is, "No, I won't obey this particular rule," but "Yes, I will submit to your punishment and will not fight back."

This is usually dubbed "non-violent resistance." Historically, this has been a very powerful method of dealing with dominators. And I admire people who do it.

In fact, I believe it is possibly the best, most realistic choice that people can make. Because when dominators punish these second level people, it usually puts a spotlight on who is the true bully and bad guy in the scenario – the dominator.

And this willingness to defy domination begins emboldening other people to also disobey the dominator. Gandhi and Martin Luther King Jr. effectively used the method of non-violent resistance.

Third, are the level three people who outright confront dominators. These are the people who use violent resistance in freeing themselves from domination.

While non-violent resistance to dominators is possibly the *best* option, it is NOT the *only* option. And you need to know this. Because dominators almost never – maybe never – lay down their power.

Dominators are never interested in lessening their hold and domination. They always want more and more control. And there are dominators who will never stop gaining and maintaining dominance until someone physically fights back.

Someone at this stage might predictably ask, "Are you advocating violence?"

To which you must learn to FACTUALLY say in response, "No! I'm totally an adversary *to* violence. I'm totally *against* the violence that dominators use to dominate our lives. If you are supporting the dominators, you are the one advocating violence!"

Dominators are deceivers. And the law of the dominance hierarchy is hypocrisy. Dominators hypocritically use violence to gain and maintain dominance. Dominators use terrorism to control people.

And what do dominators do to discourage disobedience? They call anyone resisting their dominance as "advocating violence" and "terrorists."

Hypocrisy. Moralized dominance.

Again, while non-violent resistance is the *best* choice, it will not be the *only* choice on the table. I hate to have to give you this mental preparation. But you may have to physically fight back against a dominator one day. You may very well have to use violent resistance.

One day, you might have to stand up to some form of bully and go to blows. Because there have been, currently are, and will be dominators who are not afraid of, nor impressed with non-violent resistance. In fact, non-violent resistance makes their domination that much easier to maintain.

Some dominators can only be stopped by violent resistance.

- Hitler was not going to be stopped by non-violent resistance and friendly negotiation.
- The cartels in Mexico are not going to be stopped by non-violent resistance and friendly negotiation.
- ISIS is not going to be stopped by non-violent resistance and friendly negotiation. They would be glad to chop off your head and happily move on with their mission.
- And there may be a day that the United States government's invasion into your personal life will not be stopped by non-violent resistance and friendly debate.

There are those dominant individuals and groups in this world where the only language they understand, respond to, and can be stopped by is "a punch in the nose."

To be clear, the world needs peaceful people who wisely use non-violent resistance. But the world also needs equally peaceful people who have the wisdom and moral clarity of knowing when to fight back with violent resistance – with deadly force.

There is no way around this irrefutable, historical fact. If you want to be free, you may have to risk your very life and physically fight for it.

These level three people are willing to give two "No!" responses to dominators. That is, "No! I will not obey you" and "No! I will not submit to your punishment. I will not let you hurt me anymore."

And these two "No!" responses will demand two different type of "Yes!" responses to the dominator. "Yes! I am willing to physically fight you for my freedom" and "Yes! I am willing to die fighting you for my freedom!"

Level three people remind me of Caesar on the most recent version of *Planet of the Apes*. Caesar was placed in an ape prison by his human dominators. But Caesar's mental awareness and consciousness had been awakened. He realized, "Why am I submitting to these dominators?"

On one day, when the timing was just right, Caesar was ready to confront his dominators. It was the time of day when the ape prisoners were briefly let out of their cages and placed in a contained recreation area. When the time came for the apes to return to their cages, Caesar defiantly disobeyed. He remained in the recreation area.

His prison dominator quickly entered the recreation area with an electrical shock device. He was going to use violence to force obedience. That's what dominators do.

The prison guard was shouting at Caesar, "Get back in the cage!" And the guard began shocking Caesar with his electrical weapon.

But the pinnacle moment of the entire movie (and really, the entire series of movies) occurred next. When the prison guard was just about to shock the chimpanzee again, Caesar grabbed the arm of the dominator and shouted a word that no ape had ever spoken before.

Caesar screamed, "No!"

Caesar was a level three individual. He looked the dominator square in the eyes and his word and actions said in effect, "No! I'm not going to obey you anymore!" And "No! I will not submit to your punishment! You cannot use electrical shock on me! I'm not going in your cage! Yes! I'm going to fight you. Yes! I'm willing to die to free myself and my fellow apes!"

And Caesar's defiance and disobedience to his human dominators launched a freedom movement for his species.

No one obeys their way to freedom. Deliverance from dominators only comes through disobedience. If you want to live a life that is free, and one that feels extremely free, you must learn to disobey.

Disobedience is the absolute requirement for freedom. Every incremental step toward greater freedom in humanity was the result of disobedience, not obedience.

At this point I know that others who might read this are screaming for clarifiers to be made. And I could make them.

But I'm not going to. People who possess common sense already know what the clarifiers would be.

The price of freedom is high. You must fight for it. Disobedience is required. Death may be required.

This message of "Live free or die" has been almost totally lost. Courage has currently been defeated by cowardice. Liberation has been defeated by domination. Billions of people on this planet have enslaved minds and atrophied, shriveled-up spirits due to power class dominators.

Dominators who program their dominated to shut up and stand down as a way of life. Dominators who program their dominated to value consumerism, materialism, entertainment, luxury, imperialism, indoctrination, industrialization, etc. over human freedom.

Dominators who have no real problem with the majority of their dominated battling self-destructive addictions to drugs, alcohol, sex, porn, digital screens, money, work, etc. It makes their domination easier.

In these COVID-19 lockdowns, schools, churches, and small businesses have been shut down. But liquor stores, Marijuana shops, and abortion clinics are open.

Hmm. I wonder why?

Because a population strung out on drugs, alcohol and sex are far easier for dominators to control. Dominators who supposedly care so much about them. Dominators who have stolen the diamonds of identity and inner peace from those living under their spell.

How do you feel free in a world of slavery?

1. Take back full control of the diamonds of your identity and inner peace.
2. Learn the difference between cooperation and submission.
3. Learn the difference between leadership and lordship.
4. Learn the difference between self-respect and self-preservation.
5. Learn the difference between the peace of a free man and the peace of a slave.
6. Learn the difference between being a *conscious* person and being a person with a *conscience*.
7. Learn to disobey dominators.

I really wish I could have given you more simple advice. I wish the path for being and feeling free was a softer, gentler, easier path.

But it's not.

You were born into a world of dominators. Dominators who believe they have the right to take the diamonds of your identity in your inner peace. Dominators who program your mind as they moralize their dominance over you.

You must free your mind. You must free your spirit. You must think for yourself. You must be willing to fight with your words. And if those do not work, you must be willing to fight with your body.

Believe me when I say that I do not like to bring up the place for violent resistance any more than a pacifist Quaker would. But a Continental Congress full of Quakers would have never thrown off the chains of its British dominators.

There is a time to fight back. I must confess that I have been depressed in recent days when I think of the millions who died in the 20th century in the Holocaust and Russian concentration camps. There is a large part of me that thinks, "Why didn't they fight back? Why just go to the Gas Chamber? Why just surrender to the KGB and submit to the concentration camps?

Aleksandr Solzhenitsyn said something I never want you to forget. A former soldier in the Red Army, Solzhenitsyn spent 8 years in a Soviet concentration camp after criticizing Joseph Stalin in a letter to a friend. It was Solzhenitsyn who later wrote the *Gulag Archipelago* which exposed how Stalin's rule caused millions to vanish and be placed in scattered concentration camps.

Solzhenitsyn said,

And how we burned in the camps later, thinking: **What would things have been like if every Security operative, when he went out at night to make an arrest, had been uncertain whether he would return alive and had to say good-bye to his family?** Or if, during periods of mass arrests, as for example in Leningrad, when they arrested a quarter of the entire city, people had not simply sat there in their lairs, paling with terror at every bang of the downstairs door and at every step on the staircase, **but had understood they had nothing left to lose and had boldly set up in the downstairs hall an ambush of half a dozen people with axes, hammers, pokers, or whatever else was at hand?**... The Organs would very quickly have suffered a shortage of officers and transport and, notwithstanding all of Stalin's thirst, the cursed machine would have ground to a halt!....**We didn't love freedom enough. And even more – we had no awareness of the real situation.... We purely and simply deserved everything that happened afterward.**

— Aleksandr I. Solzhenitsyn , <u>The Gulag Archipelago 1918–1956</u>

I'm not being overly dramatic when I say that you very possibly, maybe probably, will face something similar in your lifetime. Don't let any dominator drag you to a Gas Chamber. Don't let any dominator drag you to a prison camp.

Determine that they won't take you alive. Fight back. Even be willing to kill dominators and their soldiers and police.

Gasp. I can almost hear multitudes of weak-minded, dominated people being internally triggered and responding with a "You can't say things like that!"

Says who?

Dominators?

- They can kill me, but I can't kill them?
- They can destroy my family, but I can't destroy theirs?
- They can ruin my life, but I can't ruin theirs?

Wake up people. This is the law of the dominance hierarchy: hypocrisy. I can exercise power over you. You can't exercise power over me. I can make you afraid of me. You can't make me afraid of you. I can hurt you. You can't hurt me. I can kill you. But you can't kill me.

Many good-hearted religious folks from my past may respond to such a statement with, "But the Bible says, 'Thou shalt not kill.' Period. What do you say to that?"

To which I offer the following food for thought.

- By stating, "Thou shalt not kill," you have quoted to me the beginning and end of a simple four-word sentence in Exodus 20:13. Now would you explain to me the beginning and end *of the total context* that this single sentence finds itself in.
- The same people Yahweh commanded, "Thou shalt not kill," were the same people he *commanded to kill*
    - False Prophets (Deuteronomy 18:20-22)
    - Blasphemers (Leviticus 24:16)
    - Sabbath Breakers (Exodus 31:14)
    - Murders (Exodus 21:12-14)
    - Rapists (Deuteronomy 22:25-27)
    - Kidnappers (Exodus 21:16)
    - Adulterers (Leviticus 20:10)
    - Homosexuals (Leviticus 20:13)
    - Kids who hit their parents (Exodus 21:15)
    - Kids who curse their parents (Exodus 21:17)
    - Rebellious, uncontrollable kids (Deuteronomy 21:18-21)
    - Witches (Exodus 22:18)
    - Idolaters (Exodus 22:20)
    - Apostates from Judaism (Deuteronomy 13:6-11)
        - And this is an abbreviated list.

To be clear, I'm NOT saying that I agree with this execution list. I'm saying that it's abundantly clear that the "Thou shalt not kill" coming from Yahweh is NOT a universal law with universal application. Yahweh had numerous exceptions to this command. True, or not true?

- The same people Yahweh commanded, "Thou shalt not kill," were the same people he commanded to kill every man, woman, and child living in the land of Canaan that they were about to occupy (Deuteronomy 7:1-5; 20:16-18; cf. I Samuel 15:2-3). True, or not true?
- The same people Yahweh commanded, "Thou shalt not kill," were the same people he would NOT punish killing in the cases of 1) killing a robber who broke into one's home in the night (Exodus 22:2), and 2) killing someone who committed involuntary manslaughter against your loved one and failed to find asylum in one of six sanctuary cities (Numbers 35:26-27). True, or not true?
- The same people Yahweh commanded, "Thou shalt not kill," he commanded the organization of a military for protection (Deuteronomy 20). True, or not true?
- The same people Yahweh commanded, "Thou shalt not kill," celebrated the killing prowess of their first two kings (I Samuel 18:7). True, or not true?
- The same people Yahweh commanded, "Thou shalt not kill," had his priests kill millions of animals throughout their history and before the destruction of their temples. True, or not true?
- Even gentle Jesus told his disciples that the time would come when they would need to buy a sword (Luke 22:36). Yes, he balanced that with warning Peter that the one living by violent advancement with the sword, would die that way (Matthew 26:52). But it is clear that both statements are true. Jesus advocated self-defense against dominators. Jesus rejected the idea of violent, offensive domination. True, or not true?
- Even Revelation states that gentle Jesus will return and will personally kill and slaughter thousands, maybe millions of soldiers in the battle of Armageddon (Revelation 19:11-21). True, or not true?
- Multitudes of Christians fought and killed in the name of freedom in the Revolutionary and Civil Wars. True, or not true?

What is my point? Freedom must be fought for. Disobedience to dominators is required. Fighting dominators will be required. Killing may very well be required.

Dominators want to enforce this double standard: We can use force and violence, you cannot. We can take your lives. You cannot take our lives. Dominators love to moralize their dominance.

Peaceful, freedom loving people resisting domination are not the bad guys. Dominators using coercive fear, force, and the threat of violence are the bad guys.

I'm tired of being afraid of dominators. It's time for dominators to be afraid of good people who want to be left alone to live their lives in peace. I'm tired of the worthless attempts to "speak truth to power."

Speaking truth to dominators?

What a waste of time. It's time to speak truth to people…to give them back their power! It's time for humanity to be free and to feel free.

This is a book that would have historically been burned by dominators. Dominators don't like independent thinkers. Dominators hate having their phony moralized dominance exposed. Dominators don't like those who fight back. Dominators want people to stand down, sit down and shut up. They hate those who stand up, speak up, and strike back against them.

We live in a world that is afraid of its dominators. Again, it's time for dominators to be the ones who are afraid. This is how to feel free in the world of slavery.

One final thought. Learn to live with dominators, not under them. One of my favorite extemporaneous stories I used to tell your brothers was the story I made up about *Happy the Honey Badger*. Maybe one day I'll write a book chronicling his adventures.

Happy the honey badger perfectly embodies the disposition we should all have when living in a world of dominators. Happy the honey badger lives in Africa, a land filled with many more dominant animal species than himself. Happy is pretty far down the list when it comes to the dominance hierarchy. He is surrounded by dominators.

But even though Happy is surrounded by dominators, he is still in possession of his diamonds. He controls his own identity, inner peace, choices in life, and destiny.

Happy the honey badger is not afraid of anybody. No one ever told him he's only 30 pounds. Nevertheless, he fears no one. He's not afraid of the lion prides. He's not afraid of the rogue leopards. He's not afraid of Hyena packs. He's not afraid of cobras.

It's hard to control someone who's not afraid.

But Happy is also not stupid. He's smart. He doesn't go out of his way to try to confront these bigger dominators.

But when they interfere in his life, when they threaten him, and when they try to bully him – he doesn't back down. And if they attack him, he's going to fight back with everything he's got, even to the death.

Happy the honey badger knows how to live *with* dominators. But he doesn't live *under* dominators.

Be like Happy the honey badger. You can't help it that there are large dominators all around. Big religions. Government officials, military, and police at every level of existence. Rich bullies who want to reshape the world in their own image. Learn to navigate around their existence. Learn to live *with* these dominators without living *under* them.

These dominators have absolutely no right to dominate you. But be smart, they do have the might.

But never give them your two diamonds. If they come for your diamonds, stand your ground. Never have a fear of them and make sure they know it. If one day they threaten your very freedom, be willing to fight them to the death. And make them pay a price for having killed you.

As you can tell, I'm just at a stage in life where I want to speak plainly. I am not tucking my message of freedom in fiction. I'm not going to leave things to you to connect the dots. I'm going to say it straight. I'm going to say it plain. I want to give you a message that gives you the greatest chance of a free future.

The torch of freedom has flamed out. It is time that the torch of freedom is relit. It's time for a freedom movement of FREEDOM LOVERS to begin.

I encourage you to live as externally free as you possibly can. No one owns you. No one has the right to order you. No one has the right to oppress and hurt you. You were not born to be dominated. You were born free.

I encourage you to live *extremely* free – as free as you possibly can. This is my advice on how to feel free in a world of slavery.

www.ingramcontent.com/pod-product-compliance
Lightning Source LLC
Chambersburg PA
CBHW031806270326
41933CB00028B/736
9781735378800